THE DRUMS OF MEMORY

THE DRUMS OF MEMORY

They will sound distant as we grow old
       – The drums of memory –
But they echo our hopes, our loves, our fears
  Our moments of triumph, our follies, our tears.
Neither time nor desire can change their beat
  And we must follow them down the years
Till they roll at last for our retreat.

And they beat for the march of a vanishing race
       – The drums of memory –
In whom duty and service knew pride of place,
  For whom even great Empire was never disgrace.
A people redoubtable, proud and strong
  Whose bond was their country – right or wrong
Disciplined, tolerant, Christian and free
  Steeled in the forge of their history.

And I hear a warning of what could be
       – Tapped on the drums of memory –
Should fashion destroy such constancy,
  Should their children forsake their destiny,
Should they ever consent to bend the knee,
  Lost in a marsh of dependency,
God grant that my drummers may yet be heard
  Long after they beat retreat for me.

S.L.E.H. Milton, 1994

THE DRUMS OF MEMORY

An Autobiography

by

STEPHEN HASTINGS M.C.

LEO COOPER
LONDON

First published in Great Britain in 1994 by
LEO COOPER
an imprint of Pen & Sword Books Ltd,
47 Church Street, Barnsley, South Yorks S70 2AS

A CIP record for this book
is available from the British Library

ISBN 0 85052 431 8

Typeset by CentraCet Limited, Cambridge
Printed by Redwood Books Ltd.
Trowbridge, Wilts.

For Elizabeth Anne
and in memory of
The 2nd Battalion, Scots Guards

Contents

Acknowledgements

I am indebted to the following for their generous help:

Brigadier Kim Ross, CBE, DSO, and Major Edward Woods, Regimental Lt. Col and Adjutant, Scots Guards; Lt. Col I. F. Smith, MBE and his staff at Headquarters, The SAS Regimental Association; Major General David Lloyd Owen, CB, DSO, OBE, MC, Chairman, LRDG Association; Major Ion Calvocoressi, MBE, MC, (to whom all of us who served in the 2nd Battalion Scots Guards in the Western Desert owe so much); Sir Desmond Fennell, OBE, sometimes Chairman of the Wing Airport Resistance Association; Anthony Freemantle, for much research and help with the index; The Naval Historical Branch, Ministry of Defence (P. R. Melton); the SOE Advisor, Foreign and Commonwealth Office (Gervase Cowell); Miss Janet Spufford of Ayrshire Business Services for her patience and impeccable presentation; Michael Sissons of Peters, Fraser and Dunlop, for his faith in the enterprise; my publishers, in particular Tom Hartman, for much guidance and a blessed sense of humour.

Prologue

A LETTER TO ELIZABETH ANNE

I am writing this partly in homage, partly in gratitude for many hours spent on your own while I sat scribbling or gazing out of the window, instead of doing something which you had every right to think might be more useful. But partly also to complete a picture.

You said once that I had been lucky to have a varied life, and that by contrast you had spent yours mostly working or being married: that all your adventures had come in the middle and that if you'd known it was going to be so quick you'd have been "much worse".

I do understand. I have been "worse" for much longer. I'm not sure that is the best predicate for this book but it will have to do.

Once faced with a blank sheet of paper and armed with the temerity to write about one's life there is a compulsion to dig deep. Much of what is dredged up at the beginning you will already know but you do complain that it has always come out "in bits". So this is an attempt to stitch it together for you.

I arrived on 4 May, 1921, in Hans Crescent. This is not a beginning; it is a focal point because time stretches in all directions. I wonder where I came from. You will understand this question. Part of the answer lies in a tiny grain of human history, part in something more mysterious about which I am free to wonder.

People have different ideas about genealogy. I have been reminded of a passage from C. S. Lewis's *Mere Christianity*: "There was a time when every man was part of his mother, and earlier part of his father, and his grandparents . . . If you could see humanity spread out in time as God sees it, it would not look like a lot of separate things dotted about. It would look like one single growing thing – rather like a very complicated tree. Every individual would appear connected with every other."

It's a big picture and I think you'll agree there are quite a lot of them we would rather not be too closely connected with, even if the concept does provide a useful overview for God.

1

Heroic medieval attempts to link important personages direct to Adam and Eve are not very convincing, while our College of Arms even foundered trying to find bits of my family in Ireland a few generations back.

It's an imprecise science. My own beginnings stretch down so many different bits of this tree that it is impossible to say whether our family are predominantly Highlanders, Huguenots, Anglo-Irish or Danish marauders, indeed the more one looks at us the more we resemble a sort of squirrel's nest stuck in the branches.

Nevertheless perhaps it helps to understand something of ourselves and our fate if we can see a little way back down the branch.

After the first war my father bought a farm in what was then Southern Rhodesia. His passion was Africa. So, soon after I was born I was taken there by my mother together with a nurse, who disapproved wholeheartedly of everything she found. My sister was born on the farm. After two years we were returned home, allegedly because I had malaria and was ailing unto death. Thenceforth we were brought up by my grandmother in a large white house in Berkshire. My mother travelled home most years to be with us. My father appeared more rarely. He brought weaver birds' nests on sticks, primitive burnt wood carvings of antelope, strange devils and other Africana. Even then I had the feeling his visits upset our grandmother's orderly female household, and our disciplined nursery existence. We longed to know more about him.

Memories of my mother are misted with sadness. She was lovely, an only child, dominated by my grandmother who had wanted a son, and who later adopted me as a surrogate. I think this increased the tragedy of my mother's life. She must have been a girl of extreme sensitivity. Her poetry at twelve years still seems to me poignant and beautiful. George Meredith, to whom my grandmother showed it*, was said to have been deeply impressed but advised caution and delay. Perhaps he suspected that so solemn and forlorn a muse would be too delicate to survive, and so it proved. For this gentler side of my mother's nature became case-hardened by the men she chose, the powerful personality of my grandmother, and the circumstances of her life. Gradually she constructed a refuge behind walls of prejudice which effectively protected her from speculation and uncertainty. She became a Catholic convert of violent conviction, and in due course propelled my ageing father back into his long abandoned church. During the First World War she refused ever to dance out of respect for the young men she knew who fell at the front like leaves in autumn. Perhaps this was when her true heart began to break.

* It must have been just before he died in 1909.

Her first marriage ended in early divorce, a rare event in those days. The truth of the matter, or even her version of it, was veiled from us children. Indeed this silence shrouded much of our family tragedy. Questions were not encouraged and if asked only elicited dark hints and a ponderous shift of subject. The illusion of Victorian propriety had to be preserved for us, more's the pity, for the habit of enforced avoidance grows into estrangement. Taboos take root and extend. A disposition not to discuss anything awkward permeated our lives and established barriers which, alas, were never breached later on. When she was old and needed comfort there was no gate into the fortress of my mother's prejudice, and my own weaknesses, mistakes and wanderings were, by habit, too well hidden to be shared. In her last years I felt a desperate affection, bordering always on exasperation which stemmed from my own inability to help. Her sorrow a reproach, the gulf unbridgeable.

But it was not always thus, and I cherish the memory of her coming into my room when I was small, a vision in shining evening dress on her way down to dinner. I looked forward to those precious minutes. "What shall we talk about!" one of us would ask, and each time the question prefaced an adventure; such was the delight of her company and the harmony between us. Sometimes she would read glorious tales of trolls and misty highland magic from *Beyond the Border*, or later, and incomparably well, from *The Experiences of an Irish RM*, but with the long absences in Rhodesia this understanding gradually faded until the war swept me away. Afterwards it was already too late.

Neither my sister nor I were any more sucessful at establishing a relationship with our father. Of tremendous physique and appearance, he strode in and out of our lives like a whirlwind. As well as the weaver birds' nests he brought exhilaration, suspense, and uncertainty. Our confused emotions were further perplexed by my mother's prostration and my grandmother's studied disapproval of him. His was a life of stirring and haphazard adventure. Brought up a Catholic, his father had been a successful lawyer with a London practice and a complicated conscience, who committed his agonized confessions to a secret commonplace book written in Greek letters which came to me from an uncle I hardly knew. It was perhaps unlucky for him that I could decipher it; but then why did he write it? He married a stout highland girl, a MacDonald of Sleat who bore him 13 children including Theresa who became a Catholic nun of considerable eminence and my Uncle Basil, a successful playwright. His grandson, my cousin Max, writer and modern military historian, is currently the highly effective editor of *The Daily Telegraph*.

My father Lewis was destined for the Bar, but after a violent quarrel with my grandfather over some alleged scandal at Stonyhurst in which my grandfather sided with his accusers, Lewis ran away, aged 17, and took ship for South Africa where he joined the Cape Mounted Police, a corps with a considerable *esprit* and a popular starting point or refuge for young English gentlemen adventurers, misfits and remittance men. Thence he was swept into the vortex of what genuinely was developing Africa. He lived in the veld with two Boer companions shooting buck for the gangs working on the railroad as it advanced north into Rhodesia. He played a considerable part as a special reservist in the suppression of the Communist-led riots which shook Johannesburg as early as 1913 and was subsequently chosen by Smuts to help his recruiting campaign on the outbreak of war in 1914. There was much opposition. Somewhere I have an old photograph of him standing, legs astride, haranguing a vast crowd from the steps of the Rand Club in Johannesburg. He was the most powerful platform speaker I have ever heard. Then, with all the unbeatable enthusiasm of his imperial generation, he went to war, at first with a scratch cavalry unit rejoicing in the title of the Imperial Light Horse which moved against the Germans in South-West Africa. When these capitulated he came home with two companions, was commissioned into the Gunners and sent to France. Wounded and decorated, he met my mother soon after the war while recuperating in hospital from a gas attack. They were married in 1920. But Africa was in his blood and before long he was back in Southern Rhodesia. The first farm, Marangoe, somewhere in the Umvikwes, failed. A second and larger investment took place near Macheke. My godfather, Philip Gribble, played a prominent part in this. The Southern Rhodesian Tobacco Estates constituted one of the biggest enterprises of its kind in the country. My father was Managing Director. I do not know how successful he was as a farmer, but he founded the Rhodesian Tobacco Growers Association and subsequently became Member of Parliament for the constituency of Lomagundi in support of Lord Malvern's government. From time to time he returned home and certainly played a part in resisting the 1926 General Strike. His electric command of a large unruly audience must have been valuable to the Government and I believe he received much encouragement subsequently to stand for Parliament at Westminster, but the Veld and the free ways of Africa prevailed. When the 1939 war began he and his associates decided to sell up. It was a mad decision economically, brought about by Philip Gribble's conviction that we would lose the war and by my father's determination, at the age of 60 plus, to be in it.

And in it he was, first as a Gunner Officer again. I met him by chance one night on an ack-ack site in Hyde Park. I think he had little idea what his battery was supposed to be doing but he was entirely happy. Later he became a Rhodesian war correspondent, and finally the BBC's principal war reporter and broadcaster, at which he excelled. These various titles provided him with a passport to travel the war fronts almost at will and to engage whenever opportunity provided. For a few days he even commanded an infantry company which he found without officers after the Sicilian landings. He finished the war with a flourish by "liberating" Bremen Town Hall single-handed, armed only with a walking stick, with which he belaboured the Nazi officials. He was one of the first people into Buchenwald and the horror persisted for the rest of his life. After the war he continued to write, lecture and broadcast. Persuaded by a publisher to write something of his life, he produced a short book called *Dragons are Extra*. A cockney circus manager he had once known in South Africa charged "extra" to see the "dragon" which he kept in a tent. I know nothing of the aspect of the dragon but the allusion is right. My father was "extra" and "a dragon". But sadly his book was no more than a series of anecdotes strung together. It does not do justice either to a varied and exciting life or to the considerable intellect he possessed. His poetry is powerful and amusing, for he had a firm sense of rhythm and imagery, although it is sometimes spoiled by an unnecessarily bitter twist. Those who were not with him were seen to be seriously against him.

The name Hastings stems from a Danish Viking called Hästing, the horseman or knight, who harried the south coast of England for 2 years until finally seen off at Pevensey by King Alfred. Indeed I think he was the cause of the burnt cakes. Hästing and his men retreated to France, and if you visit the chateaux of the Loire valley you will find recorded in more than one guide book that the place was assaulted and burned by "*Le féroce Hästing*" during his passage up the river. Genetics work in strange ways and I can picture my father standing in the prow of his longship, battleaxe in hand, with the horned helms behind him. Some of Hästing's people must have developed a bridgehead on the south coast and who can deny the possibility that his bloodline spread into the Midlands where the Hastings family established itself. When I look at the fine portrait of my father by Robert Purvis I feel sure it did.

My sister Anne marked his death with a poem, given to my mother and subsequently lost. I retain one memorable couplet:

"His laughter paid the dues of God
We should have lit a ship".

The third and greatest influence over my childhood was that of my grandmother, Edith Isabella Lumsden, the eldest daughter of 13 children, born to Henry Lumsden, Laird of Pitcaple, an ancient fortress in the village of that name some 25 miles west of Aberdeen. It was a legendary boast in the family that Lumsden in their heyday could put 500 men into the field; hardly a match for Forbes or Gordon, but a useful contingent in days when the rich lowlands of Aberdeenshire lay under constant threat of assault from the Lords of the Isles, or subject to treacherous rivalry between resident magnates and clans. Every major holding in Aberdeenshire was built for defence and Pitcaple, eventual headquarters of the Lumsden clan, is no exception. Constructed on the Z plan, the Thane's Tower with its grim coronet, the hanging tower, certainly stood in the 14th century. The walls in places are 5ft thick. Originally a Leslie stronghold, Pitcaple passed to Lumsden by marriage in 1757. The Leslies were good royalists and Pitcaple provided the scene for a sad incident in the last days of Montrose's life. After his defeat at Carbisdale in May, 1650, the Marquis was run to ground like a fox in the heather. Exhausted and without hope, he was trussed to a pony and brought down to Pitcaple by his Covenanting escort. The Laird, John Leslie, was away, but his wife, Agnes Ramsey of Balmain, was a loyal and resourceful lass. She and her servants plied the guard with whisky. When they were besotted she slipped alone to the second floor where she had arranged that Montrose should be lodged. There she showed him a shaft connected to a tunnel through the walls by which he could have escaped. Montrose, surely conscious of the fate which would have overtaken this brave lady had he gone, thanked her but said he preferred to take his chance in Edinburgh, whither in due course he was carried, bound, through the silent gaping crowds, unsuccessfully imported to jeer at him, and beheaded. The end of this tunnel was found not long ago in a bank by the burn near the castle, and there is no question that it provided an escape route.

My Victorian forebears peopled the place with ghosts which were much in fashion at the time and Montrose's room was supposed to be a certain haunt. I have slept there several times without success but nonetheless I lay awake imagining the tension and tragedy of that last hopeless decision.

From this granite background my grandmother Edith Isabella emerged, beautiful and imperious. Much sought after, she fell in love at nineteen with a Captain Brooke of the Gordon Highlanders. Her father considered him unsuitable and was unwise enough to tell her so while she sat at the piano in the drawing room at Pitcaple. She slammed down the lid, and rose in wrath: "Very well, Papa, I shall marry the next man who asks me". The next man turned out to be my grandfather, Neil Benjamin Edmonstone. The family of Edmonstone emerged from the mists of lowland Scottish history. I have an extract from an ancient genealogical table which records the marriage of a daughter of King Robert III to Sir James Edmonstone of Duntreath in

Stirlingshire. My great-great-grandfather, also Neil Benjamin, had been the fifth son and as such he took one of the few options open to him. He set sail for India where he served the East India Company with distinction, became secretary to the future Duke of Wellington and made a fortune. I have a picture by Chinnery of his enchanting children. There are also Anglo-Indian Edmonstone cousins from some earlier and unrecorded liaison. Alas, no contact survived with them.

After his return from India, Neil Benjamin and his descendants were frequently at Duntreath and my grandmother loved the place. It was there she met and sat at the feet of Alice Keppel (born Edmonstone), already Prince Edward's favourite. Alice set a fast and glittering pace in the Prince's circle and encouraged my grandmother to join in. To no avail. "But, why didn't you Grangran?" I once asked. "My dear, I really couldn't be seen about with those sort of people!" was her puzzling reply.

Colonel Neil Benjamin, my grandfather, went to South Africa with the Fourth Hussars, survived the siege of Kimberley and eventually arrived with his regiment on garrison duty in Ireland. They led a sporting life. My grandmother hunted four days a week mostly in Meath. She was an exceptional horsewoman and thus was laid the foundation of so much of my beginnings, indeed of my life as it has turned out. This happy state of affairs was brought to an abrupt conclusion by the investigations of some newly appointed English General, whose ill-mannered ardour led to an unscheduled inspection of the 4th Hussars barracks in Cork. No officer was to be found, nor any senior NCO. One corporal presented himself and, in response to the General's furious questions, confessed that everybody else was out hunting. The unfortunate Colonel of the 4th Hussars was dismissed the service and most of his brother officers, outraged at such ungentlemanly behaviour on the part of this upstart General, made the only protest open to them: they sent in their papers. Thus ended my grandfather's military career. I have his swords, his silver-plated revolver and a Martini Henry rifle he carried at Kimberley, also a faded photograph of a tall thin figure with a drooping moustache and a strangely haunted face. His life sank soon after into tragedy. "Poor Dear Neil", as he was always referred to by my grandmother went off his head, became violent and died in a nursing home some time in the early twenties. At least that is what we believe. His fate became yet another closed subject for us.

Edith Isabella was quite fearless. There is a story of her during the troubles at the time of the Curragh Mutiny. Three Irish roughs broke into her house in Cork while my grandfather was away with his regiment. This was the equivalent of the IRA and they were surely bent on serious trouble. The Irish servants melted away. She stood at the top of the stairs facing her assailants with my grandfather's 45 revolver in her hand. There were no bullets and in any case she had no idea how to load it. "Get out," she said. "I'll count to three and if you are still here I'll fire." They wavered until she reached two, then fled. God knows what would have happened to her if they had stood their ground. I still cherish that revolver.

My debt to my grandmother is great indeed. I loved and admired her. I think she spoiled me thoroughly and probably at my poor sister's expense, but she was my guardian and mentor, and she was our home. The most exciting times may have been when my parents returned from Africa but "Grangran" provided the background to our lives.

Most of our childhood was spent where we belonged, well out of sight upstairs. The nursery itself was a large square place, the linoleum floor of which tilted toward the outer wall thus providing a useful slope for rolling things. We had a Peruvian guinea pig called Jimmy in a hutch, a charming little black and white fellow with long silken hair. I can still hear the scratchy noise he made as he scampered about. He made very small messes about a quarter of an inch long, solid and beautifully rounded. They fitted into my toy cannon and I fired them indiscriminately. One Christmas my sister was given a splendid dolls' house. I got lead soldiers to add to my existing and extensive army, and also a clockwork engine. None of the grown-ups were interested in the parade I organized for their benefit, or indeed in my engine, but all cooed ecstatically over the dolls' house. I was furiously jealous and mounted a secret attack with my entire force from behind a sofa. When nanny and the grown ups had withdrawn I bombarded that dolls' house with a mixture of Jimmy's turds and matches until my sister was reduced to tears of fury. She was always capable of retaliation, but this time she played a master stroke: she seized my engine and hurled it straight through the nursery window where it fell with a shattering crash through the conservatory roof, covering the gardener's boy with broken glass and bringing general retribution upon us both.

It was a country life, amid dogs, chickens, cattle and, very soon, ponies, for horsemanship was to be our first real challenge in life. My grandmother placed us in the care of Mr Prince, a famed riding master who kept an establishment on the edge of Windsor Park. To Prince we owe much. His gift with animals and children was founded on humour and kindness, balanced by absolute firmness, indispensable qualities when dealing with both. "Now children," said Mr Prince, "I am going to take you into fairyland," and so it seemed in the great park, unravaged then by ploughshare or picnic site. There we learned our first paces on the lead rein with Prince and his assistant, Mr Gaiter, both immaculate in stiff collars, bowlers and, appropriately, gaiters. "Sit up straight, Master Stephen. You don't and I shall put this stick behind your elbows, you see if I don't." "Now you remember Miss Anne, you have a sixpence between your knees and the saddle and that stays there until you get off." We loved Prince and we did learn to ride. Indeed if we had no other attainment as children we were the terror of the local Pony Club.

The time came for me to be kitted out for school and from that day my apprehension increased until I was driven off with my mother down to Langton Maltravers, a small grey stone village near the Dorset coast and dumped at the mercy of an enormous, rotund, and to me immensely terrifying being with bulging eyes and gaping mouth who waddled rather than walked towards me leaning on a stick, and laid a vast and hairy hand on my cringing head. This was Tom Pellatt, proprietor and headmaster of Durnford, one of the leading and, I believe, more expensive preparatory schools of the day. Judged by modern standards, I wonder how any of us survived the experience of Durnford. Yet "TP", as he was always referred to, was an eminent educationalist, on good terms with the great of his day who dispatched their boys to him in apparent confidence. One of my earliest memories of the place was a visit by Lord Cranborne, then a Conservative candidate in the 1929 election. His son Robert had preceded me at Durnford and this was my first tenuous contact with a family I was to know, respect and love much later in life. The school was paraded for his inspection and told to give three hearty cheers for good measure. It was clear whose side we were on.

TP had written several successful plays and a book called *Boys in the Making*, hailed in its day as a profound statement. By the time I got there I think he must have been losing his grip, yet there was a benign quality about this enormous shambling figure and a glint of perpetual humour behind his rheumy eyes.

Otherwise, benign qualities were in pretty short supply at Durnford. The food was execrable, even to a small nine-year-old scavenger, anxious to keep alive. The only way I could get anything down was to mash up a sort of dog's dinner of whatever grey and unidentifiable substances were dumped on my plate, smother it with salt and pepper and stir hard. I have often been accused since of ruining good cooking by dousing it with dynamite of one kind or another. I have to plead guilty. It is because of Durnford. The staff, or most of it, seemed to operate on the basis that growing boys, even small ones, were best left to their own devices. Discipline was harsh when they were present but liberty was otherwise virtually unrestrained and this combined the worst and the best of the place.

Every morning we were wakened in our dormitories by a piercing whistle. Twenty or thirty boys tore off pyjamas and stood naked and shivering in a queue at the door. Two minutes later a great bell clanged and the whole school, some seventy of us, converged around the draughty corridors and corners of that great wandering building to what was called "the plunge", a 12ft-long miniature indoor swimming bath well out of a small boy's depth. If you had the strength and courage to leap you could just make the other end without going under. If you were too small someone hauled you out. In either case your heart stopped. The chill was supposed to be taken off in winter but the house was unheated except for coal fires, and the greatest prize obtainable was to be excused "the plunge". You had to be at death's door to achieve it.

Bullying was fearsome. Left to themselves, small boys are capable of setting up a lifelike imitation of the Nazi party or the Mafia. The victim was selected, beaten up and harried without mercy. I remember one such, a small inoffensive boy with the unusual name of Lionel Queripel who was persecuted for weeks on end and for no apparent reason. It happened that my mother came down to take me out during the course of his ordeal. I was smitten by his misery and invited him to accompany us. He was pathetically grateful, and for weeks afterwards I went in constant dread of retribution from minute to minute round any dark corner. It never came; I don't know why. I was a successful small boxer, but could never have defended myself against the assault of this particular gang, headed, I remember, by one Humphrey Gilbert, whom I have often wished to meet in later life so vivid is the memory of his reign of terror. He may well have become a Bishop, but so far as I am concerned there is still an account to settle.

To compensate for much else there was the Dancing Ledge. Some two miles from the village across open fields a path ran to the edge of steep cliffs and thence wound down to a broad flat ledge of rock jutting some thirty yards or more into the sea. At low tide you could jump off the edge into deep water. The place belonged to the school and by dynamiting the rock they had cleverly created a sea-water pool which was washed and renewed at each flood tide. Thither we marched in summer, three or four times a week and there the small ones were dangled in the pool on the end of long bamboo poles with canvas loops attached. We learned to swim like fish. It was that or drown.

On winter afternoons on the rare occasions when the weather made games impossible we constructed a hair-raising form of speedway. This took place in a vast L-shaped room which normally held three or four classes. All the desks and benches, which must have been virtually indestructible, were piled up in the middle of the room, thus leaving a circuit round the walls about three yards wide. The corners were sharp and to make them more hazardous water was sprinkled there. Then the bigger boys strapped roller skates to each foot. An atlas or other suitably stout book was fixed to a third skate on which the competitor sat, holding the strap between his legs. The small boys were then divided into teams of pushers and allocated arbitrarily to each contestant. The dust, the noise, and the excitement were tremendous. Wild skids and thunderous crashes were frequent. The roar of many steel wheels on the wooden floor was interspersed by yells of "pusher" as the last exhausted little slave could no longer keep up. It was not so good while you were a pusher but the final experience as a racer was well worth the apprenticeship.

Somehow we were taught enough to assail the common entrance exam and thus depart to our various public schools, well prepared at least for the roughest of receptions. Eton for me proved a positive haven of security and peace by comparison.

I went back to Durnford some years ago. The great stone house is gone. A garage stands where once we roared round on our roller skates. There is no trace of our playing fields. But the walk to Dancing Ledge is the same and the precipitous sheep trodden path to the sea. The ledge itself is now the haunt of tourists and holiday makers, but the gulls wheel and cry as they did when we scrambled down, and the wash of the sea brought a grateful recollection of that rough but very human place.

My memories of Eton are almost entirely happy, although I did little to distinguish myself and even less justice to the efforts of a series of "beaks" who did their blameless best to strike some academic spark out of me. I did what I had to. My house master, Cyrus Kerry, managed to induce a temporary panic when it came to what was then the School Certificate. I strove hard and got eight credits. After this unexpected triumph my intellect relapsed happily back into neutral.

The wide and varied life which was such a precious attribute of Eton was bound to create opportunities to bend or defy the rules. One such was "bicycling leave". On whole holidays (*Non Dies*) you could apply for this concession, ostensibly to visit some place of interest outside the boundaries of the school. The business served me well.

When I was around fourteen, a farm near our home was taken over by a racing stable. I used to follow the string on my pony day after day fascinated with the beauty and excitement of thoroughbreds in training. One day, it was winter, a sheet fell off one of the horses and lay unnoticed in the road. I picked it up and returned it to a fat man on a bicycle who turned out to be the trainer. "Would you like to sit on a racehorse, sonny?" Would I! So I was hoisted up while the lad led my pony. All the way back to the yard I sat perched on a racing saddle entranced by the spring and stride of a real racehorse. Before long I was riding work regularly for Joe Davis, first lot at six in the morning clinging on for dear life, with the wind whistling past and the pounding of hooves in my ears. I would pull up almost unable to lift an arm but the exhilaration surpassed any other experience in my short life. It was not a distinguished stable, indeed, from what I could gather, even a fairly dubious one, but I shall always be grateful to them. Later, fired by this my grandmother bought me a racehorse. He was a nine-year-old tubed steeplechaser called Redford who had won a few races but had clearly lost the taste for it. If he was not in the mood he would simply down tools, but if he felt like it he could gallop and jump like a stag. We did fairly well in point to points and I rode him in a number of steeplechases, including Cheltenham. He was trained by a family friend near Ascot and the trouble was that his best engagements generally fell when I should have been at school. What to do? "Bicycling leave" came to the rescue.

I would join the queue, explain to Cyrus Kerry my intention to follow some fictitious scenic route, get the necessary chit and be off to hire my bicycle. From then on the operation worked with military precision. I would bicycle innocently up Windsor Hill in my school clothes and out into the park, where I hid the bike in some thick bushes near the Ascot lodge gates. My grandmother's chauffeur, Langley, a stout ally, met me at this rendezous and drove like Jehu to the races while I wriggled into breeches, boots and jersey in the back. I remember one time arriving at a point to point and running all the way to the weighing tent while my opponents were already in the paddock. As a matter of fact this occasion was nearly my undoing. My great friend Tommy Peyton, (killed in the commando raid on St Nazaire in 1941), had preceded me by some comparable subterfuge and had backed me. I was two lengths clear over the last fence, but got caught on the run in and beaten into third place. Old Redford was carrying a 7lb penalty and was definitely not in the mood that day. I don't believe even Fred Winter could have galvanized him.

The drama of these forays lay in getting back to Eton in time to answer one's name at "absence". I once did it dressed in a top hat and overcoat over my breeches and boots. Anyway on this occasion I just made it. So did Tommy, who, to my consternation, had clearly lingered in the beer tent, doubtless drowning his sorrows. Swaying about at the back of the crowd he was complaining loudly to several fascinated listeners about how he had been "done". Security was destroyed. Tongues wagged. Next day at what was called "boys' dinner" one of those inexplicable silences fell on all 40 of us boys. Kerry chose his moment with precision. He leant forward. "Stephen, you know what happens to boys caught riding in the races?" I was speechless. "Well, they are apt to get sacked. I thought you ought to know. Now Smith minor," he added turning to some goggle-eyed boy, his knife and fork frozen in midair, "What are you up to this afternoon". The clatter of cutlery became instantly deafening, but that was the last I heard about the matter. As the extent of my escape sank in so my gratitude and affection for Cyrus Kerry grew. From then on security held, but it was just as well my house master didn't take the *Sporting Life*.

My grandmother was an essential co-conspirator in these adventures. Anything to do with horsemanship could not in her eyes be wrong. But she also took a serious interest in my future and about this time began to think about what would now be called "career planning". "What do you want to do when you leave school, darling?" she asked. I had no idea apart from an inclination to remain associated with horses. "I had always hoped that you would have a Place," she said. "A Place" meant an establishment with broad acres to match. I think my grandmother had long harboured hopes that from the scattered domains of Lumsden or Edmonstone something would turn up for me. I do not know upon what calculation this was based but clearly it had proved unsound. "But since this seems unlikely," she went on, "there are two things I believe you can do. Horses go well for you and I think you might make a trainer. I can arrange for you to be apprenticed to a good stable; or you can go into the Regiment." Not, be it noted, the Army, the Navy or the Air Force, but "the Regiment". It turned out to be the Scots Guards in which her brother, cousins and friends had served. My grand-father's choice of the 4th Hussars did not, understandably, commend itself. I cannot say that I considered the alternatives all that deeply. I think I was grateful for the suggestion. Certainly it never entered my head to challenge it. There were rumours of war. Most of my forebears and relations, known or legendary, seemed to have been soldiers. Race-riding and hunting were encouraged in the Army. I chose "the Regiment". "Very well I'll speak to Albi Cator (then the Lt-Col Commanding) about it," and, good as her word, she did. My future was sealed, fortuitously as it turned out. War was not long delayed.

And so, my darling, this is the visible bit of the branch and the first tremors of the twig which gave rise to me.

Now I shall tell what I can about what happened.

———|———

1

OVERTURES TO WAR

Chamberlain had already returned from his notorious negotiation with Hitler, waving his worthless piece of paper, by the time I arrived at the Royal Military College, Sandhurst.

The initial excitement evaporated almost as soon as I got used to the smart uniforms. After the freedom of Eton I thought it a terrible place, ridden with petty constraints. I had a healthy respect for the NCOs, mostly from the Brigade of Guards, into whose tender care we were delivered. "Now Sir," bellowed a drill sergeant in the Grenadiers, his face six inches from mine, "you're 'Sir' to me, Sir, and I'm 'Sir' to you, Sir, you see, Sir!" I saw. Here there was clearly no nonsense tolerated or expected. The psychology was less sound among the Under Officers or senior cadets, whose exhortations were, if possible, best ignored. There was real satisfaction in parade ground drill performed in true unison. We drilled and drilled until the unison was true all right – or else. I enjoyed the horsemanship. My occasional race riding continued unrestricted and I spent a good many hours and a few quid trying to ingratiate myself with the girls of Camberley. This proved unrewarding since they were well rehearsed in means of defence against the approaches of gentlemen cadets.

Then, one morning in my second term, war with Germany was declared. I regret to say we greeted the news with unrestrained enthusiasm. After all that was what we were there for, was it not? I remember how disappointed I was with Chamberlain's faltering and melancholy tones. This wasn't the clarion I felt we had the right to expect. So some of us decided to mark the occasion with what would now be called a demo. Fortified by more drink than we could safely hold, we danced about the parade grounds shouting defiance at Germans in general and Hitler in particular, together with ribald insults at our least favourite Under Officers. This display of martial spirit got rather out of hand. Next day the ringleaders, of which I was held rather unfairly to be one, were harangued in the strongest terms by our seniors, and if it had not been for the general trauma brought about by the outbreak of war things would have gone hard for us. As it was our term at Sandhurst was brought rapidly and mercifully to a conclusion. We were the last regular intake of so called Gentleman Cadets. For some reason the "Gentlemen" finished with the war; our successors, young volunteers fresh from university or the city, and much better behaved than we, were made to wear battledress instead of our smart uniforms and referred to simply as "cadets". The rest of us soon departed for our regiments and a real world began to take shape.

I was sent to the training battalion at Pirbright Camp, an insalubrious hutted cantonment in the middle of a waste of pine trees, birch, gorse bushes, patches of heather and sand, in which we did our training. Much of this was more relevant to 1914–18 than to anything that subsequently happened to us. We would spend hours at night sitting in a dug-out at the bottom of a carefully constructed first war trench opposite another similar earthwork full of "the enemy". Patrols crawled about no-man's-land in the moonlight. A good deal of port was drunk. Instead of machine guns, which didn't seem to be available, we were given wooden rattles of the kind that used to be popular at football matches before the bovver boot and the black-jack supplanted them. We rattled away happily, firing an occasional and severely rationed verey light into the sky for effect. By day we spent hours on the rifle ranges, crawled about among the gorse bushes and drilled and drilled. The food in the Officers' Mess exceeded in excellence anything I had yet encountered. I went back there some years ago to give a talk of some sort and the standard, I was happy to find, was still the same.

Even more unexpected was the presence of a Chinese officer. I remember this diminutive figure stoutly haranguing a rank of guardsmen about three times his height. Kung Ling-chi had passed out of Sandhurst before me. A distinguished and important foreign student from Chiang Kai-shek's China, he was due to spend some months with a British regiment before returning home. When asked what arm of the service he preferred, he selected the Scots Guards. It was pointed out that this regiment unavoidably bore certain tribal connections. How about the Blankshires, an excellent regiment without the same unfortunate restriction? But he was adamant. Nothing would do but the Scots Guards. The needs of Anglo-Chinese relations dictated acquiescence and he duly appeared at regimental headquarters before our Colonel Bill Balfour. This formidable figure was near to retirement and unused to diplomatic niceties. Confronted with Kung Ling-chi standing stiffly to attention, and lost for anything suitable to say, he fell back upon a series of conventional questions, already well out of date. "Well now Mr Kung Ling-chi, I must ask whether you have sufficient private means to maintain yourself as a young officer in the Brigade of Guards?" he growled. "Oh yes Sir," was the reply. "My plivate means are quite unlimited. I am the son of the Finance Minister of China?" That settled it. (He was also, in fact, the nephew of Chiang Kai-shek).

Before long he left us and I have often wondered since how poor Kung Ling-chi fared in the ceaseless warfare which engulfed China and the Kuomintang.

We were in the midst of what was known as the phoney war. The French sat in the Maginot Line. The British Expeditionary Force hung about in Belgium, and the Germans went on building tanks and aircraft. Life at home changed little and my racing innterest was suddenly and unexpectedly reinforced. Christopher Soames, my friend and a fellow conspirator from school days, and I were at Windsor races. We watched a selling chase won by a 9-year-old chestnut and fairly capable handicapper called "Sea Trout". After the race, with no plan that I knew of, we stood by the sale ring. "Sea Trout" was led round. No bid. The war was well underway. No one was anxious to buy racehorses, least of all an ageing gelding. "Five pounds," says Christopher suddenly. There was a titter round the ring. The auctioneer suppressed a grin and ignored us. "Sea Trout" was led away. Christopher looked vastly relieved. "What did you do that for?" I asked. "I don't know," he replied. At that moment a diminutive stable lad tapped me on the shoulder and I turned to find "Sea Trout" standing beside me still blowing from his efforts. "Was it you what bid £5 for this 'orse, Gov?" he asked. "No, it was him," I said ungallantly, pointing at my companion. "Well you can 'ave 'im. We want to find 'im a 'ome" We looked at each other and without further thought, which was surely necessary, we fished in our pockets and between us conjured up £4.17.6d. It sufficed. "Yer got a box Gov?" We need the rug for the next race." And with that our client whipped the sheet off poor "Sea Trout" and disappeared in to the crowd. Now at that time strict pre-war rules still applied to young officers in the Brigade of Guards in uniform. (Christopher was in the Coldstream.) You might not carry parcels in London. You might in no circumstances walk arm in arm with a girl, etc. We were far from clear how this might apply to horse-coping in a public place. We had no horse box and no rug. We took "Sea Trout" to the stables entrance and did our best to hitchhike him. In the end a merciful driver stopped and agreed to take him off to a yard not far away and known to us, whence eventually he found his way to Peter Thrale at Epsom who trained for Christopher's father. We were full of hope. "Sea Trout" was entered shortly afterwards at, I think, Market Rasen. Christopher had first turn. The horse ran well and they finished fourth. I was much looking forward to the next ride when we were informed that poor "Sea Trout" had died of some mysterious disease. To this day I suspect foul play and the finger points at a combination of Christopher's father and Peter Thrale. There had been some doubt as to who was going to be responsible for the training fees and perhaps our optimism had been less well founded than we thought.

It was during this autumn of 1939 that the Soviet Union launched its treacherous attack on Finland. Divisions of the Red Army lumbered across the frontier into the forests of Karelia that October expecting little resistance and ill-equipped for the bitter winter to follow. The Finnish Army, just 10 divisions strong, all that could be scraped together from a nation of 4 million people, blunted the attack, then brought the Russians to a halt as the snows enveloped the battle. By night the white-clad Finnish ski patrols struck silently at their clumsy ill-equipped enemy, then vanished into the forest. Sympathy for the Finnish cause and admiration for their heroic resistance was intense in Britain. Churchill sanctioned support and a volunteer battalion, the 5th Scots Guards, was formed. This consisted of two companies of regular Guardsmen and two companies of officer volunteers drawn from all arms and regiments. Skiing experience was, not unnaturally, a desired qualification. I had none, but, fired by the romance of the enterprise, I tried to volunteer. My application was summarily dismissed and I was reminded that I was a very young and inexperienced officer who had best pay more attention to his present duties. Many of my friends of later years, George Jellicoe, David Stirling, Carol Mather and others, joined the 5th Scots Guards which was dispatched of all places to Chamonix for ski training. Now the Alps near Chamonix bear about as much resemblance to the Finnish forest as the technique of downhill skiing does to the ability to cross the frozen wastes in Karelia, as I was to discover myself after the war. Mercifully for the 5th Scots Guards, this discrepancy was never discovered. They got no further than embarkation on a Polish vessel waiting in the Forth to transport them to Helsinki when the Winter War ended. The Finns had held the overwhelming numbers sent against them for four months throughout that bitter near-polar winter. They had destroyed two Red Army Divisions, horse, foot and gun. They held a line 1000 miles long from Lapland to the Gulf of Finland; but at last, their supplies at an end with no hope of support from their Swedish neighbours or elsewhere, they capitulated. Later, when Hitler marched on Russia, the Finns became his ally. As I learned to appreciate after the war when posted to Helsinki, they would have joined the Devil himself if he had agreed to fight Russians. This time the Finns raised no less that fifteen front line divisions and, with the support of four German divisions, flung the Russians out of their country and surrounded Leningrad.

The Russians have never forgotten the pounding they got from their diminutive western neighbour and it is to their courage in 1939 and to the leadership of the remarkable Marshal Mannerheim that the Finns owe their postwar years of liberty. The modern term "Finlandization" and the inference drawn from it are a gross injustice to a brave people.

It can scarcely be said that the advent of the 5th Scots Guards would have saved the situation, but it was a brave gesture and a merciful deliverance, for a number of its officers played gallant and leading parts in the saga of the commandos, the SAS and SOE.

Then came Dunkirk. It was hard for a young officer brought up on the notion that the British were never more than mildly inconvenienced in warfare to hoist in the extent of the disaster. I drove through Camberley one morning where I noticed a rabble of some 100 soldiers outside a pub. They were filthy dirty, had no officers and no arms; some were blind drunk. The publican had either taken pity on them or been forced to open up. It was clear where they had come from. This was the face of defeat. Gradually news of friends filtered through. Julian Fane, whom I had known so well at Sandhurst, lay wounded in a military hospital nearby. He must have been nineteen years old at the time. I hurried to see him. Undaunted by his experiences and just decorated with the Military Cross, he made a heroic figure. His story of the overwhelming superiority of the German equipment and the irresistible momentum of the blitzkrieg left me wide eyed. "We've got to get back there" he kept repeating. I left him full of admiration and unease, painfully aware that we at Pirbright, with our indulgent messing arrangements, our port decanters and our rattles, were still very far from war.

I was soon transferred to Chelsea Barracks, a wing of the Guards Depot serving my regiment and the Coldstream Guards. Hither came the raw material from which Guardsmen were fashioned. One would watch them slouching through the gates in little groups, half-curious, half-rebellious and utterly unconscious of the ferocious and exigent discipline about to envelope them. By the end of that first day they were scurrying, squad after squad, as fast as their legs could carry them from one store to another, hung about with items of uniform and gear like ambulant cloakrooms. The foundation for these regiments is laid by the non-commissioned officers and the depot was the place to see it done. Later in battle the officer played his part, but here scarcely at all. With an amazing blend of psychology and iron firmness, flotsam from the Gorbals, remote, almost alien highlanders, and awkward, querulous Lancashiremen were moulded, in days, before our eyes, into men with a common cause and a common pride. They were chivvied and hounded mercilessly when they failed to smarten up, and sometimes (for good measure) when they did. I came to understand the harmony and confidence which the hours of mechanical drill on the square bring to all manner of men, and I have often pitied those who have never known it. Only two beings do I recall who simply could not manage physically to conform. The first was a highland gypsy. They say the gypsies teach their children a long stride by making them step along a railway track. At any rate this poor recruit had a loping gait which probably carried him effortlessly across hill and heather, but he just could not keep in step. His sergeant instructor, quick to recognize the lad's anxiety and disability, spent hours arm in arm with him, a pace stick by his side. 'Left, right, left, right.' It was no good and eventually the lad was given some menial job in the stores. The other was a professional boxer who, strangely, suffered from feet so flat that he could not march properly either. He, too, was sidelined. We became friends, he and I, and later when the bombing started we formed an unofficial rescue team together. He was quite fearless and distinguished himself among the rubble and gruesome remains of what had been Sloane Square underground station.

But first came the assault of the Luftwaffe upon the RAF and its airfields. The drone and whine of straining engines, the distant splutter of machine guns and the wheeling midget aeroplanes far above our heads were a daily experience and marked a drama the significance of which we could only guess looking up from among the squads of recruits prone in the gardens of the Royal Hospital learning their Bren-gun drill. Sometimes an aircraft dived out of control, with engines snarling, below the London horizon. There was an instant of silence, then the dull explosion and slowly billowing smoke. Sometimes, not always, the parachutes swung lazily down. In the evenings, off duty, I and my friends went out into London to seek adventure. There was a tavern near Piccadilly Circus, much frequented at the time. At a big table in the corner sat a group of young pilots in RAF blue, wings on their breasts, the striped ribbon of the DFC already much in evidence, shirts open at the neck and coloured scarves round their throats, asserting a lack of convention which we had no excuse to copy. Drunk they were, and full of laughter, for they had lived another day. The girls had no time for us when they were there, "the few". How humbled one felt, unable to share the gaiety which stemmed from a nearness to death in that wheeling ballet in the sky. What were we doing stamping ceaselessly about the parade grounds in our stilted and virtually peacetime existence? My friend John Bowes Lyon and I heard the RAF were short of rear gunners. Apparently it took little time to learn this trade, so we volunteered. Again no success.

We listened to the news and read the evening papers eagerly to get the day's score, as if it had been a test match. So many Germans shot down, so many of our aircraft missing. The figures were almost always encouraging, often, as we now know, wholly inaccurate, but however computed, victory belonged to those lads in the bar. Their names were soon household words to us, just as those of their opponents were to our enemies, for there can surely be no distinction in Valhalla between Hillary, Pease and Bader and Heinrich Sayn-Wittgenstein, German night fighter ace of the 80 victories, who sometimes took off in his dinner jacket. He died over Berlin in 1944. These were true knights. Not for them the squalor of a creeping earthbound campaign.

Then came the bombing of London. Having failed to pulverize the RAF, Göring resorted to terror, presumably expecting to demoralize the British to the point of surrender. There was little sign of this. With hindsight it seems to me the bombing of the cities can have had no clear objective at all since it was no longer geared to invasion and its effect at best was unpredictable, but this first attack on a civilian population changed the course of warfare and brought a terrible retribution upon its perpetrators. For us young officers in London it served to heighten the reality of war. A stick of bombs straddled Chelsea Barracks one night, killing two ATS girls; otherwise we were unscathed.

One got used to the wailing sirens, the slowly weaving searchlights, the pounding of the ack-ack guns and the drone of the bombers. The German engines made a sombre pulsating noise, unmistakable, quite different to our own aircraft.

In the evenings off duty some of us would go out into the streets and try to make our way to the nearest shambles in order, so we hoped, to help with the rescue. We were not much use. The firemen and rescue workers went about their grim business with such bravery and certainty that we were often, I suspect, more of a hindrance. We would watch the firemen silhouetted on top of their long ladders against blazing, foundering buildings playing the flames, while the droning engines passed repeatedly overhead and the bombs fell. If the first explosion was followed by another closer, and another closer yet, there would be a moment of horrible tension while one waited for the rest of the stick. But we were lucky. Sometimes we set to scrabbling at the rubble under which we were told people might be.

I remember helping a Red Cross man one night. He had come upon a body crushed below tons of masonry and, as he scraped slowly at the dust-coloured flesh, he gently and discreetly covered the remains with a blanket, inch by inch.

If we found nothing useful to do we would make off to the night clubs which remained surprisingly cheerful and as expensive as ever. Those below ground in the West End must have made a fortune.

In November, 1940, I was posted to the 2nd Battalion in Egypt. Perhaps my attempts to escape the ponderous rhythms of the Guards Depot had persuaded regimental headquarters that I was better dispensed with. I left good companions behind. There was Anthony Lyell. I never saw him again. He won the VC in North Africa making a single-handed assault on a German machine-gun post and died in the process. There was Peter Carrington. I laughed so much with both of them, and the memory of shared laughter lasts well over the years.

I said goodbye to my mother and grandmother in the big white house. I saw despair and resignation in their faces, for they had known it all before. My sister came down the drive with me as far as the gates where I was to catch a lift for the war. Neither of us could find words to help each other. Of course I felt sorrow at leaving those I loved and the familiar things, but there was also the silly embarrassment of the schoolboy when parents or family betray emotion. I could not quite believe in any drama or the possibility of being killed. It was just that I was going off on an adventure. All young men did. My head was filled more with romance than sense or sensitivity.

I reported to the Adjutant at the Tower of London to join a draft awaiting passage. I had no idea where I was going or how I would get there. Allocated a platoon, I was told to prepare for garrison duties. The bombing was nearer and more menacing here toward the east. The crash of bombs, the droning engines, the thump of flak and the livid glow of the fires filled our nights.

Garrison duty consisted principally of the Ceremony of the Keys which dates from Norman times. The high point of this is a confrontation between the sentry by the Bloody Tower and the Yeoman carrying the keys. As he and his escort emerge, jangling, from the arch of the Tower, "Halt!" cries the sentry. "Who goes there?" "The keys," replies the Yeoman in a sepulchral bellow. "Whose keys?" demands the sentry. "King George's keys," comes the reply, or it did in those days. "Pass the keys, all's well." Tramp, tramp – dignified departure of keys and escort into the gloom. The trouble was that neither I nor my guard had been properly rehearsed. The poor sentry, a lad from Glasgow, never having expected to be involved in such momentous historical events, and very nervous, got his rituals in a twist. Instead of "Whose keys?" he called out, "Advance one and give the countersign," an entirely appropriate challenge for all other circumstances but not for the keys. Nobody had said anything like that to them in living memory. They didn't know the countersign. There was a long moment of ghostly silence, followed by some tentative jangling. I and the sergeant looked at each other aghast. I had the feeling that I had inadvertently stopped the war. Gathering his wits, my sergeant clattered over the cobbles and gave the correct challenge. The keys sprang into resentful action and stamped off into the night. The unfortunate sentry was returned to the guard room in disgrace and I eventually went to my bunk certain that retribution would fall upon us in the morning. But fate intervened decisively. Before the Yeoman's complaints had time to develop those of us awaiting draft were told to get our kit together.

We left the Tower in a small convoy that morning, splashing through dirty pools, over the snakelike pipes and cables of the fire brigades which lay across so many streets. Fires from the previous night's attack still smouldered and the reek of rubble lay heavy in the air.

———|———

2

UP AND DOWN THE DESERT

We were driven to a transit camp in Liverpool and told to stand by for embarkation next day. My last evening on English soil was spent at the Adelphi Hotel, something of a shrine because of its connection with the Grand National. I harboured an ambition to ride at Aintree, but this was not to be. The shrine turned out to be a gloomy place, full of grumpy waiters. We did our best to cheer it up. I think our efforts were rather overdone and, so far as I remember, we had to beat a retreat to the transit camp just ahead of the provost marshal. Next day we embarked on the *Britannic*, an imposing Cunarder built for the North Atlantic passage, a fact which became ever clearer the further into the tropics she sailed. Our small contingent of eleven junior officers in the regiment got aboard early and I stood at the rail with some of my companions watching our future shipmates climb the gangway. Suddenly, to our surprise and delight, a group of twelve army nursing sisters appeared at the quayside. One by one they came aboard. Each in turn was carefully scrutinized and each given the thumbs down. Surely there had to be one pretty one – but no! I have often reflected since how a man's measure of female attraction changes with his age, but I never experienced such a dynamic revolution as happened aboard the SS *Britannic*, bound for Suez. Within days those girls were raving beauties and the competition intense!

Our convoy was one of those ordered expressly by Winston Churchill to reinforce Wavell's Army in Egypt. They bore his initials; ours was WS.5.B. The offical report reads:-

"sailed in three parts from Bristol (4 ships), Liverpool (6 ships) and Clyde (11 ships). The Bristol and Liverpool section were obliged to anchor in Moelfre Bay before proceeding to Belfast Lough for water. Final sailing and rendezvous with Clyde section took place 12th January 1941".

After hanging about at anchor in Liverpool roads for several days, spent sorting our kit and developing the sea-going routine we were to follow for the whole of that long two-month voyage, we crossed the Irish sea and awoke in Belfast Bay. Here was an impressive array of shipping. Tugs chugged busily about. Naval launches plied between ship and shore. It rained and the Irish coast had a forbidding, lowering look. That evening, after dark, *Britannic* slipped her moorings and throbbed out to sea. Early in the morning we were paraded on deck in our life belts for inspection. We stood there in our ranks and looked out at a scene still vivid. Ahead, astern, on either side and quarter, as far as the eye could reach into a sullen grey Atlantic, sailed the convoy. Ships of every size and description; great liners such as ours, tankers, cargo vessels, humble tramps; a massed flock of the defenceless carrying the men and materials of war; and on the flanks, some near at hand, some hull down below the horizon, steamed the escort. There was a battleship, two aircraft carriers, five cruisers, many destroyers, weaving and cutting their way across the course of the convoy, and the ubiquitous corvettes, the sheep dogs, small sea-scarred hulls, bucking past within hailing distance of *Britannic*'s long flanks, their officers and ratings duffel-coated, swathed in jerseys, bearded and unsmiling as they clung to railing and companion ladder, rows of depth charges lashed ready astern.

"Air cover was provided by *Naiad* and *Phoebe*. Ocean escort consisted of *Ramilles*, *Australia*, *Highlander*, *Harvester*, *Witherinton* and *Leopard*, *Lincoln*, *Vansittart*, *Fearless*, *Brilliant*, *Watchman*, *Beagle*, *Jackal* and *Leamington*."

We knew nothing of this litany, but for many days, and in all weathers, we watched our Armada sail north towards the Newfoundland coast, thence south along America's eastern seaboard before turning east and south to re-cross Atlantic. It was a great demonstration of sea power and how insignificant I and my thousands of land-lubbing soldier companions seemed by comparison. The lesson of the U-boat losses had been well learned and we beheld the answer. From time to time the flashing Aldis lamps and ships' sirens signalled the presence of U-boats dogging our progress. The mighty convoy would swing into a ponderous zig-zag. Destroyers darted about and the distant thud of the depth charges told of a contact somewhere astern. No attack was pressed home, no ship was lost. It was as though one was watching the very flow of our seagoing history. How could such an enterprise fail? How could we be overcome? We learned soon enough!

The food on board had been laid on for the New York run; standards were high. Before lunch most of us collected at a bar on the afterdeck; drinks were free and in consequence much was drunk. Most days at this time an amiable, corpulent and somewhat senior person came lumbering around the deck in a praiseworthy effort to get fit for war. He made an unlikely military figure and each time he passed the bar we raised a cheer. Nothing daunted his determination or his serene good humour; we all liked him. Later he became Lord Chancellor. His name was Captain Quintin Hogg.

Gradually the weather warmed and the northern mists gave way to a long blue swell. Flying fish skittered before *Britannic*'s bows and on 25 February – landfall. Palm trees along a white beach, shipping at anchor – Freetown. Cheerful black people in small boats offered exotic fruit. Small boys dived into the shining water for coins. After four frustrating days aboard in this haven we put to sea again.

It was reckoned a dangerous passage down the West African coast. Five new warships joined the escort. There were several U-boat alarms but we reached Cape Town on the 8th, Durban on the 11th. Here we were allowed ashore for four days and, as each of us young officers stepped through the dock gate, a limousine drew up driven by some kind and lovely lady who had volunteered to comfort the troops. South African hospitality proved boundless and those days are hard to forget.

The streets of Durban were haunted by drunken Australian deserters who had found the beer too much and had missed their ship from the previous convoy. You could hire rickshaws in the town pulled by Zulus in splendid feathered headdress. For obvious reasons the passengers were limited to two and the Zulu balancing against the weight behind proceeded by great loping strides at a surprising speed. I watched four Australians try to board one of these vehicles. After an altercation the rickshaw boy won his point, temporarily. Two got in, but as soon as they were underway the other two jumped aboard as well. The Zulu touched down once, but then the shafts swung heavenward dumping him from a great height on top of his surplus fares.

On the passage up the Red Sea the drink on board *Britannic* finally ran out. The withdrawal symptoms were painful. One hardened merchant captain travelling as a Naval Reservist Officer was reported to have been confined with delirium tremens. The convoy reached Suez on 3 March, 1941.

We joined the 2nd Battalion encamped at Tel el Kebir, scene of the British victory over Arabi Pasha in 1882 from which flowed our occupation and equivocal relationship with Egypt.

Long lines of white tents and bronzed guardsmen in sunbleached caps. It was clear the solar topee, headgear of the Empire, which all of us had been instructed to buy, had gone clean out of fashion.

Here was the same iron discipline, smartness and familiar routines of Chelsea and Pirbright transferred to this arid and windswept wilderness. Piped out of bed in the morning by the familiar monotonous notes of "Hey Johnny Cope", we watched our Battalion come daily to life and go through a hard training schedule. None of us newcomers had a command as yet but we were allowed to accompany our comrades on a fifty-mile route march along the Suez Canal to Kabrit on the Bitter Lakes – more lines of tents; more training, and talk of a possible invasion of Rhodes.

On 31 March Rommel struck. All the gains achieved by General O'Connor during his spectacular destruction of the Italian Army in January and February '41 were lost and the Africa Korps recaptured Cyrenaica. Rommel invested Tobruk and was already consolidating his forward positions along the Egyptian frontier south from Sollum. The British were caught dangerously off balance and all thoughts of Rhodes were abandoned.

The 3rd Coldstream departed first for the Western Desert and there was much resentment in the Battalion when it was learned they had come through a minor but victorious action against Graziani's temporarily rejuvenated Italians. But the Scots Guards did not have long to wait. In early April, 1941, the Battalion was driven off in trucks to join the 22nd Guards Brigade consisting of the Coldstream, the Durham Light Infantry and ourselves.

To our chagrin the new draft of officers was left behind. The chagrin was much mitigated by visits to Cairo and in due course my friends and I were posted to join the Regiment at a place called Buqbuq to the west of Mersa Matruh.

Soon after our arrival we experienced our first Khamsin, the dreaded sand storm blown on a scorching south wind from deep in the Sahara. Visible several miles away, a dark impenetrable wall of sand and dust two or three hundred feet high, it travelled towards us at fifty m.p.h. or faster. It was evening. The cookhouse was already in action. Orders came to dig in and under no circumstances to eat. With a roar it was upon us. The sky turned black. Visibility was down to two or three yards. Breathing was difficult. We lay in whatever shelter we could find, our heads under our blankets, and panted.

After half an hour of hissing fury it passed. Our relief was short-lived. Several men in a neighbouring company had disobeyed orders and eaten their evening meal. Four were unconscious with heatstroke.

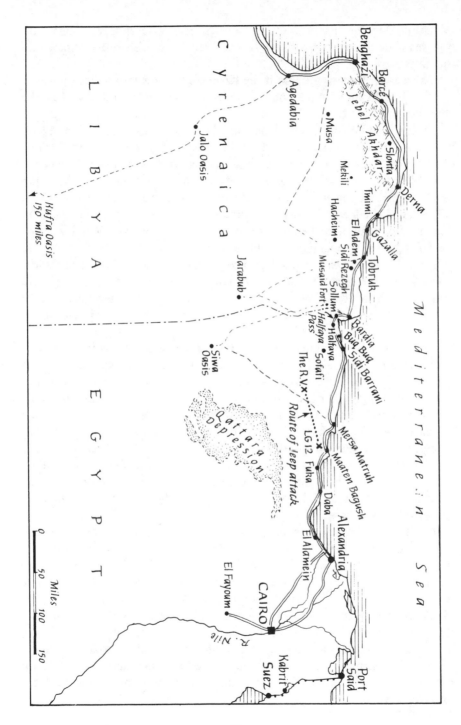

What to do? No medical officer was present. We dragged them into the sea and dunked them. To our great relief they recovered remarkably quickly.

There is an Arab saying that if the Khamsin lasts for four days or longer a man is free to murder his wife. I doubt whether we would have had the strength.

At last I commanded a real platoon, No.9 to be exact, in Right Flank Company of what I was convinced was the best battalion in the British Army. It therefore had to be the best platoon and for a time I believed it was, due solely to the fortuitous presence of my platoon sergeant, Ian Stewart. He told me gently what to do and ensured that everyone else did it, all accomplished with such tact, firmness and efficiency that he was soon taken away, commissioned in the field, and later won a Military Cross commanding a Company in a Highland regiment.

Right Flank was commanded by a somewhat forbidding Highland Officer called John MacRae. I and my brother officers in the Company held him in some awe. The awe didn't last but he remains a legendary figure in the Regiment, his name recalled in a pipe tune still played in his honour.

John was a born soldier and the guardsmen under his command worshipped him. He could be nice to his young officers and we solicited and valued his praise. But he was a strange unsettling character who seemed to seek sanctuary in the rigours of his calling. Sometimes he would overcome his own internal tensions by sneering at the fears of his juniors. And he had his favourites. We each enjoyed our turn basking in his indulgence, but his capacity for isolation and subtle bullying drove most of his officers in the end to something near despair. He was killed by a bullet in the brain while on patrol just before the Battle of El Alamein. The Company swore a bloody vengeance and for all I know they took it. Had he lived he might have commanded armies.

Life at our company headquarters, in whatever dugout or desert hole it happened to be, was a spartan affair. When things were relatively calm we platoon commanders were summoned to dine with MacRae. There was no attempt to improve the bully-beef, but there was whisky in plenty. After what passed for dinner he would call for his piper, Sergeant McConnell, and whenever I hear the strains of "Loch Duich's Side", song of the lands and hills of MacCrae, I can still conjure the lone figure of our piper against a livid desert sunset. And we sang. I had inherited Highland songs. My great friend Alec Ramsay, 2nd in command of the Company, and of course John himself knew many more. How we sang. Those were evenings, rare enough, of great comradeship.

But what a contrast and delight it was to be invited to the headquarters of Left Flank Company commanded by Johnny Drury-Lowe who was as kind and companionable as MacRae was veiled and unpredictable. His platoon commanders included my friends David Butter and Ion Calvocoressi. Left Flank was merry. Everyone laughed and Johnny fussed over us. It was a different world. Drury-Lowe had his headquarters staff fashion entrée dishes from the flimsy disposable petrol cans which littered the desert and from which millions of British gallons brought thence at great cost in lives and money must have leaked into the sand. It was a scandalous waste but they did make good entrée dishes and represented one of Johnny's untiring efforts to maintain civilised standards.

"Come along Stephen, you are late again. Hurry, you'll miss your sherry."

Wherever we were Johnny Drury-Lowe managed to convey the atmosphere of a Regency drawing room, that is until some gun or other went off. "Oh, the noise these tiresome people make," was a frequent comment on our circumstances.

Always impeccably smart, Johnny led his company courageously, complaining gently and constantly about the discomfort and vulgarity of war. He was well served and not surprisingly his officers loved him.

Just after my 20th birthday, on 15 May, the Battalion was ordered to attack a place called Musaid Fort on the Libyan frontier. This lay on top of the great escarpment which runs parallel to the coast from east to west closing northward to the sea at Sollum. The coast road winds up to the frontier through a pass called Halfaya, inevitably known at the time as "Hellfire" pass.

This was Operation "Brevity". The 22nd Guards Brigade, supported by twenty-four Matilda tanks, was supposed to improve the situation on the frontier and interfere with the arrival of Rommel's 15th Panzer Division. It failed in both. Our subsequent hold on this frontier position proved only temporary. 15 Panzer duly arrived at the beginning of June.

Our Company was carried in lorries belonging to the Indian Division and dumped on top of the escarpment at a place known on the map as Sofafi. We set off on foot following a compass bearing in the general direction of Musaid. For a long time nothing happened. There was some desultory shelling in the distance and then near at hand the occasional crack of a rifle.

"Are we in action?" I asked Alec who was nearby. Alec had been with the First Battalion in Norway and was thus omniscient. He seemed to think we were. I felt greatly relieved. Whatever happened, I could now say I had been in a battle. Presently we came upon some dugouts; empty tins and debris lay about. The place was clearly inhabited and some frightened Italians came scrambling out of a hole with their hands up. Our first prisoners. My platoon sergeant told them in stentorian tones to "Go to the rear!" The message was not fully understood, so Sergeant Todd pointed in the general direction of what we thought was the rear and fired his pistol over their heads. They ran off. Other startled people were emerging from the dugouts. Clearly we hadn't been expected. The Official History claims we captured 320 Germans and Italians from a supply depot. It didn't seem so many to me, but we had had a minor success.

After walking on for half an hour or so we came to a small hillock covered in lumps of distorted masonry. This seemed to be Musaid Fort. My platoon was ordered to dig in a quarter of a mile to the north. We couldn't. The place was solid rock. All we could manage with what we carried were shallow trenches about two feet deep. There we crouched until evening when McRae appeared.

"I've just been told," he said, "that 15 Panzer Division is advancing through your position, you'd better dig deeper. You'll be all right. You've got your anti-tank rifle." With that he left.

The Boys anti-tank rifle was one of the more useless pieces of equipment, (and there were a good many) issued to the British Infantry at the time. It was heavy, clumsy, nearly broke your shoulder when it went off and failed to inconvenience any armoured vehicle I ever saw. There was quite a competition in the platoon not to carry it. We had never yet met the Germans, but I had of course heard of this dread formation and felt a little uncertain about the capacity of No. 9 platoon to stop it. We lay gazing through out field glasses across the shimmering waste; nothing happened. In the evening we were told to leave our holes. The Battalion was to be relieved and taken back to the rear. Just as well. German armour, though not yet 15 Panzer Division, did arrive next morning, mauled the unfortunate Durham Light Infantry at Sollum and chased them off the escarpment.

Thus ended our first action. My friends and I were pretty perky; if this was war it didn't seem beyond our capacity. The feeling didn't last long; within a few days one of my favourite brother officers, Hugh Stirling, David's* youngest brother, was killed out on patrol with another unit, and Peter Fane-Gladwin wounded by dive bomber attack. We also learned of the ease with which the German Army had swept through the positions we had so fortuitously left. Nothing seemed so simple any more.

On 15 June, after three weeks' rest by the sea, the Battalion was sent forward again. Operation "Battleaxe" was supposed to destroy Rommel. It dented him a bit, though that is probably the best that could be claimed.

* David Stirling, founder of the SAS, see Chapter 3

Along the Egyptian/Libyan frontier from Sollum south towards the Siwa Oasis there stretched a high barbed wire fence which then hung in drooping festoons. What its purpose had been goodness knows for it could scarcely have deterred anything but a wandering camel. Nevertheless it was necessary to cut holes in it in order to pass through. The Battalion got mixed up with some headquarters vehicles at one of these gaps and paid for it. We were heavily strafed more than once by the Luftwaffe. We lost one of our senior officers, Harry Knight, and the Regimental Sergeant Major, Fred Leiper. There followed a somewhat muddled advance during which we were told we had to recapture Musaid Fort, this time from the west. There were supposed to be tanks and guns in support but they never appeared and finally we were launched into a night attack at around 4.00 in the morning.

We shuffled uncertainly forward over bare stony desert, bayonets fixed. No one knew if the place was occupied or not. A dog barked and kept barking. Then a murderous fire broke out; you could see the tracer bullets slashing the night in coloured arcs to both sides of us and mercifully well over our heads. Clearly the sooner we got to grips the better. We ran on. After about a hundred yards we reached a line of trenches. A figure rose out of the gloom, raised a rifle, and missed me! In we went and my particular opponent ran off screeching, helped by a bayonet in his backside. The night was full of flying figures as we stumbled into trenches and dugouts.

Dawn found us in undisputed possession of the same mound of broken masonry and debris. A few grisly corpses lay about. Musaid was ours and a bedraggled and terrified collection of Germans and Italians was herded away. It seemed we had captured over 80 and killed about 20. By mid-morning G Company had captured Sollum barracks as well. More prisoners. We felt pretty good for the next 24 hours, but then the German Panzers, supported by the 5th Light Division, came thundering down on the desert force and a day later we were again withdrawn, this time under heavy fire. So ended Battleaxe, or the Sollum *schlacht* as the Germans called it.

It turned out that the Prime Minister was furious at this failure, having risked a large convoy carrying 240 tanks through the Mediterranean in order to reinforce the desert army. The unfortunate General Wavell was sacked and replaced by Auchinleck. We returned to El Daba, another relatively hospitable place by the sea, in order to be turned into a motor battalion and, as such, to travel in support of the armoured formations. The transformation took most of that July.

There was little to prevent Rommel from advancing to Alexandria except the garrison still in Tobruk and the overriding dificulties of his long lines of communication. For it was patently clear, even at our level, that the British Tanks were no match for the German Panzers. Of our tank strength of 190,

92 had been lost by enemy action or breakdown in "Battleaxe", and only 12 of Rommel's destroyed. It was a depressing factor which weighed increasingly on all of us as the months went by. British tank design and our anti-tank guns were inadequate. The Matilda infantry tanks were heavily armoured but carried a small two-pounder gun whose shells bounced impotently off their opponents; while the cruiser tanks, although faster, seemed to break down regularly and had nothing to defend themselves with except the same small gun.

Against them the Panzers mounted a 50mm gun and used their formidable 88mm anti-aircraft guns in an anti-tank role. They could penetrate anything we had, even the Matildas. We considered ourselves lucky to be on our feet.

In August we were back at the advanced tip of the desert force position below Halfaya. It was the time of the patrols. None of us knew why, nor who had ordered them. Some said it was from Cairo, even London. We occupied a defensive position, which is to say we scratched and dug slit trenches, strung out from west to east in the narrow plain between the Sollum escarpment and the sea. One company lay along a ridge above the beach and across the salt marsh to a further ridge some quarter of a mile inland. Another, mine as it turned out, occupied more shallow trenches amongst the rocks on a further ridge some two miles to the south and midway to the escarpment, the dark forbidding cliffs of which stretched away to our front and eastwards behind us. The German and Italian positions were concealed in its folds below Halfaya Pass.

We were told we were a "spring". If seriously attacked the Battalion was to recoil, so to speak, into alternative positions near Sidi Barrani, to the east. This concept inevitably created a mood of jumpy uncertainty.

For several weeks that August nothing happened; then someone sitting far away behind a desk, and wishing doubtless to appear active, began to initiate these patrols. The day came when they picked on me. My Platoon Sergeant, Tubby Henderson, my soldier servant, Guardsman Bleakley, and I were to make a reconnaissance patrol in order to locate the enemy position. We set off in gym shoes, faces blacked, at dusk, armed with an assortment of offensive weapons. The night came still and moonlit, the face of the desert shining dully, like old bones. We marched, stumbling not infrequently, on a compass bearing for about 10 miles by my reckoning. The great ribs and folds of the escarpment loomed ever closer. If the map was accurate we had to be near the enemy. Nothing to be seen. On we go another mile or more. The ground grew steeper. Still nothing. We shuffled upwards losing a heartbeat every time a pebble rolled. Gradually there came upon me a creepy and indefinable certainty that we were not alone. Yet still no sign.

Just above us was the outline of yet another rock-strewn ridge. I signalled to climb on and as I did so looked up and saw an arm, silhouetted against the sky, in the act of clipping a magazine on to a machine gun. We froze. A second later a long burst shattered the silence. It was not aimed at us or we should have been blown to bits. The gun was laid on what was called a "fixed line", covering a narrow arc on a likely route of approach by night, and clamped there. The noise was deafening; streams of tracer shot far into the night, too far to be any threat to us. Presently on either side of us more machine guns opened up. Wild shouting in the distance, then the crump of a mortar shell behind us.

Sergeant Henderson whispered hoarsely in my ear, "Shall I throw a grenade?"

I said, "No." We had to get back with the news. That was supposed to be our objective.

I agonize over this decision even today. I thought that, in spite of this magnificent display, no one had yet seen us; if we exploded grenades they surely would and escape seemed problematic to say the least; thus no report on the enemy positions. The heroic thing would have been to throw it and quite probably wipe out a machine-gun crew. I was probably wrong. Tubby Henderson, with whom I'm happy to say I am still in touch, luckily can't remember what he thought at the time. Had he thrown the thing we might all have got a medal, or we might all have met our Maker then and there. Anyway, I chose caution and, after a minute or two to get a bearing on the proceedings, we ran for it.

To my amazement our enemies, Italians surely, continued their pre-set pyrotechnics. We leapt and tumbled down the slope and ran. The night sky was full of lead; great looping streamers criss-crossed above us and on either hand; nothing came very near. Then, as we pelted away, I heard the unmistakable and unwelcome sound of field guns. Shells whispered over us and crumped in the distance on our path back to our lines. I felt sure we must be running through a minefield but if so we were lucky. The shells fell nearer, but we were spared.

Exhausted and well after dawn, we staggered unchallenged into our own positions, to everyone's amazement. We had been given up for dead and no wonder. Seen from the east the entire enemy front from the escarpment to the sea had opened up with everything they had and kept it up for half an hour. We must have cost the Axis a great deal of money if nothing else and at least anybody seriously interested in our doings no longer had any doubt about where the enemy front line was located.

Some weeks later Right Flank Company was switched to the saltmarsh and the inner of the two coastal ridges.

As night fell on 14 September, from my platoon headquarters under the ridge I thought I heard the distant throb of engines. Many engines. Could it be the wind? The ominous rumbling rose and fell above the great escarpment whose distant outline we could still just make out. We were connected by telephone cable to our Company Headquarters some seven miles behind us. I reported to McRae. His voice crackled back.

"Nonsense, it's the sea."

I telephoned Johnny Critchley who commanded the next platoon to the seaward ridge.

"Do you hear a noise?"

"Yeah, sure do," came his cheerful Canadian accent.

"McRae says it's the sea."

"First time I ever heard the sea change gear," replied Johnny.

It turned out to be a reconnaissance in force led by Rommel himself with the 21st Panzer Division in attendance, moving along the top of the escarpment.

Next morning, soon after dawn, they started to shell us. From the fall of shot they were unsure where our positions lay, but half an hour later we, that is myself, Tubby Henderson and Bleakley, a dour but faithful Lancastrian heard the chatter of a Bren gun and small arms fire along the ridge ahead of us. I again telephoned McRae whose faith in the marine theory seemed to have evaporated.

"My forward section is under attack, I'm going up there."

"Stay where you are," he said.

I had told my lads I would join them if anything happened, so I put down the telephone and ran along the ridge with Bleakley. It was a ten minute scramble to reach them. We crossed to the south side and ran crouching along the edge of the saltmarsh. The firing had stopped. Now I could see the heads of the men in the section above the parapet of their little trench. They were signalling us to get down. We did so just in time. A light machine gun opened on us from a few yards above on the ridge. There was an abandoned petrol tin some three feet from my head and I watched it jumping as the bullets cut through it. When the firing stopped we ran for the trench. I made it, but poor Bleakley didn't. He fell immediately, shot in the back. I tumbled into the trench to see my Section Commander, my friend Sergeant Todd, propped against the parapet, a bullet through his head. His corporal had a jagged gash through his tin hat. The enemy were above and behind us, so we were effectively pinned. Presently we saw some of them running back over a fold in the ridge and opened up on them without hitting anything as far as I could see. When they had gone I went back to Bleakley who was conscious and in shock. I decided to try to get a carrier, a small lightly armoured vehicle of which we had several in the battalion, to pick him up.

As I dodged along the ridge I must have been visible to the enemy observation post on the escarpment some miles distant and gave them some interesting target practice. Three thumps in the distance and the whispering flight of the shells. I lie flat. The whispering swells to a roar and three shells burst fairly close. I run on fifty yards. Three more thumps, but all was well. I was, after all, a very small target.

We got Bleakley out and later that evening came the order to withdraw to Sidi Barrani.

For some reason this massive enemy foray came to nothing; they turned back next day, 15 September, instead of invading Egypt, to everyone's relief. The option was surely open to Rommel.

The unexpected success of the patrol brought misfortune on our heads; devising these expeditions became a popular pastime in Cairo. My friends and I were sent traipsing around the desert at night to discover if anyone was sitting on such and such a trig point, hill or ridge. Mostly they were not, but the ambitions of the patrol-mongers grew unabated. We were propelled on fighting patrols to attack enemy posts and I was ordered to prepare a dozen men for one of these useless provocations. We were supposed to advance along the beach until we bumped into the enemy and then charge them. I knew the ground and had the deepest misgivings. Then the Company was relieved and this dubious assignment transferred to John Bowes Lyon of F company. John, nephew of Queen Elizabeth, was a favourite with all of us, a charming aesthete. Even in the desert his toilette was a most elaborate affair with bottles of aftershave and lotion of every description set out on a plank by his adoring soldier servant, Guardsman Pearson. The Battalion still buzzed with stories of his escapades before the war. John had been a wild one.

He arrived in my position the morning of the scheduled patrol full of enthusiasm which I did my best to quench. I showed him where he could lay up on the distant ridge and advised that he go no further until he was quite certain where the opposition was. That night, 18 September, he disappeared into the gathering dusk, never to return. He had led his men straight along the beach, where they bumped into an enemy post. They were Germans, alert and waiting. John charged forward armed only with his pistol and a hand grenade. He was, of course, riddled at short range. They had to drag Guardsman Pearson away. Months later the Battalion found his grave. The Germans had identified him. It was all written on the little cross they had made.

At the end of September the Battalion was relieved and I reaped a splendid dividend. I was sent for a week as a patrol instructor to a South African battalion, the 2nd Transvaal Scottish, who were new to the desert. I had a hilarious time with them. I don't know what they learned from me but I picked up a smattering of their lilting Afrikaans song, bits of which have stayed with me to this day. It was a good exchange.

The Battalion became great friends with these South Africans and presently a day of Highland games was held between us at El Daba. The South Africans won every event with the single exception of the piping, for which, as I remember, we provided the judges.

On 18 November the great operation known as "Crusader" began. The Desert Force had metamorphosed into 8th Army. Most of the infantry, supported by First Army Tank Brigade, were to comprise 13 Corps, under General Godwin-Austen, while the armoured and mobile forces, including 4th Armoured Brigade, made up 30 Corps under General Willoughby Norrie.

In our new role as a motor battalion we were supposed to protect the supply columns of 4th Armoured Brigade, part of the 7th Armoured Division which now disposed of 150 tanks. These were light American Stuart tanks known for some reason as "Honeys". In contrast to our own they at least seemed mechanically sound and went very fast across the desert, but they were still armed only with a 37mm gun which was unlikely to inconvenience the German Panzers unless at the closest range.

The object of "Crusader", we were told, was to relieve the garrison at Tobruk and drive the Afrika Korps out of North Africa. After an uneventful advance of about 50 miles towards Sidi Rezegh we came under shell fire. We had been accompanied until then by two cheerful and voluble American instructors sent to 4th Armoured Brigade in order to teach them how to work the "Honeys". A shell fell fairly near us and the top sergeants took an instant decision that their job had been accomplished, described a definitive U-turn and were seen no more.

We climbed on to the tops of our vehicles and gazed into the distance, vainly seeking to establish who was shooting at whom. Fresh orders came to dig in. It seemed we had bumped at last into one of the two dreaded Panzer Divisions. It turned out to be a battle group comprising 5th Tank Regiment of 21st Panzer, supported by field artillery and an infantry regiment.

The little Honey tanks sped past us, each in its own billowing cloud of dust, one young officer blowing a hunting horn and waving an imaginary whip. Then far away on the top of a long uneven ridge we could just make out the sinister black shapes of the Panzers, like squat beetles occasionally spitting a small twinkling flame, as the horde of little tanks came at them. The effect was devastating. One after another the Honeys were struck. There would be a flash and then a slow oily cloud of black smoke rising and drifting with the wind. Somehow the cavalry of 4th Armoured Brigade managed to destroy some 20 mighty Panzers by driving virtually against them. They fought until well after dark; their own losses were horrendous. We had watched them picked off like driven partridges.

There could no longer be any doubt that our armour was hopelessly outgunned. The only effective weapon we had against the German Mark III and Mark IV Panzers was our faithful 25-pounder field gun firing over open sights. It did nothing for morale. Frustration and resentment grew against those who had sent us into battle so ill equipped. It was a scene I could not forget and years later as I sat through defence debates in the House of Commons listening to our Labour opponents making their regular and repeated case for defence cuts, I remembered those little tanks broken and blazing, with the charred bodies inside.

The "Crusader" battle swung backwards and forwards. The Battalion was suddenly ordered to support Armstrong's 5th South African Brigade which was dug in three miles south of the Sidi Rezegh escarpment and expecting attack. They didn't have to wait long. There was no time to dig trenches. We crouched among our vehicles in foot-deep scoops in the ground. In the far distance with my field glasses I could make out a billowing cloud of dust to the south, and through the mirage a column of tanks and transport. A South African gunner officer came up to me.

"What do you make that lot out to be, man?"

"Germans," I said.

"That's what I think but we've been told they're ours." This discussion ended with the arrival of the first German shells. In fact this was the whole of 15 Panzer Division under General Cruewell, supported by the Italian Ariete Armoured Division. One by one our own armoured cars, part of the reconnaissance screen ahead of us, gradually withdrew through our positions, always a bad sign.

The next hour was the most unpleasant I think any of us who survived it had yet experienced. A grizzled South African sergeant told me subsequently that it was like what he remembered from World War I. All was confusion, dust and lead. The German tanks came right through us. A good many were destroyed by the admirable South African gunners but the weight of the attack swept on. In the thick of it McRae appeared in his pick-up truck shouting about a counter-attack. Upon whom or in which direction was unclear, but since he disappeared into the melée as quickly as he had come there was not much I felt I could do about it. With dusk came a lull; most of the South African guns nearby were out of action. I told our sections to follow and drove back through burning vehicles belonging to both sides. After half a mile or so we came upon remnants of G Company together with "Shrimp" Coghill, their bland and ever placid commander. We decided to make a defensive position there and sit it out for the night. Shrimp had a radio and soon we were told to join up with Battalion Headquarters not far away.

It was days before the Battalion collected itself and during this time we drove, as it seemed, aimlessly in a gradually swelling column consisting of fragments from various units, back and forth across the desert. On the way we scooped up an enormous armoured headquarters vehicle containing a Brigadier complete with his staff. He had no idea what had happened to his brigade. At one moment a German petrol tanker joined the column and it was a surprisingly long time before either we or its crew noticed the mistake. It was during this intermission that the apt phrase "swanning around" was coined and seems to have passed into the language.

The Germans were in comparable confusion. Without telling either General Cruewell or von Ravenstein, commanding 21 Panzer, Rommel highjacked a tank regiment together with as much of the Afrika Korps as he could collect and made for the Egyptian frontier. It was a bold if somewhat desperate move. He now threatened the supply bases upon which 8th Army entirely depended.

Meantime, though we didn't know it, Cunningham, whose nerve seems to have gone, sent for Auchinleck in order to explain why he thought retreat was inevitable. The "Auk" overruled him. Soon after this Cunningham was replaced by General Ritchie.

The British situation was critical, but thanks to the determination of the New Zealand Division, supported by 13 Corps, the battle continued on and about Sidi Rezegh and El Adem. Rommel's supply position became impossible and he was forced to retreat.

Order and counter order. The gallant New Zealanders were eventually driven off Sidi Rezegh leaving their field hospital, full of casualties, behind. Who should suddenly appear there but Rommel who carried out a rapid inspection, asked if anything was needed and promised to send further medical supplies to the New Zealand doctor. I don't know if they ever arrived, but there was no doubt of his good intent.

22 Guards Brigade was now sent to retake the airfield at El Adem at dawn on 29 November.

The Battalion's objective was again Sidi Rezegh. This had been the centre of the battle so far, originally captured by 4th Armoured Brigade, retaken by 15th Panzer Division and retaken again by the New Zealanders on their march to relieve Tobruk. The situation there was quite unclear and we did not know what to expect.

We advanced across the airfield in open order. Fighting had been vicious here and the 60th Rifles in particular had lost heavily in a gallant action a few days before.

I thought I heard an aircraft engine. German fighters were active in the area. Simultaneously I noticed a figure lying prone nearby; instinctively I crouched, looking for the plane. The noise died away but the figure didn't move. It was a sergeant in the 60th, a bullet through his head.

We crept on westwards in among some sangars, rough stone and sand defence works. Everywhere signs of flight and abandon. All was eerily still, yet somehow the air still reeked of the smell and clamour of battle. The order came to halt and brew up for breakfast. Our 15 cwt trucks arrived and the men set to digging and clattering cans and mess tins. Through my field glasses I could see an odd shape on the near horizon. I went to check. It was a two-pounder anti-tank gun, the barrels sloughed sideways, the shield riddled with bullet holes. Slumped over the breech was the dead gunner. The body was as stiff as a board; he could only have been dead a few hours: a New Zealander. The yellow-grey face looked absurdly young. I found a wallet with his paybook and went back to my Company to organize his burial. In the paybook were pictures of his smiling parents, outside a farmhouse, and a girl.

A livid sky began to light up the grim still life of Sidi Rezegh; somewhere to the west I heard the rumble of gunfire; vehicles were moving a mile or more away, their dust clouds lit by the rising sun. I couldn't make them out.

Operation "Crusader" was approaching its unexpected end. Further attacks by the Afrika Korps were not particularly successful, but when 7th Armoured Division under General "Strafer" Gott advanced again towards Mechili on 19 December Rommel considered he was about to be enveloped and, in spite of Italian objections, decided to abandon Cyrenaica and to withdraw the Afrika Korps beyond Agedabia. He moved too fast to be caught and Gott's armoured cars entered Benghazi unopposed on 23 December. A few days later the Battalion found itself digging in on the sand dunes and ridges by the sea facing south towards the Arab village of Agedabia. The Italians and the Afrika Korps occupied a position at El Agheila on a ridge on the opposite side of the village. Rommel's communications were now telescoped and his supply problems greatly reduced. For the 8th Army the reverse was the case.

After this long and confused battle we were tired, many of the vehicles and much of the equipment in need of repair. The enemy position at El Agheila was certainly strongly held. We were ordered to attack it by night.

Around 8.00 pm. in the evening of 26 December we moved off south along the coast in our trucks. After two or three miles we got out and started to walk. The idea was to creep down the shore until we were well past the enemy frontline and then take them in the flank from the west. Whoever devised this plan had decided to bombard the enemy positions with our 25 pounders and thus effectively to abandon surprise, that not wholly insignificant principle of war.

For some five miles this march by stealth continued. It was viciously cold, column upon column shuffling through the mud and dust in the moonless gloom. No one spoke and only the occasional ring of steel on stone or the clatter of accoutrements marked our passing along the desert shore. To our right hand loomed the darkness of the sea, the heft and slap of waves hissing on the sand. At last we wheeled inland and stumbled on through wind and sleet over rock and scrub. The land lifted in a series of stony ridges. Then we heard the first distant thudding of our guns and the bursts of the strike ahead of us. Crouching instinctively, we followed the path of the barrage and the singing flight of steel and rock. I felt deeply grateful we did not have to face our own 25 pounders.

The inferno moved slowly but steadily across the ridges; all ranks carried rifles, bayonets fixed. At any moment surely we should be among them. Then abruptly the barrage ceased and there was only the noise of our boots. Far behind us sweating gunners, amid the reek of cordite, must be straining their ears for the sounds of battle. For us only muffled curses, the clink and crunch of our advance towards a vanished enemy.

On we go into the first hint of this deceitful dawn, with the desert horizon picked out in rose and ochre, jerking shadows like the ghosts of men groping forward. Then they see us. From away to our right come a few tentative rifle shots, a burst from a light machine gun. The entire battalion was wandering across empty desert in front of a strong position whose defenders had been well and truly woken up by our useless barrage. Only the extreme right hand platoon of my Company under John Clarke bumped into the opposition and, together with McRae and his Company HQ, performed prodigies that morning and took a number of prisoners, proof of the blow we could have struck if surprise had not been sacrificed and the information on which this plan was based had proved anywhere near accurate. Instead of the daft enterprises on which we had been despatched at Sollum surely this was a case when reconnaissance patrolling would have paid.

We struggled back to our positions near Agedabia, under heavy fire while we were still in range. Johnny Critchley, our tough and cheerful Canadian comrade, was killed. My friend Ian Weston-Smith wounded, about 30 casualties in all. It had been a sad morning, but nevertheless McRae and Clarke on the extreme right wing of the battalion had taken the same number of prisoners and killed a fair number as well. Both were subsequently decorated.

Bitter cold, rain and sand storms, the desert at its worst. We hung about north of Agedabia with nothing to defend ourselves with but our small arms. Field guns and anti-tank guns had all been taken away to the south. On 21 January when our water cart made its daily journey to the well in the village it was greeted by three German 8-wheeler armoured cars.* It beat a hasty retreat. The battalion in turn was ordered back. There followed a general helter skelter retreat known locally as the "Msus stakes" because there was a temporary halt on the perimeter of a depression of that name in which were located Headquarters 30 Corps and supply dumps of almost everything. All was confusion and the Battalion had unquestionably done well to maintain its cohesion. Most units had been scattered.

We were ordered to hold the rim of this depression. I happened to be the right-hand platoon of the Battalion. Having established some sort of defensive position, I walked off westward into the gathering dusk to see whether I could locate the 60th Rifles who were supposed to be somewhere near us. Dimly I made out a single figure walking towards me. The situation was to say the least uncertain. I drew my revolver. Out of the gloom came James Lees, my best friend at Eton, with whose family I had often stayed in Dorset during the holidays. I had no idea he was in the desert. We repaired hastily to my truck where I had cached a half bottle of whisky. Together we listened to the low rumble of guns to the south and east, watched the dim flashes over the skyline and the long arcs of tracer shells. But no one bothered us and we had much to talk about. I saw James only once more, in Cairo, before he was killed on a raiding party in Yugoslavia.

We did not know it but this retreat caused almost total confusion in our high command. Auchinleck bullied Ritchie. Ritchie issued order and counter-order. Godwen-Austen of 30 Corps, supported by other commanders, sent blunt explanations why what was ordered was impractical. He won his point and immediately resigned his command. Churchill meanwhile was advocating the recapture of Cyrenaica!

Rommel, nimble as ever, had appreciated the weakness of 8th Army's supply position and, reinforced to a strength of 84 German tanks, struck while the going was good and without telling his superiors, who were advocating caution. He made a sorry mess of our 1st Armoured Division, just arrived and inexperienced, and this precipitated further retreat.

We wound up eventually, not far from the start point of Operation "Crusader" in what was known as the Gazala line.

From February to April the lines of battle were more or less static between the Gazala positions stretching from the Free French at Bir Hacheim in the

* This wing of the German counterattack was led towards Agedabia by Rommel himself.

south to Tobruk on the sea. The Germans and Italians stopped on a line roughly north-south from Tmimi to Segnali. This left an extensive no-man's-land some fifty miles broad or more.

Preparations were already in hand to recapture Cyrenaica. Churchill, worried about the threat to Malta, besought Auchinleck to advance the date for this initiative in order to cover the sea approaches. They were still arguing about it when Rommel struck again in May.

Meantime, 201 Guards Brigade, our new title, prepared an elaborate defensive box in the Gazala line at a location known as "Knightsbridge", with the Battalion, somewhat isolated, in its own box on Rigel Ridge.

We were despatched by companies or platoons on what were known as the "Jock" columns, an idea generated by General Jock Campbell with the object of harassing the enemy. The column would consist of a troop or battery of twenty-five pounders with a detachment of motor infantry – that is to say us – with, if we were lucky, an armoured car or two. We would lumber off at dawn from our leaguer with the gunner's observation post (O.P.) truck well in front looking for targets. If he found one it was gun trails down, a sighting shot and then several rounds "gunfire". What time we tried to scrape or dig trenches in case of trouble. The noise was tremendous, the effect on the battle negligible, so far as I could see, and the trouble fairly frequent. We were attacked by air or sometimes chased off by German armour. Perhaps we upset their breakfast.

Jock Campbell was a man of frenetic action. He had been about to take command of 7th Armoured Division when he was killed in a staff car crash. My friend Roy Farran, his ADC and later of SAS fame, was driving. The desert coast road of potholed tarmac was covered in ridges of blown sand. The general kept ordering Roy to go faster. They hit a sand ridge and turned over. It took Roy a long time to get over this, but the crash was certainly not his fault.

Before one of these expeditions, this time with the whole battalion, we were told the objective was to distract the Luftwaffe because of an approaching Malta Convoy. In plain language this meant get ourselves bombed. We duly obliged.

On the return journey from this exercise I was appointed Battalion Navigator. This had to be done by dead reckoning with an oil compass. You took a bearing on some desert feature and then checked the direction constantly while standing up in your pick-up truck on the move. As far as I could see, on either hand, sped the vehicles of the Battalion and our accompanying guns each followed by feathers of billowing sand and dust. It seemed an awesome responsibility and I was intensely relieved when we fetched up after 70 miles at exactly the same group of rocks we had left several days before.

Apart from these occasional expeditions, life settled down in the Gazala line while the Sappers laid acres of mines in front of us. It was here that MacRae struck up an extraordinary friendship with Simon Elwes the painter, who for some short time held a staff appointment with General Lumsden, now commanding 1st Armoured Division. Whenever the General came to our sector Elwes would appear outside the dugout which served as our Company Headquarters, strike an attitude, sweep his fore and aft cap off in a theatrical and singularly unmilitary salute and demand audience. MacRae welcomed him. Much whisky was drunk. It would be impossible to encounter two more utterly different people: the extrovert, uproarious artist whose subsequent love affair with Farida, Queen of Egypt, scandalized Cairo (he didn't last long on Lumsden's staff) and this strange introverted Highland soldier.

It was at this juncture that Alec Ramsay and I learned that David Stirling, also a Scots Guards Officer, was recruiting for his SAS Regiment, then known as L Detachment. We volunteered and were accepted.

It was an exciting prospect; the success of David's attacks on enemy airfields behind the lines was already legendary. But there was another reason. We had both had enough of MacRae. We had served him longer than any other officers in his company.

Admiration of a kind persisted. It always will. John MacRae was a very brave man, but while other Company Commanders offered understanding to their junior officers, MacRae dealt in tension. Charm he had in abundance when he chose to use it, but all too easily it could turn to a morbid sarcasm, and that is hard to live with in the midst of war. Colonel Brian Mayfield, our much beloved Commanding Officer, sympathetic as ever, offered us alternative jobs, but we had made our decision.

From Buqbuq Alec and I got a lift to Cairo where, to my bewildered concern, Alec fell gravely ill. In just a few days his towering 7 foot frame began to buckle. At that time there was no defence against TB and they sent him to hospital in South Africa. It would have been hard indeed to support life in Right Flank Company for so long without his companionship. We laughed, we sang, we cursed a lot and got drunk together. We were as close as two young men at war can be. Indeed he was like an elder brother. I believed he must recover, but on my return from operations two months later, I got a message that he had died. Intelligent, sensitive and brave, this was a happy warrior whose life promised much.

Memory, even of one's friends, dims with the years, yet there are a very few who remain as vivid as ever they were. I hear his voice now, see him walk into the room as if it were yesterday, his face suffused with fun, enquiry and mischief. We laugh again, it seems to me. Perhaps in time, who knows, we will.

———————|———————

3

SAS

"Postern of Fate, the Desert Gate, Disaster's Cavern, Fort of Fear,
The Portal of Baghdad am I, the Doorway of Diarbekir."

"Pass not beneath, O Caravan, or pass not singing.
Have you heard that silence where the birds are dead
Yet something pipeth like a bird?"

From "Gates of Damascus" by J. E. Flecker

(Chapters 3 and 4 were compiled from notes made some three months after
the event and somehow survived, in a stained and yellowed typescript.)

My first impression of L Detachment, or the first SAS Regiment as it was
shortly to become, more or less stood the test of time.

Here was an idiosyncratic collection of people, officers and men with the
minimum distinction between them, whose only bond seemed to be a
reflection of their extraordinary commander's personality. It was all very
different from the enveloping tribal hierarchy of the battalion.

Six foot five inches in his desert boots with a slight stoop, an eager open
face with beetling eyebrows beneath a battered service dress cap, David
Stirling radiated urgency and confidence. His eyes carried a penetrating
directness and a hint of impish humour. Here was no welcome for affectation.
His expression could shift with bewildering suddenness from an intense
almost puzzled concentration, rather like a schoolboy who ought to know the
answer, to one of uproarious irreverence. This change of mood often followed
some reference to the doings and denizens of GHQ whom he held in ribald
and more or less permanent contempt.

It was clear why David could never have settled into regimental duty.
Administration bored him and was left in other capable hands. Ruthless he
was and needed to be. He demanded absolute loyalty and adherence to his
own concept of discipline, yet one always sensed an underlying kindness and

humanity. It was not difficult to respond to him. Here was an inspired and merry warrior whose hour had come.

About him was a hardened group of those who had survived his first six months of operations. Paddy Mayne, a huge soft-spoken Ulsterman, capped several times for Ireland as a Rugby forward whose tally of enemy aircraft was already legendary;* Bill Fraser an ever cheerful Highland officer and accomplished saboteur. Bill Cumper, engineer officer, and manufacturer of bombs; Johnny Cooper, Pat Smiley, Bob Bennett, about twenty-five in all, proud veterans of L Detachment.

Among recent recruits was Fitzroy MacLean, soon to become famous as Head of Churchill's mission to Tito, and after the war as Member of Parliament, author and much travelled authority on Central Asia and Russia. Fitzroy had been a Parliamentary candidate already, not so much from political ambition, rather because it was the only route by which he could escape from the Foreign Office into the Army.

Then there was George Jellicoe, whose spectacular raid on the Cretan air base had already cost the Luftwaffe twenty-one planes and whose later adventures with David Sutherland in the Special Boat Section (merged with the SAS) among the Dodecanese islands and in the Aegean cost the Axis a heavy toll in casualties, destruction and morale.

He, David and Carol Mather of the Welsh Guards, years later my colleague in the House of Commons, had been with Stirling in the Commando Brigade sent out to the Middle East in 1941 and subsequently disbanded. Mercifully they all survived – and friends they remain – whose subsequent achievements stand as vivid testimony, and whose laughter and companionship have enhanced my life ever since.

The base of L Detachment lay in a tented camp back at Kabrit on the Bitter Lakes.

The SAS was David Stirling's brainchild and he led it with matchless bravery and imagination. The war spawned many good ideas but I can think of no enterprise pursued against all the odds which proved more astonishingly successful. He had to cheat his way into Headquarters Middle East in order to sell it to the Director of Military Operations. His first operation was a disaster. Men and equipment were given grudgingly; even his eventual success bred jealousy rather than gratitude but in the end he could not be denied.

There was a striking resemblance between Rommel's approach to warfare

---

* Paddy's exploits have been properly recorded in a biography published after his death in a motor accident in 1970, *Lieutenant-Colonel Paddy Blair Mayne – Rogue Warrior of the S.A.S.*, by Roy Bradford and Martin Dillon, John Murray, 1987.

and David's. Both were superb opportunists. Both believed in high risks and both led from the front. So far as the comparison could be stretched, Rommel used his formations as David did his squadrons. I think they would have got on well together.

Like all good ideas David's original concept was simple. The Sahara is a large place, airfields are difficult to guard so let us convey ourselves behind the enemy lines, sneak on to the dispersal area and blow up his aircraft with home-made bombs: blobs of plastic, as it happened, mixed with magnesium filings placed in a linen ration bag with a simple time pencil stuck in the top. The problem was how to contrive the journey. Parachuting seemed the answer, but the technology was still in its infancy in the Middle East. Little help or advice was available and the first two unfortunate volunteers to jump at Kabrit were killed. Shaken but undaunted, David fitted a new shackle to the strong point in the old Bombay bomber, took off again and jumped himself. This time it worked. But parachuting had no future in the Western Desert. The wind, the vastness and the night scattered David's men on this first operation beyond contact or cohesion. Only David and about 25 returned safe, rescued by Jake Easonsmith's patrol of the Long Range Desert Group. David Lloyd Owen, who commanded the Yeomanry patrol, witnessed their arrival and it was he who subsequently persuaded Stirling it was both safer and more practical to go by truck with a Long Range Desert Group patrol acting as navigator and taxi.

Thus, with the essential support of the LRDG, a tiny group of men enjoyed unparalleled operational success. The number of aircraft destroyed well exceeded the number dealt with by the RAF. The Germans were forced eventually to consign their infantry battalions resting from the Front, together with Italian units, to guard the perimeters against these Will o' the Wisp raiders. Entry by stealth thus became more difficult. Greater strength in men and equipment seemed necessary and this led to the second recruiting campaign to which Alec and I had responded.

Life at Kabrit was animated to say the least. Together with other newcomers, I did my parachute training, which at that time consisted of jumping off the back of a moving lorry. Having survived this we were taken up in the Bombay bomber for our first descent. There was a hole like a large funnelled loo in the centre of the fuselage. When it was your turn you had to sit bolt upright on the edge, your feet dangling in space, then launch yourself forward into the void without looking down. If you so much as glanced towards the ground you were certain to bash your head on the rim as you went out. This took a lot of self control and those who failed were apt to land very sore, if not half conscious.

I shared these experiences with George and Carol. Paddy was also at

Kabrit. I held him in some awe. He had an occasional weakness for the whisky and the trouble was that his bouts led to outbursts of truly berserk proportions.

Soon after my arrival he went to Cairo for a few days' leave. On the second day there was a call to George, who was in charge, from none other than the Provost Marshal.

"Did we know a Major Mayne?"

George owned up, expecting the worst.

"Well, you'd better come and see him, he's under arrest."

George sped to Cairo where he found a dishevelled and deeply penitent Paddy incarcerated in the Provost's lock up. It seems he had had a difference of opinion with some Australians in a bar. There was nothing surprising in this on either side. The astonishing part of the affair was the extent of the damages, both to the Australians and to the furniture. Six stout Aussies had been laid out cold and the list of broken chairs, tables and other missiles read like a sales catalogue. The Greek proprietor of the bar had to close and was understandably hysterical. A Court Martial loomed but before it had time to loom any nearer George hurried to see the Director of Military Operations.

The temporary incommoding of six gallant Australians and the complete destruction of a Greek café was a serious matter; but the destruction of enemy aircraft was even more serious. Paddy was already responsible for more than fifty of these. The DOM took a view based on strict wartime priorities and Paddy was spirited away in a jeep. What happened about the Australians I never learned.

The day came when we were summoned to Cairo for a final briefing before departure on our first jeep-borne operations. By this time we owned a train of supply vehicles which had been assembled on the quay at Port Said, such was the priority afforded to the SAS.

We also had our own navigators: Mike Sadler, seconded from the LRDG, and Corporal Johnny Cooper, ex-Scots Guards, David's driver, minder and right hand man.*

Sadler's military career was unusual to say the least. At the outbreak of war he was learning farming in Rhodesia so joined the Rhodesian Army. He soon made sergeant but was reduced to the ranks by some pompous officer for allowing his men to stand to in gym shoes instead of boots. (He argues they got there quicker). Later he was commissioned "in the field" by David, or to be precise "in Cairo". David simply said, "I want you to be an officer, Mike; go and get yourself some pips". Mike found some in a bazaar and

* Lieut. Col. John Murdoch Cooper, MBE, DCM, author of *One of the Originals – The story of a founder member of the S.A.S.*

established himself as a lieutenant. All was well until he returned to Cairo after David's capture and enquired about his pay. GHQ had not caught up with this rapid advance in rank and its author was no longer available. But in the end all was resolved. There is no doubt Mike's record helped.

The briefing was to take place in David's brother Peter Stirling's flat in Garden City. Peter was Second Secretary at the British Embassy at the time and his apartment was a focal point in many respects for officers in the Scots Guards and the SAS.

It was a surprising scene that morning. In one corner of the large and somewhat battered drawing room a group of SAS officers were pouring over a large-scale map of the western desert clearly marked "Top Secret", while George Jellicoe described to them the route they were to take behind the enemy lines. Across the room an animated drink party was in progress, consisting mainly of people going to Gezireh races in the afternoon. It included several pretty girls, and the "va et viens" between the two groups added much spice to the proceedings. The briefing was late, so I subsequently learnt, because Mohammed or "Mo" as Peter's incomparable sufragi or butler was universally known, had hidden the secret maps in the bathroom in a praiseworthy if vain attempt to tidy the place up.

The SAS was still essentially an amateur army and security a constant hazard. Indeed, one prominent personality and fairly useless officer who had infiltrated himself into the unit was taken on a hazardous reconnaissance behind the lines simply because it was reckoned he could do less damage to the cause there than by chattering in Cairo.

While the briefing continued David's army was assembling in the street outside: a line of some 20 jeeps bristling with Browning machine guns, and their supporting 30cwt trucks. Even in wartime Cairo such a concentration of armament was an unusual sight, particularly outside the British Embassy which lay immediately opposite. The Egyptian police on guard were visibly disturbed.

In early afternoon of 2 July the consultations broke up and we dispersed, some to the races, the rest of us to our date with the desert.

Because of the heavy traffic on the Cairo/Alexandria road we were routed through the Delta. The Front, by this time, lay only forty miles along the coast from Alexandria and the build up for the battle of El Alamein continued along the desert road by day and night. We were to pass through the crowded Boulak quarter, over Zamalek island and then south through the cultivation. Somewhere in the labyrinth of the Boulak the convoy ground to a halt. The streets had become progressively narrower as we neared the embankment of the Nile, and the crowds ever more pressing. We were surrounded by a river of humanity, camels, donkeys and little carts, on either side the pitiable dwellings of the poor of Cairo, rickety balconies, threadbare rags of linen hanging in rows like the tattered flags on Bedouin shrines. The gutters ran with filth. To my European ear the constant babble of Arabic had a quality of sustained hysteria. It was punctuated by the bellowing of camels, the honk of ancient motor horns and the barking of dogs. Half-starved and mangy dogs ran everywhere. I got out of the jeep to see what was causing the hold up and was instantly surrounded by a crowd of children and adults, hands thrust towards me.

"Backsheesh, Backsheesh," they whined helplessly. One move to give alms and I knew I would be overwhelmed. I shook my head, trying to avoid their eyes, but the people stood their ground, thrust against each other, gazing listlessly, lips parted, features distorted by disease and malnutrition, flies crawling unheeded about their half-seeing eyes. They picked and scratched and gaped. Beyond pride, beyond even resentment, they represented shameless animal want like the furtive curs running between their feet. What was it to them who marched across their land, made war, lived or died? It had always been thus. I glanced at the men on the jeeps; like me they were trying to ignore the misery about them, their faces a mixture of disgust and pity.

Suddenly I was aware of a small man in shabby European clothes standing in front of me. I hadn't seen him approach. I watched him put a cigarette between his lips, then without looking up he spoke to me in excellent English.

"Have you got a light?"

Relieved perhaps, in the middle of this foetid poverty to be able to grant some service, I reached for my lighter and struck it. The man mumbled his thanks and stuck the cigarette end forward. As he did so he looked up sharply; for an instant I saw a wizened nut-brown monkey's face, the eyes fixed and squinting, not at mine but at something above my forehead. Then the small figure was gone, melted as suddenly as he had come into the crowd. As he disappeared I had the sudden conviction I had been tricked, but what was it? The man had wanted something more than a light. Then it hit me. He had looked not at my face at all but at my cap star. The British soldier, unlike most of his foes, carried the identity of his unit proudly, if unwisely, displayed in his cap. That was it.

For a second I contemplated pursuit. Impossible; in any case the identification of my cap star would be of no use to the little spy. I wore the Scots Guards' badge. The SAS had not yet designed their Winged Dagger. But of his purpose I had no doubt. The scene is vivid still. I reported it of course, but no one took much notice; there were weightier matters afoot.

Presently engines revved, the blockage dissolved and the convoy eased slowly forward over the Boulak bridge, through the plush suburban streets of the island and over the little Zamalek bridge. Once over the Nile the human tide closed about us again, seeming at moments to be thrust aside like a bow wave by the bonnets of the jeeps and trucks, the gabble rising to a crescendo as we passed.

Gradually the streets turned into simple tracks. The ramshackle houses gave way to mud brick hovels interspersed with date palms, pomegranates and prickly pears. Then we were in the cultivation, vegetable crops alternating with rice and cotton fields, criss-crossed by irrigation canals carrying the life-giving waters of the Nile. We drove past lines of eucalyptus, acacia and groups of tall stately date palms. High overhead wheeled the kites, watching for death and unlikely to be disappointed.

We passed through several villages causing much screeching and running of children, barking of dogs and a rout of scrawny chickens. A mile after the village of Fattach the burgeoning black soil began to fail and the smells of wet earth, rotting vegetation and dried dung faded. Dust came on the wind. For a while patches of cultivation persisted, screened by breaks of sticks and blackened palm fronds struggling to hold back the sand. Then, abruptly, the track ceased. Ahead lay the desert. In the distance we could see a line of telegraph poles along the Cairo/Alexandria road, at right angles to our route; beyond, like black beetles, passed the trucks, bren carriers, tank transporters and water wagons of the 8th Army's supply line silhouetted against the westering sun.

Our business awaited us more than 200 miles to the west of this road and we must pass along the rim of the great Qattara Depression to the south of the southernmost patrols of Rommel's armies.

The passage through our lines was uneventful. We were escorted by the Military Police. Three days later, guided by Robin Gurdon of the Long Range Desert Group, we made a pinpoint rendezvous with the Guards Patrol of the LRDG. Waiting for us there was my friend Alistair Timpson, also from the Second Battalion, Scots Guards, who was in command. He had already found a likely area for us to hide in. We were now some 60 miles south of the coast and around 150 miles behind the German lines, to the west of the track from Mersa Matruh to Siwa Oasis which in better days had carried a telephone line, now looped disconsolately between broken poles. The desert climbed gently westward and upward to a series of ridges some 30 or 40 feet high, under any of which it would certainly be possible to conceal a vehicle.

David selected a place and we drove along beneath, looking for suitable holes and crannies to hide in. This place, an infinitesimal crease in the vast dead face of the Western Sahara was to be our refuge for the next two months.

The raids began. Our target was the coast road, Rommel's main line of communication along which crawled his supplies day and night towards El Alamein.

My first expedition was far from successful. George Jellicoe, Carol Mather and I were despatched in three jeeps with two gunners each aboard to attack the road and anything else we came across in a general area some thirty miles behind the German/Italian lines.

We set off full of high intent at about midday aiming to reach the great escarpment before dark, lie up until it was safe and then descend towards the action. We had been warned that, because of our previous activities, a flight of Italian Macchi fighters regularly patrolled the escarpment in the evening.

As the sun began to drop we were nearing the edge. George called a halt. The jeeps were on a particularly exposed plateau. About half a mile distant was a patch of camel scrub which could serve us well until dark came. We decided to make for it. Half-way there I spotted three menacing shapes weaving and diving above what must be the edge of the escarpment in front of us. We stopped, hoping against hope. Hope failed. The planes roared over us in triumph, wheeled and came in to attack. We had time to get about 20 yards from the jeeps before they opened up. When they had run out of ammunition my jeep and Carol's were burning fiercely. George had the presence of mind to drive his into a small crevice in a broken ridge some few hundred yards away. We collected ourselves, amazed to find that no one had been hit, and were inspecting the damaged but still mobile jeep when we heard the sound of aircraft engines. Back they came; there were four this time, including a bomber, but before they were above us we had put a good 100 yards between ourselves and the blazing jeeps and lay among the little thorn bushes covered in as much sand as we could scoop over ourselves. Interminably the Italians searched for us while it grew steadily darker. At last they gave up and were gone.

There was nothing to be done about the burning jeeps and it was likely the enemy would send patrols out after us at dawn. George's jeep had been repeatedly hit but miraculously still functioned. There were several bullet holes in the radiator which we plugged up as best we could with plastic explosive taken from our Lewis bombs. There was some uncertainty as to whether it would explode when started. It didn't and the nine of us set off back for the rendezvous 70 miles to the west. Progress was slow; every quarter hour the radiator boiled and we had to open the bonnet and turn the jeep into the wind. Water was, as ever, precious, particularly since our future seemed problematic, so we took it in turns to pee into the radiator. For biological reasons this course was also limited, but somehow that jeep limped back to within a few miles of the rendezvous before it died. By his quick action George had saved us a very long walk, if not indeed our lives.

Ours was not the only adventure during these raids. Mike Sadler, again a sergeant, set off under command of a nerveless officer called Russell. Their objective, like ours, was to destroy transport and any other worthwhile targets in the enemy rear area. Their night approach was more succesful than ours. They managed to sneak in among a lot of German transport and field guns upon which they began discreetly to distribute their Lewis bombs. But at this critical point Russell's jeep sprang a puncture. Moreover, their pump turned out to be broken. Russell, who spoke German well enough, so he claimed, to pass as a Bavarian, decided to try to borrow a pump off the Germans. He told Mike, who couldn't speak German at all, that if he was approached he should simply say, "*Ich Weiss Nicht*". Off he went. Several Germans wandered past, but mercifully Mike was not called on to declare his unspecified and general ignorance. Russell returned complete with pump and the repair was completed. They made off slowly westward when a series of loud bangs disclosed that the Lewis bombs were duly exploding. Russell counted the bangs. In his estimate they had not all gone off and, to Mike's dismay, he decided to go back and investigate. This time, instead of the loan of a tyre pump they were met with machine-gun fire. They turned and fled, eventually returning safe to their RV.

Tragically on another of these early raids Robin Gurdon was killed. His patrol was on its way to attack a target near El Daba when they were spotted by German fighters which attacked repeatedly. Typically Robin had fired back and died in his burning truck. He had been about to join David as second in command and his loss was a grievious blow.

After three weeks of this activity supplies were running low and David decided to return to Cairo to organize the replacement of lost vehicles and replenish food and ammunition. He left with a small party comprising George Jellicoe and Sandy Scratchley, across the Qattara for the sake of speed. They got badly bogged in the salt marsh but made it safely. The main party was to follow, making the best time they could, while a small detachment would be left behind to guard the RV.

There we lived for the next three weeks, Carol Mather, Malcolm Pleydell the SAS doctor and I, like rabbits in a bank, our six or seven vehicles driven into the crevices made by dried water courses in the side of the little cliff and heavily camouflaged with nets and scrub. We had about thirty men with us and a party of Free French, including three officers, Jordan, Martin and Zirnheld. The French detachment had joined us about the same time as I did and were already close friends.

Further down the escarpment and living a somewhat separate life was the New Zealand patrol of the Long Range Desert Group.

All of us had been out in the "blue" for about a month and most were burnt black except for the few unfortunates who stayed bright red. Most wore a pair of shorts, sandals or boots with rubber soles and either bush hats or big khaki handkerchiefs over their heads like the Bedouin. We all had beards. We were a wild-looking lot.

If you climbed the escarpment and looked east towards the enemy lines there was nothing but yellow-brown gravel with grey pebbly patches sparsely covered with the little black bushes of camel scrub. The ground shelved away and visibility was limited. To the west it was the same except that the ground rose gradually to the next ridge some two miles distant. North and south were the bays and promontories of the escarpment stretching into vague featurelessness.

It was blazing hot in the daytime and cold at night. The best moments were at dawn and dusk. There were no flies then and the desert was transformed from minute to minute, drawing pictures in itself with long purple and brown shadows of castles, cliffs and ravines. Everyone cheered up. We cooked our evening meal in dixies placed on the ubiquitous petrol cans with their fires of fuel-soaked sand, a little bully beef mixed with biscuit and dried vegetables. There wasn't much but it was difficult to eat without water and there was not enough water. We made about a mug and a half of tea a day for each man and there was a little drawn every evening and put into the water bottles. The wise ones buried their bottles at night. The water was near iced in the morning and as one always woke up thirsty this was a good moment.

Carol and I lived in a small cave with mosquito nets hung over the entrances. They failed to deter the flies. We sweated and cursed and swotted by day, read and re-read the two tattered novels. The heat dulled one's thoughts and in any case these seldom varied:

"When would the others get back? Would they miss the rendezvous? If something went wrong how long could we last before going back to the Nile Delta?"

Every evening we watched the sun crawl down, a great orange ball, its progress eventually perceptible to the human eye as it dropped below the far escarpment, now turned black, the outline of every rock standing sharp against a livid sky. Slowly the hated thing disappeared, leaving the whole desert bathed in colours so rich, hard and brilliant as to defy the painter's

1. "The third and greatest influence over my childhood was that of my grandmother, Edith Isabella Lumsden" (p.5).

2. "Memories of my mother are misted with sadness" (p.2).

3. Lewis Aloysius MacDonald Hastings: "He strode in and out of our lives like a whirlwind" (p.3).

4. "Later he became... the BBC's principal war reporter" (p.5). A Nazi caricature of my father. Clearly his broadcasts were hurting.

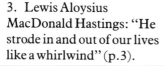

MAJOR HASTINGS

Auch dieser Krieger im Büro weiß stets genau „warum", „wieso" und macht das mittels Kommentar dem wundergläub'gen Leser klar. „Der Nazis Unglück", schreibt er, ist im G...

5. Pitcaple Castle in the 16th century, my grandmother's home (see p.6). Mary Queen of Scots is said to have danced round the tree.

6. Duntreath, home of the Edmonstone family (see p.6).

7. The author in Cairo, 1942.

8. Alec Ramsay, 2nd in command of Right Flank Company (see p.28).

9. John McRae, Company Commander, Right Flank — "had he lived, he might have commanded armies" (p.28).

10. "Johnny Critchley, our tough and cheerful Canadian comrade" (p.40), killed in action at Agedabia.

11. "... my friends David Butter and Ion Calvocoressi" (p.29).

12. The approach of the Khamsin (see p.26).

brush. Now we talked, mostly neither of home nor war but of "Comfort day". This project covered our activities during the first day we should get back to Cairo. It was a wide and wonderful subject. It started with a shave and a Turkish bath, led on through visions of long glasses, iced drinks, exotic restaurants, the air-cooled cinema and thence to the open-air night clubs of Cairo filled with ravishing belly dancers. Our evening ration of rum and lime helped a lot, so did the French. We spent several cheerful evenings by their cave singing the songs of the *Infanterie Coloniale* and listening to André Zirnheld's accounts of his adventures. Clearly French exploitation of Cairo's delights had been more successful than our own.

We posted a lookout all day on a rise above the escarpment and everyone took turns for a long hour gazing through field glasses all around the compass into the shimmering dun-coloured void. Sometimes there would be lizards or black beetles to investigate, or the sentry could walk backwards and forwards to another rock nearby, two minutes there and two minutes back, one minute to search the emptiness. It was too hot to walk much so most of the time the sentry just sat on his little cairn and throbbed in the glare. The others were hidden below and it was like being alone on some alien planet.

At last another small figure would crawl over the ridge and make its way slowly up the slope. The glasses would be exchanged.

"Anything doing?"

"No," and the relief would climb down again to his patch of shade.

Sometimes a plane was heard. There would be a shout of "Aircraft" from the sentry. Everyone lay still under the escarpment and strained to catch the tiny pounding in the distance. These were anxious moments for enemy aircraft were the principal fear as well as the prey of the SAS.

The buzz of flies, the thwack as someone struck at them, occasional voices, otherwise the great silence, thus day followed blazing day.

It was afternoon around 4 o'clock when the sentry came running to our cave.

"There's vehicles in sight, Sir, coming from the east."

"What are they?"

"Can't make them out yet, they are a long way off."

He looked scared, although he knew the column was due. We scrambled up to the top of the escarpment and focused our glasses. Far away in the shimmering mirage which constituted our horizon we could see several little black dots. Their shape kept changing; now some appeared elongated as if reflected in a bent mirror; two would merge into one and then part again. They were certainly moving. We brought the Bren gun onto the escarpment and lay gazing at the little black dots. Sometimes they seemed to be coming nearer, sometimes to stop. The minutes ticked by and then suddenly they emerged from the mirage, quite close and recognizable – jeeps and several 30cwt trucks. It was the column from Cairo.

They had left base three days before: Cairo and the fleshpots, hotels, dinner parties, traffic, trains and teeming humanity. They had pressed through the British lines, the ration dumps, Naafis; hundreds of thousands of men, tents and vehicles; out past TAC Army headquarters, through the divisional lines, to the forward troops and finally the last armoured car patrol. Then to the edge of the Qattara Depression with its stark black cliffs falling 500 feet sheer to a sea of soft sand and salt marsh. West through the rocky broken country with its crags and tors that mark the shores of this prehistoric sea bed. South of the southernmost enemy patrols and then west-north-west across level desert to this tiny stretch of escarpment 130 miles behind the enemy front line where a few ragged beings awaited their arrival. That seemed eminently satisfactory.

The leading jeeps drew ahead, the feather of dust growing larger behind them as they accelerated.

A figure climbed out of the first and strode towards us. Immensely tall with slightly bowed shoulders, beetling eyebrows under a battered cap. David was back and life had returned to the escarpment.

———————|———————

4

A NIGHT TO REMEMBER

We were now a party about 50 strong. Fresh fires flickered up that evening in the failing light. There was much to talk about; three brews of tea with rum and cigarettes afterwards. The Wyndham radio aerial was erected on the escarpment for the evening contact with Cairo. The officers gathered around David, drank some of the precious supply of whisky and pored over the map.

As the fires died the buzz of talk and laughter gradually stopped. Groups broke up and the men went off to their trucks and kit to find soft places for their bed rolls. The glow of cigarette ends faded and there was only the fut-fut-fut of the petrol charging engine to break the silence.

Two days of hurried preparation followed. On the first morning a further column arrived; the heavy section, 3-ton trucks loaded with water, petrol and rations, explosives and ammunition. There was even a recovery vehicle piloted by two grimy experts in oil-soaked shorts. We now had over 20 jeeps on each of which were mounted a twin Vickers K machine gun on a steel upright in front, with another in the back. The magazines consisted of steel drums containing 50 rounds attached above the barrels. These guns had a very quick rate of fire and when both were discharged together it was impossible to detect the individual shots. There was just a roar. Windscreens had been removed to give a clear field of fire over the bonnet. Jerry cans of water and fuel were lashed on the footplate, the bonnet and on the back. Each jeep had a crew of three, a driver and two gunners.

This profusion of men and vehicles was new. No sabotage operation on this scale had been attempted by the SAS before. Gone were the days of the silent approach on foot. Every airfield along the line of communications was now surrounded by a defensive ring of troops.

All day trucks moved up and down our escarpment dumping supplies. The skeletons of two jeeps were propped up on jacks minus most of their entrails, near the repair truck. In one bay was a group of men making up explosive charges amongst a littler of black adhesive tape, time pencils, fuses, primer cord and heaps of strong-smelling sticks of plastic explosive. Overall was a constant din and clang of hammers. The moving vehicles raised clouds of yellow dust and those of us who had waited behind remembered the stillness and anxious moments when enemy planes were heard. Luckily there was too much to do to allow the imagination undue play and no aircraft spotted us.

A busy and ever-changing group of officers squatted in the sand around David outside our little cave. As soon as his briefing was complete each sought his men and jeeps. Every vehicle moved from dump to dump to collect its load of water and petrol, emergency rations and escape kits. The guns were stripped and tested; at the end of the first day we knew what lay ahead.

Along the Egyptian seaboard from Mersa Matruh to Sollum the features of the coast are much the same. The coastal plain stretches up to 50 miles south from the sea to a high escarpment rising some 500 feet and running roughly east/west until it turns north to join the coast at Halfaya and Sollum. Above this escarpment the plateau stretches south indefinitely. It was on this coastal plain and in the area bordering the escarpment that the ebb and flow of the desert battle took place. About 50 miles north of our position and just above the great escarpment which here approached within two or three miles of the sea, the enemy had established a large airfield at a place called Fuka near Marten Baghush, known as LG 12. It was a staging area for all planes approaching or leaving the front and air reconnaissance had reported this particular field constantly full of aircraft. This was to be our target. It was said to be guarded by about two battalions of Italian infantry.

There were to be 12 jeeps in the attack. We were to approach by night and assault the defences in formation, 10 abreast and one flanker behind on each side of the line. As we got through the defences we were to change formation on a Verey light signal from the centre and close in two lines, following each other in pairs, this in order to bring all our fire to bear. It was vital that no jeep should break formation, for if one drew too far ahead it would certainly cross its neighbour's line of fire. Officers were to drive.

Towards the end of the second day our 12 jeeps drew away from the escarpment to practice formation. We drove up and down some half a mile from the camp. First attempts were muddled but eventually distances and drill were more or less perfected and the idea of the jeep charge became reality. After dark we carried out a dress rehearsal. There was a quarter moon and visibility was good. David decreed live ammunition. The noise and the pyrotechnics were spectacular. We wondered what the enemy, only 50 miles away, might make of it. Anyway it gave us a lot of confidence and all went well.

Next day there was little to do but wait. I tried to sleep but lay wondering what it would be like. It was comparatively easy to keep formation on a known piece of country with no enemy. But what about the defenders? Would they be dug in? Was there any wire? With luck we should have surprise on our side. The danger could be when the planes came to look for us. Never lie up near a known track or in isolated bush cover. We should be safe if we could get far enough away before dawn. But if they did find us – first black dots in the sky chasing hither and thither like insects – hard to tell if they were coming towards you or not. Finally the realization they had seen you as they banked into attack. The steady calculating run in and the feeling of impotence as the roar of engines got louder and the planes came into head on silhouette. Seconds of suspense and then the guns. Little spurts of sand, the sighter, then the long burst as bullets kicked up around you. The cracking and popping of burning vehicles. We had known it all too recently.

Flies buzzed; the heat beat down; the hours passed. At last shadows began to creep along the escarpment and the colours deepened. We were ordered to move.

A last look around for things forgotten. Quick "goodbyes" and "good lucks" from those left in the RV.

The jeeps pulled out, bumping through the soft churned-up sand at the foot of the escarpment, guns rattling and swinging on their mountings, out into the firm desert. A halt while the navigator checked his bearing, then off due north across level sand gathering speed. Twelve menacing little shapes gliding through the dusk with the livid rays of the sunset filtered through the dust clouds rising in their wake.

It was easy to see at first. The jeeps kept no particular formation; we picked our own way a little to right or left of the man in front, and following his dust. Occasionally you hit a rock or a bad bump; gun mountings would rattle; the cans and ammo boxes clash in the back. Mostly we rolled along at a good 20 mph over flat shingle or sand. Every now and then we had to negotiate small escarpments. There was a halt until someone found a way up or down. The dust rose thicker, engines revved as we changed gear to pull up one after the other and fan out again on the level.

In about an hour the moon was up. We stopped and switched off while Johnny Cooper fixed up the tripod of his theodolite to take a shot. We saw his torch moving as he bent over the instrument. Meanwhile, our course was double-checked by Mike Sadler at the rear of the column. Cigarettes glowed and there was talk in low voices. Dust slowly settled over us.

The face of the desert changed. Of all her fickle moods the moonlight is the most unreal. Before us, to the north-east, the horizon showed sharp and black, it could have been a range of mountains 20 miles off or a ridge 20 yards away. About us glowed a sea of dull unearthly silver, broken by long shadows and the black masses of rocks and ridges. Above, the millions of winking stars, like a night at sea in the tropics.

Engines started. We moved off east of north and close together. The pace was slower now. Clouds drifted up from the south across the moon; it was hard driving, especially as the country had become more broken and it was impossible to see the rocks and ridges until you were on top of them. We came to a cliff that appeared impassable. David sent two jeeps out to find a way up. It turned out there was a passage about a quarter of a mile away. The little convoy swung right-handed. The pass proved to be a wadi running up about fifty feet and very steep. It was pretty dark. The first jeep got about half way up, hit a rock and slithered to the bottom. There was a grinding of gears as the drivers reached for the booster. The next car made it, engine racing, and one by one we crashed and bounced up the slope and on through the night like a pack of mechanized wolves.

After another hour, with two short halts to deal with tyre bursts, we sensed we were in regions used by men. The change was scarcely perceptible but most of us had been in the desert long enough to know. The front jeep's progress would slow suddenly and the dust increase. We would bump over a series of ridges, like a ploughed field, then the surface settled again. That was a track. Shadows round about took on a new significance. Half an hour before, that strange humped shape on the skyline would have passed unquestioned as a rock. Now it looked like a pile of old ration boxes. Cigarettes had long been put out and there was no more talk. Hands stole almost unconsciously to the double pistol grips in front of them, thumbs reaching out to touch the safety catch. The moon emerged again, etching the desert in silver and shadow. What was that sticking up on our left? Just a post? But that lump beyond was surely a pile of discarded petrol cans.

It came suddenly, over the horizon. Proof positive, rising slowly, seeming to hang interminably in the air then slowly flickering back to earth – a Verey light – German. After five minutes or so we stopped. Word came back and we all gathered around David's jeep. He and Cooper were bending over the map with a shaded torch. Our position was pin-pointed. The airfield lay about 4 miles due north. We should halt once more to get into formation when we were close enough and sure of our bearing. Five minutes to make a last check on equipment and we would be ready to go in.

We moved back to our vehicles and the gunners busied themselves with the arrangement of spare ammunition, making sure it was well within reach, settled themselves into position and swung the two thin barrels this way and that. A few of us stood in a group silently watching the horizon. There was the muffled sound of men working on the jeeps, and the wind in our ears.

"Did you hear that?"

"What?"

"Vehicles."

We listened. Far away, so that it might have been an effect of the wind or even of the silence, there was a faint growling murmur – or was there? Our group split up and after a few minutes engines started and twelve dark shapes set off again into the night.

The face of the desert here was pocked and lined with dips and ridges; progress was slow. We could see little, but it was evident the litter of man lay about us. We passed a burnt-out truck.

Then the horizon changed; a hard irregular skyline ahead gave way to a grey lightness, stretching beyond it and fading into darkness. We were coming to the edge of a bigger escarpment and could distinguish the plain beyond, probably the beginning of the broken country leading up to the great coastal cliff some 20 miles away. As we drove cautiously to the edge the moon came out again and with it the smell, familiar enough, but nonetheless disturbing, the sour-sweet smell of rotting flesh.

"Look there," my gunner pointed. There was just time to glimpse it before the dust of the front jeeps closed in. About 30 yards away was a small burnt-out vehicle, wheelless and squatting in the litter of its own charred entrails. A few yards beyond it in a patch of moonlight they lay, two of them, one on his back, arms and legs spread, the other just a hump. The battle had passed this way many weeks before and it had been a British truck. We bumped, slipped and braked out way down the rocky side of the escarpment into the grey uncertainty beyond.

The desert levelled again. The dust increased and tracks were everywhere. We no longer bothered to drive on a bearing for we knew we must be close. Two Verey lights rose on our left, hovered and sank below the horizon. No noise but the growling of the jeep engines rising and falling through the slow curling dust. Two more pinpoints of light appeared ahead. One moved some distance to the right then both flicked out. They were below the horizon. The feeling of imminent action began to grow. Surely we had surprise on our side. More lights appeared. The jeeps closed up and stopped. David appeared out of the dust.

"We'll get into formation now. I reckon we're practically on top of it but I'm not sure of the direction exactly."

Another figure ran up.

"I've burst a bloody tyre, they're working on it. It won't take a minute."

He turned to go.

"Oh Lord, Bill, we haven't time to wait for that. We may have to go in any minute."

You could feel the man's dismay through the darkness.

"OK then, but for Christ's sake hurry up."

He sped off, stones rattling behind him. Presently we heard men wrenching at the wheel and the clink of metal tools. Some of us got out and stood talking to one another in low voices:

"What the hell are you eating?"

"Benzedrine tablet. Do you want one?"

"No thanks, I woudn't mind chocolate."

"We've run out. Chewing gum do?"

"I suppose this is right. It seems damn quiet if there are two battalions of troops about."

"Must all be asleep."

Two more Verey lights flickered ahead, green over red.

"What are they doing with all these Verey lights?"

"What do you think?"

"What? The lights? How the hell should I know?"

David reappeared, unlighted pipe stuck upside down in his mouth as usual.

"OK, they're fixed. We're leaving Mike's jeep here with Sergeant Almond. He'll wait for stragglers and you can use him as a rendezvous if we get separated. We'll go in now, form up on my jeep, it's that one, and for God's sake keep in formation. Don't waste ammunition." He turned to Carol and me, the two flankers.

"Remember your job at the back is to look after the defences."

The jeeps backed and shunted into position, the dust was thick. Carol and I pulled out to the flanks, he to the left, I to the right. We were on the move again, engines revving unevenly in low gear. The wireless car with a solitary figure standing beside it faded away behind us.

We moved at snail's pace now because of the need to keep line. First one and then another jeep would pull slightly in front, change down and drop back into formation. The moon was up again and all 12 vehicles were clearly visible. The gunners sat tense, thumb on catch, guns levelled in front of them. The ground was pitted and broken, every now and then a wheel would crash into some unseen cavity. The noise of the engines seemed louder than ever and surely impossible to miss. Probably the enemy were watching us, yet there was no indication we were on the edge of a large airfield, not even a light. The line crawled on slowly. A big cloud moved over the moon. Our progress was now concealed but the strain of keeping formation over uneven ground with vision limited to 15 dusty yards was considerable.

Suddenly, above the noise of the engines, there came another sound. A great roar. It passed over us. An aircraft.

Almost before the wits had adjusted we saw in front of us and slightly to our right a long line of double lights a mile ahead. The runway! Our line swung round, straightened out and drove forward. The noise of the incoming aircraft was very loud. Two lights, green over red, broke out in the sky and described a graceful parabola.

"It's his recognition signal."

The noise of the aircraft died away and presently came again louder and lower as the pilot levelled off to land. Two little lights appeared close together, floating down towards the runway. They flattened out, bounced and continued along the flare path. The plane was down.

The pace was faster now and drivers strained to keep formation. My jeep crashed into a trench of some kind. I changed gear and the little vehicle just pulled up the other side. I trod on the accelerator to catch up. Then it happened, the flash and crack of a rifle. The line of jeeps slowed and seconds afterwards our guns opened. First, one tentative burst, then the full earsplitting cacophony roaring and spitting. Streams of red and white colour shot through the darkness, struck the ground and cascaded upwards in a thousand crazy arcs, criss-crossing each other. Some of the incendiary bullets caught fire as they hit the ground and burnt with a brilliant little white flame. Figures ran before us, or rather seemed to lumber away. Another white stream shot through the night and two of them slumped into the ground. The darkness enveloped us again.

A few more bursts were sprayed in front of the line and then David's green Very light signal broke from the centre. The landing lights had been switched off, so also the deep motors of the aircraft which had just touched down. In fact, not a light of any description was to be seen. No shot except that from the solitary sentry's rifle had been fired at us. We were through the defences.

Again the impatient rising and falling note of jeep engines as drivers changed down and clouds of dust as we worked into attack formation. The leading pair drove forward slowly, the rest following until Carol and I came together at the rear of the column. Gradually the pace increased again. The ground was flat now, as flat as a tarmac road. We were on the airfield. The guns smelt heavily of burnt powder; empty cartridge cases rattled about at the driver's feet.

After two or three minutes firing began again. First the roar of the guns on the leading jeep. Then the whole shattering belching medley as pair after pair of Vickers guns opened up down the line. I was crouched over the wheel, striving to concentrate on the squat, slowly moving forms in front of us silhouetted every few seconds against the crazy flashing streaks. Behind we could only catch glimpses of the direction of fire but the guns had opened up along the right-hand column, drivers and gunners shaken by the blast of their own guns and by blows from the ejected cases. A great shape loomed up about thirty yards to my right. A twin-engined aircraft, Junkers 52. The bullets were ripping through the fuselage with a curious swishing sound audible at the same time as the detonation of the guns. Just as our own guns came to bear the interior of the aircraft glowed red for a second; there was a dull explosion and the whole body burst into flames.

The heat and blast of the explosion struck the nearest crews forcibly and little sparks flew everywhere. The shooting died down again and our line moved on leaving the big aircraft crackling and blazing. I could hear the noise of liquid pouring on to the ground and the smell of aviation spirit was strong.

Gradually in the flickering light of the burning aircraft and as the gunners perception tightened, the forms of planes hove up on both sides. We were in the middle of the dispersal area.

Two more big Junkers caught fire on the right of the line. As I passed the nearest I saw long red crosses on the wings – unfortunate but no chance to consult the Geneva Convention. The second plane was burning furiously and beneath it about 15 yards from the wheels lay two figures flat on their bellies, head and shoulders slightly raised watching the line of jeeps. My rear gunner saw them.

"There's two Jerrys."

"Well, shoot at them; go on shoot at them."

The rear gunner leaned well out over the side of the jeep and the guns opened again.

"Did you get them?"

"I don't know, Sir."

We had to shout. Voices were drowned by the guns.

The line of jeeps twisted to the left and the forms of more aircraft became visible on that side. No mistaking the two clawlike wheel guards and hooked nose appearance. These were Stukas, the hated German dive-bombers. Burst after burst shot out in their direction, coloured streams waving about them and then intersecting on the fuselage – the ripping noise, the flow and burst of leaping flames and the hot blast of air.

Planes were going up on both sides and the dispersal area was illuminated for some distance by the fires. This gave our gunners a chance to spot aircraft parked further away. It also meant we could be seen.

The line stopped suddenly beside a big Dornier. Unintelligible orders were shouted from the head of the column. I saw a man run out to the aircraft, reach high up on the wing, plant a Lewis bomb and snap the fuse. As he ran back to the jeep the figure was unmistakable; Paddy Mayne was adding to his prodigious score. We moved on.

Just as my jeep passed the Dornier there was a tremendous explosion which momentarily stunned us. One wing sagged to the ground and the big aircraft caught fire.

We heard more explosions above the noise of the guns as burning aircraft, some of them probably "bombed up", started to detonate behind the column.

We drove on for some minutes, the gunners ranging continuously about them. Two or three large tents appeared ahead. Scarcely had they begun to receive the same attention as the planes when there was a swift whistle followed by the thump of a mortar shell slap in the middle of the line. Two more shells followed; then a heavy Italian Breda machine gun began its slow tattoo from a position a few hundred yards dead ahead of us. Ponka-ponka-ponk – the big 20mm red tracer bullets flashing over the heads of the jeeps' crews.

The firing was regular but luckily high. A few rifles cracked out, another shell arrived uncomfortably close. In the front of the line some jeeps had stopped and were shooting steadily in front of them. The tail end of the column telescoped and all our vehicles were bunched awkwardly close. In front I could hear confused shouting; ahead of the leading jeeps and to their right was a Stuka, already on fire, the bunched vehicles silhouetted in the leaping light of the flames. Tracer from the two Breda guns now began to play about us.

After a minute's delay the line began to move again; crowded and out of formation, we ran the gauntlet round the nose of the blazing bomber and turned back across the airfield with the enemy defences pounding away at us. As we escaped the betraying flames, gunners on the front jeeps gradually stopped firing to conceal our course. The defences were our job. The Breda opened up again.

"Do you see where that is coming from?"

"Yes Sir."

"Well, shoot."

The guns roared. A few seconds later we were rewarded by a long burst from the Breda. Big red streamers shot past and sailed away into the night. Then they hit us. I felt something hot pass most uncomfortably close beneath my seat. Clang! My face and my gunner's were doused in oil. There was a moment of blindness. I wiped the oil out of my eyes, the jeep swerved violently, hit a bump, recovered itself and miraculously continued.

"You OK?"

"Yes, I think so."

The rest of the convoy was temporarily lost. I stood on the accelerator and after a few anxious seconds struck them again at a sharp angle and fell into place behind.

After some minutes of uneventful progress we pulled up. I heard voices in front and David came towards the last jeeps. It turned out his had been knocked out. He and Corporal Cooper had been picked up by Sandy Scratchley.

"Everyone all right?" he called.

"Yes!" came several answers.

He reached us.

"You OK?"

"Well we've been hit, but it's still running."

"All right, we'll have one more go over this side of the dispersal area then beat it. How much ammunition have you got left?"

"Two drums."

"Well don't fire unless you're certain of getting a target and watch out for those bloody Breda guns."

Behind us and to our right the stricken aircraft were burning and crackling. Otherwise neither light nor sound from the enemy on the far side of the airfield. The jeeps moved away again right-handed and for some distance we saw nothing, then the guns opened up at the front of the line and at right angles. There was a plane some 200 yards to the right. A few bursts struck it but it failed to burn. A Messerschmitt 109 appeared to our front. More firing. Bullets from the rear jeeps were passing those in front at a narrow angle.

"Look out, that's not your target."

The fighter succumbed easily and our line hurried on out of the light of the flames. One of the heavy Breda guns, guided by this fresh fire, opened up but the bullets passed wide behind us.

The shooting ceased for some minutes until we passed between some ruined stone outbuildings which received a generous quota, coloured ricochets darting in all directions. The line turned gradually left-handed, the pace increased and our flight began.

We were soon off the smoothness of the runway and crossing rough desert. After a few minutes the jeep in front of mine stopped. As we drew level the driver was struggling to restart her. Two of the crew climbed out and ran over to us while the jeeps in front pelted away into the darkness.

"Hang on; we've seized; our bloke's putting a bomb in her."

The last member of the damaged jeep's crew was dragged on board and I got going in a hurry. We bumped crazily off in the general direction the others had taken and it was with some relief that we found them.

David stopped about a mile south of the perimeter, having failed to find Mike Sadler's jeep, and summoned the officers. We were to split up into three parties and make for the rendezvous independently. The idea was to get as far as possible from the airfield before dawn, due in another two and a half hours, then camouflage down before daylight should betray us to an angry enemy in the air. The exact direction of our flight was of little importance, provided we checked our course, but we should all try to cross west of the track with the telegraph poles which led from Baghush to Kara at the north-western tip of the Depression. Did we remember the track? We did.

We were to lie up all the following day and then make our way back to the escarpment after dark.

"Now refill your tanks and get going."

It transpired that several jeeps, besides mine, had been hit, but these would have to take their chance; they were all still running. Hurried orders were passed to the crews and while the tanks were being filled some of us stood watching the aircraft still burning behind us. We tried to count the fires.

"I make it twelve."

"We shot at a hell of a lot more."*

"Yes, I reckon there will be plenty won't take off tomorrow."

"Did you see anybody hit?"

"Yes, there were one or two to begin with before we got onto the runway and did you see those bastards running about in their pyjamas among the tents? Could have been pilots. One of them got it."

Far away behind the fires two streams of tracer from the Breda gun cut through the night. The opposition were still understandably nervous.

Sandy Scratchley joined our group. Sandy, old Harrovian and ex-steeple-chase jockey, was something of a hero of mine, an irrepressible character with curly red hair. We talked racing together. He had ridden an old steeplechaser of my grandmother's on which I had begun my very short race riding career, and had a disappointingly low opinion of it.

"You OK Sandy?"

"Yes, but my rear gunner was killed."

We looked towards Sandy's jeep; one man was leaning over the petrol tank; another figure was slumped in the back seat by the guns. Johnny Cooper was standing beside it.

"What happened?"

"Got one through the head, poor chap. I think it was a Breda bullet. I was shouting at him to shoot and when nothing happened I looked and saw him slumped on the guns. It was just before we picked up David and Cooper. They got one through the engine."

Chastened, we made our way back to the jeeps. The three parties soon

* The official count was 40 destroyed.

split. For some minutes the various dust clouds were dimly visible moving parallel; then they faded into the night.

David's party consisted of four jeeps including Sandy's with the dead gunner. Mine and another had been hit. We drove south-west fast now through thick camel scrub which swished oddly along the running boards. It was uneven going. In front was a vague dark horizon and the swerving lurching forms of the leading jeeps visible through their dust; behind, the stricken airfield with fires still flickering in the distance.

We climbed a small escarpment and rattled away over a loose rocky surface heading well west of south. The fires disappeared; we were alone again in the darkness.

The pace was hard to sustain and the interval between us grew longer. We sped on for about a quarter of an hour before my jeep failed. The engine coughed and stopped. Several cylinders seemed to have gone, but there was not time to verify the damage and no possibility of repair. Kit was hurriedly slung on to another vehicle, a Lewis bomb placed in ours with a 10 minute delay fuse. We and the four men we were then carrying dispersed to other vehicles and on we went. We now had three extra men on each of the remaining jeeps.

For two hours we sped on, only stopping occasionally to make a rough check on our bearing. We missed the track, but after some 30 miles on a course south of west we reckoned we must have passed it.

At the first suspicion of dawn we found ourselves, 14 men and the dead gunner, in three jeeps clattering slowly over a loose stony surface. Our estimate of the distance to the enemy airbase was, with luck, about forty miles. The Germans and Italians would put every plane they could in the air. They would start their search at dawn and forty miles was a matter of minutes. In the faint increasing light we could see a desert of flat stone and rock outcrop promising ill to our hopes of concealment. Mercifully a thick ground mist lay about us so for some time after first light we were hidden.

The same mist undoubtedly saved Mike Sadler and his party that morning. He had waited for stragglers until nearly dawn, then driven southward. As light came they found themselves on a wide sand track churned by many vehicles. Shapes suddenly loomed up through the fog. It was a column of German infantry, halted. The Germans, collars turned up against the cold, were standing in groups by their vehicles. They peered at Mike's jeep as it bumped past them. Mike and his men peered back. No greeting was exchanged. No challenged offered. No sign of recognition. Deeply relieved, Mike drove on into the mist.

Ground visibility for us was not much more than 20 yards. We continued slowly on course, only turning away to follow any hint of a gully in case it should develop into a wadi deep enough for refuge. The face of the desert did not change. Now and then the level rose or sank slightly but there was nothing to conceal our nakedness. The fog gradually lifted and uneasiness increased. We listened for that faint humming of engines we had learned to dread.

Suddenly and unexpectedly the desert befriended us: the fog cleared and we found ourselves on the edge of a small escarpment dropping about 15 feet. Below was a large bowl-shaped depression a quarter of a mile broad, its walls cut by fairly deep wadis with thick scrub up to 3 or 4 feet high. We bumped our way down towards what appeared to be the thickest patch of cover. No one needed orders, we heaved and manoeuvred the jeeps into the centre of the dry water course amongst the tallest bush. It was a matter of minutes before enough scrub had been wrenched up and thrown over them, together with our camouflage nets. In their sunken position they were virtually indistinguishable from as little as 50 yards.

Relief. Once the jeeps were hidden it would be easy for each man to run for cover on the noise of aircraft. We looked at each other! A ragged-looking bunch, faces, hair and beards covered in a thick yellow-grey film of dust, eyes red and strained, our dirty open-necked battle dress and loose overcoats hung upon us like scarecrows. Sandy was trying to scrape dried and sand-caked bloodstains from his trousers with a stick, the blood of the dead McKay who was lying on his back under a blanket nearby. Our mouths were dry and ill-tasting. There was a burning behind the eyes. But for the moment we were safe.

"All right," said David. "Brew up."

He turned to Sandy:

"We'll bury McKay here. There's nothing else to do."

Two men went back to the jeeps for spades and set to work a little distance away in the scrub. The rest of us sat down and lit cigarettes. The relief which follows action and escape loosened tongues and there was much talk of our success. Behind us our crews squatted round the brew, two charred old tins, the bottom one full of burning petrol-soaked sand and scrub, the top one with the water. A little way away two figures bent to their task. Every now and then came the clink of steel on stone. A certain amount of mist still hung about; it was 5.30 in the morning.

Presently tea was ready. Black, practically unsugared and brewed in brackish water but still hot, strong and unbelievably refreshing. The two men returned with their spades.

"The grave is ready, Sir."

"Have you got his paybook?" David asked Sandy.

"Carry him over then."

69

We got up and stood gathered round the grave while the body was lowered, sand and rock heaped upon it. There was no cross; some of the men were trying to make one from the scrub and a piece of old ration box, but it was not yet ready. We stood bare-headed, each with his own thoughts. Most of us had scarcely known this lad who had only joined us shortly before the operation. I remembered a cheery red face and a shock of black hair. There must be someone, parents, a girl, going about their ordinary business far away at home. It would be weeks before the pathetic little message filtered back for all the pent-up sadness of this desert moment to be loosed.

I looked around at the loneliness, the vague shapeless loneliness stretching for so many hundreds of forgotten miles. Probably no living thing would ever pass this grave again except perhaps the gazelle; even the map reference we recorded might well be inaccurate after our flight from the airfield.

It was a strange burial, just a two-minute silence and the thoughts of his comrades gathered around. Yet for this fraction of time there was dignity and sorrow. Slowly we went back to our tea. Orders for the day were simple; the minimum of movement, minimum consumption of water; keep away from the jeeps and try to get some sleep.

Scarcely had we begun to settle down when someone gave the familiar warning:

"Aircraft."

Those still on their feet dived into the scrub. We lay listening. Soon we could hear the engines. They were coming nearer, the first patrol, the first of many during that long day. There were several planes but they passed away to the east, probably flying down the track, angry pilots dragged from their beds on the neighbouring airfields where they were quite possibly resting from operations to search for these *Sabotage Scheisse* who descended on them in the night.

The sun rose and the heat beat down in great waves upon us: flies appeared from nowhere, buzzed and tormented. It was difficult to sleep. We peeled off our filthy clothes and made pillows with them in the tiny patches of shade. Few words passed. Someone discovered bits of sandy chocolate in a pocket and these were shared round. There were one or two tattered fragments of magazines to be read but most of us simply lay silent hoping for sleep. The hours dragged by. Several times we heard aircraft, but saw nothing. Once, after a patrol had passed us away to the south, we caught the sound of machine guns, muffled and far off but unmistakable. Someone was catching it. Later we learned it had indeed been one of our detachments.

The sun began its snail-like descent. I caught myself looking at it every few minutes, speculating as to exactly which spot on the horizon it would eventually touch. Twelve hours passed, leaving us still sleepless. At last the cursed orange ball sank below the ridge and we began to assemble about the jeeps. David decided on half a mug of tea each before dark. No more could be allowed as water was short and our future uncertain. Scarcely had the men set up the tins and kindled the fire when we heard them.

"Aircraft!"

We were caught. One of the jeeps was half-uncovered. We dived for the scrub and flung sand over the little fire. Someone wrenched the camouflage net over the vehicle. We were scarcely still before they came – three Stukas flying at about 400 feet, their mottled greenish-brown camouflage and the big black and white crosses on their wings easily visible. They flew from the south-east, an unexpected direction. We lay face down and waited for it but the snarling roar passed overhead and away, flying on serenely to the north-west in formation, their shapes clear against the blood-red sunset. Thankfully we brushed off the sand and returned to the jeeps.

The protecting darkness was almost upon us and it remained only to find the rendezvous, probably the best part of a night's drive away.

Overcoats on against the chill of the night, our little party clambered aboard; the men squashed themselves into as comfortable a position as possible and we were off. I was driving again and waiting my turn to climb the escarpment. I took a last look back at our refuge and that forlorn little cross in the midst of the scrub.

Our route back to the RV had been discussed during the evening. It was clear that because we were unsure of our position we must try to find a point on the map, whence we could work out a bearing. The only sure landmark was the disused Kara track along which the aircraft had flown that morning. It lay 15 to 20 miles east of our present position and ran north-south. This was uncomfortably close to the scene of the previous night's work but the risk of ground patrols was negligible and had to be taken. Johnny Cooper stepped out of the leading jeep and lifted his luminous compass; then we were off to the east. We drove slowly out of respect for our jeeps. Two of the three engines were knocking and we had already suffered tyre bursts.

After about an hour and a half we found the track – a line of poles and twisted broken cable crossing our path at right angles. We turned south along it, sure at least of something and undeniably on our way back.

The track wound away through broken rock country with deep, scarred wadis at right angles. After a quarter of an hour a slow puncture on one of the jeeps finally burst. The inner tube proved on inspection to be in ribbons; there were no spares left and it was too far gone to patch. A disconsolate little group stood in the darkness round the stricken vehicle. Nothing to be done. The other jeeps were overloaded as it was. They must keep going. Forced to curtail our speed the two jeeps with four good tyres had to stop often to let the lame duck catch up. The men were crouched swaying on top of the kit, hands and necks sunk into their overcoats. After about an hour and a half's progress David's jeep stopped. Cooper got busy with a map and a torch while the rest of us gathered round.

"You see what I mean Sir, that straight bit for a mile or so through the scrub, then the hills appear again, then there's those two sharp bends and it's flat again. That's where we are."

"Where?"

"There."

Cooper bent over and made a small pencil mark. We all looked at the map then turned and stared into the gloom. Before us stretched a plain; the moon was up and the ruts of the track shone dully as they twisted away through patches of black scrub. We could see telegraph poles diminishing into obscurity. Behind we could dimly make out two hump-backed hills between which we had passed. A thin cold breeze stirred the scrub; otherwise all was still.

"Might be," someone said.

"Well, where do we go now?"

"We'll go on to this next bend," said David.

"After a mile it leads to the left; you see? Then if its the right one we'll pinpoint and work out the bearing. We should be back by daylight."

A mile and a half further the track unmistakably bent to the left. We stopped. Cooper busied himself with pencil and protractor again while David held the torch. From the pinpoint our bearing was 263°; 36 miles to the RV.

We turned away in single file. It was very uneven difficult country and we had to stop frequently for the third jeep. Each time we stopped our navigator walked a few paces, lifted the little compass and tried to find a landmark in the vague darkness ahead. Presently we emerged from the gravel and scrub onto a hard rock-strewn surface. Here we could see further. Cooper bent over the map again and marked our position as best he could. We transferred this bearing to our maps.

Our slow progress continued for a further two hours. The men fell asleep on top of each other at the halts which grew perceptibly longer. Just as the sky was beginning to lighten the lame jeep burst another tyre irreparably. They were out of sight when it happened and it took some time for them to appear. We stood round in silence, past cursing.

"Well, you'll just have to keep it going, Bill. Is it overheating much?"

"Not too bad."

"Where are we?"

"Cooper thinks we should be back soon after daylight."

Our hopes rose with the dawn. We came to several long straight escarpments rising from flat stony open desert. Visibility was good but no feature was familiar.

The lame jeep was retarding us hopelessly and David decided to go ahead with the other two to the RV. The third was to carry on along the bearing and we would send out to pick them up. After a short rest we moved on; the lame jeep soon disappeared over a ridge behind us, its rattling dying gradually away.

Everyone was now fully awake and we scoured the desert for any familiar mark, driving faster now that we knew we must be near the RV. The country continued flat and covered in pale shingle. Wide wadis of level yellow sand dotted with the familiar little bushes crossed our track. It all looked vaguely familiar. Those two strange-looking brown hills shimmering in the mirage on the southern horizon, surely we had seen them before.

"Where have we got to, Johnny?"

We pulled up and David spread the battered map over his knees.

"About here."

"Then that might be those hills?" A finger pointed to some uneven contours. There was a short silence.

"It might."

"Oh well, we'll go on."

We crossed a wide wadi. Three gazelle jumped out of the bush a few yards to our right. The little buck, loping along, easily outdistanced the jeeps, swung right-handed over a ridge and were gone.

Another hour and Cooper was sure we must be almost on the RV. We searched the desert all round with our field glasses. Nothing. Miles of nothing. Fawn-coloured waste with here and there an apparent rise or depression. No landmark, nothing familiar. We were on the edge of a small plateau with an escarpment which dropped unevenly for 20 or 30 feet below us but it was not ours.

"I think we might have a brew now but don't any of you touch your water bottles."

Silently one of the men swung a shovel and poured a tiny amount of petrol into the sand. We measured half a cup of water each into the tin, dropped a match on to the petrol and sat around the little fire in silence.

The sun rose slowly to its crescendo above us. We half-expected the lame jeep to join us, but it didn't turn up. Johnny Cooper, whose accuracy and good sense were generally unquestioned, insisted upon our position. He repeated the reasons for his deduction. Everyone agreed, but no one could sense the RV.

After some discussion David decided to continue on the bearing for a few miles then start a square search to the north, there being some reason to believe we were further south than we should have been. After three or four miles we began to search the unfamiliar ground in earnest. Every escarpment was followed in case it should prove to be an extension of our hiding place. Once we discovered faint traces of tracks which certainly seemed to resemble jeep tyres. Full of hope we followed them for half a mile, only to lose them hopelessly in a broad patch of rock outcrop. After a further two hours' fruitless search we returned to our point of departure on the original bearing. The country ahead was completely strange; we sat in our jeeps mutely gazing about us, eyes puckered against the sun, faces coated with dust and sweat. There was a strange noise in the distance. Clankety-clank bang, clankety-clank bang, over the ridge to our right came the third jeep; with one last scrunch and clank it came to a halt. The driver folded his arms and leant on the wheel, while the crew stared gloomily down at us. Everyone started to laugh.

After a short discussion it was decided we should keep together. Indeed this was now inevitable since we were no longer sure of our position. Accordingly we turned north and continued at our former slow pace, the two sound jeeps keeping well apart, climbing to the top of any high ground to get a view of the country ahead. By midday it seemed from the map and Cooper's calculations that we must have passed the RV, yet we had seen no recognizable feature. Some of us knew the country around the RV well and were ready to swear we had not passed near. Halts became more frequent and the afternoon passed without more than five or six square miles of desert searched. Even taking it in turns we could not drive much farther without sleep.

Towards five o'clock we came to rough rocky rising ground which we crossed in a north-easterly direction. The surface flattened, then ended abruptly in a steep cliff. We got out and stood silently gazing out before us while the broken jeep bumped up behind. The cliff fell steeply 200 feet or more and below us the desert stretched away into nothing. The lengthening shadows cast from the escarpment lapped down towards a large, winding bush-covered wadi. We could see other wadis criss-crossing each other and stretching into the distance, wavy ribbons of dotted yellow sand. The cliff was a clear and obvious feature and should have been well known to us if it lay near the RV. It was utterly strange. We looked at the map in turn and then back at the horizon. Slowly the uneasiness which lurks in those who use the desert grew, the fear which is denied to the last moment of plausible uncertainty. We were lost. Before us, behind us, all about us stretched the loneliness we knew so well and yet did not know, the waste which sometimes befriended, sometimes betrayed. The long gathering shadows, the rock, the sand, the cliff, the watercourse, the vagueness of the coming dusk, all seemed to mock us. For a minute no one spoke; then someone voiced a thought which must have occurred to us all.

"It can't be the coastal escarpment?"

There was no answer.

It looked so much like it: the steep, apparently continuous cliff and the flat plain sailing away out of sight – to the sea? If this was so we must be at least a hundred miles adrift and had we a hundred miles of petrol left? Yet how could this be? We had been travelling south along the track, and it had certainly been the track we knew, last night. It could not possibly be: yet when you are lost in the desert, anything seems possible.

"I think we'll find a way down and doss for a bit," said David.

We turned back to the jeeps and after a ten-minute search found a route. The three vehicles slithered to the bottom accompanied by showers of stones. The men dragged themselves painfully out and stood about.

"OK, we'll spend the night here and start again at dawn tomorrow. There's to be no more water drunk except what you've got in your bottles. Bill, check the water and petrol will you? Steve and I will take this jeep and just have a last look over there." He pointed across the plain.

The men slowly dragged their blankets and overcoats off the jeeps and lay down; they were alseep immediately. David and I drove away over the plain in search of some high ground. I was too tired to watch the surface properly and the jeep kept bumping and crashing into the uneven ruts of the wadi. We were almost out of sight of the others and no high ground appeared.

"OK I'll take over now."

David drove round in a wide circle, then back to the little group around the jeeps. We climbed out, wrapped our coats about us and were alseep.

The sun was already up when we awoke. We brewed a small measure of tea and ate some biscuits. It was reckoned we had water for five or six days if we were careful, food for a little less and the petrol would last us something like 50–60 miles. We had no idea where we were. Moreover, one of the good jeeps now had a puncture. We tried to repair it but it wouldn't stay properly inflated and soon burst on the stony surface. With difficulty we set off up the cliff and retraced our tracks of the preceding day. Progress was even slower than before and spirits were low. All now believed we were lost and the refreshment afforded by sleep only served to tighten the certainty. At not much better than walking pace our little party clattered uncertainly over the rock surface. After about 80 yards the leading jeep stopped. There appeared to be yet another escarpment in front, although no one remembered having passed it. Johnny Cooper trudged forward, hands in pockets and looked over the edge, looked for about two seconds, then whipped round and started running back.

"Hey! Hey!" he shouted hoarsely to the rest of us. We were up with him now and saw for ourselves. Below to the north and south stretched the headlands of the escarpment. In front the ground shelved to a wadi then rose to another ridge in the distance. There were vehicle tracks in the wadi and foot marks in the sand. Stuck into a cleft below us about 50 yards away was a three-ton truck. About it sat a little group of our comrades, brewing up.

We were back, but only to discover the RV had also been attacked from the air with the loss of several vehicles. We had to move our hideout.

Relief was tempered by sad news, particularly for Carol and me. André Zirnheld was dead. He and Martin had fallen behind their comrades on the way back due to punctures. When the morning mist cleared they had found themselves on the dreaded Siwa track about which we had all been warned. There was little time to get away and they had tried to hide their two jeeps in a small cliff nearby. Three Stukas flying low and searching every crevice had found them. We had heard the noise of their attacks and the planes that flew over us were almost certainly the same. André, our friend, had been hit twice and died before Martin could get back to him with the doctor. They buried him there beside the track next day with a cross to mark his grave –

Aspirant André Zirnheld
Mort pour la France
27 July 1942

Further raids were projected but had to be curtailed. David got a signal summoning him urgently to Cairo. The SAS was needed for some grandiose and secret operation dreamed up by GHQ. Nothing GHQ planned could be good news. David protested strongly, to no avail. He must come at once, all would be revealed. This turned out to be the prelude for the disastrous Benghazi operation.

GHQ proposed to send two old Bombay bombers of 216 Squadron to pick up the main force. There was a disused landing strip about twenty miles away from our RV which was deemed suitable. We had with us a cheerful RAF officer, Flight Lieutenant Laurie Pike, known as "Rafy", whose job it was to cope with such an eventuality.

Rafy found a flat piece of desert somewhere near the RV. Whether or not it was the landing strip I have no idea but we all set to work filling cans with sand soaked in petrol which were placed along the runway as landing lights. There was to be a recognition signal flashed by Aldis lamp. The great night came; nothing happened. We subsequently learnt that the pilot got lost. The second attempt was successful. The plane spotted us, turned in to land and bounced precariously to a halt amid billowing clouds of dust. In a matter of minutes David and those destined to return were aboard. The pilot turned in to the wind and lurched off in the direction of the single distant petrol can which had remained alight. It wobbled into the air and gradually the roar of engines gave way to one of the most profound silences I have ever experienced. Those of us who were left behind found it difficult to believe these goings on had not been clearly audible to the enemy and for some time the desert seemed a very lonely place.

As soon as we had collected ourselves, cannibalized a few of the vehicles which were about to die and loaded our kit, Sandy Scratchley, Carol Mather and I with the rear party set out to make the best of our way back to the Delta via the Qattara Depression, an impressive journey well to the south of the German lines. On the way I became ill. I had been coughing for some time and began to lose consciousness over the wheel of the jeep. This was a distinct disadvantage for my passengers and a kindly sergeant reported it. They found I had a high temperature and I was strapped on to the top of one of the 30 cwt trucks and treated as cargo. I remember being laid out in a small tent under the great cliffs of the Depression where we camped to wait for nightfall, for enemy air activity ruled out any passage over the salt marsh by day. That first night we missed the narrow Quneitra Crossing and had to return to the cliffs. Successful at the second attempt, we at last encountered a troop of the 10th Hussars guarding the southern approaches. We were back among friends and I was more or less recovered.

For two more punishing days we limped back eastwards between El Fayoum and the Wadi Natroun. Towards noon on the second day there appeared in silhouette to the south a long line of laden camels, wending towards the Delta. Slowly the nodding heads and swaying burdens sank below a ridge, the first welcome signal that Cairo was not far. Then above the dust haze looming closer than seemed natural or possible, massive symbols of a dead age, the tops of the pyramids of Cheops and Cephren, and that of Mycerinus beyond.

Another ridge and we lifted the squat outline of the stepped pyramid oldest of them all, and below it the dark green sweep of the Delta stretched away to the vaguely defined chalk-like cliffs of the Jebel El Hamsa on the far side of the Nile.

Our bearing drew us towards and then below the Cyclopean ruins of the temple complex of Djoser. A last jolting mile over one of the giant causeways that once linked Memphis to the Cities of the Dead brought the convoy to the first tufts of coarse grasses and along a fringe of date palms into the cultivation.

Now we were among the maize fields, the cotton and the lemon groves. We passed the familiar crooked arm of a shadouf, the wooden well rig as old as man along the Nile. A small boy in a dirty galabieh swung the balance and raised a brimming pail of brown water. Nearby a blindfold donkey turned a creaking water wheel. We reached the first canal and turned east down the dirt road alongside. The turgid stream wound past clumps of reeds and mango trees. We bumped along in the shade of Nile acacia, dun palm and tamarisk. Here were giant water buffaloes with shining flanks led by tiny laughing brown children. There were people at the roadside and on the bridges, talking, smiling, gesticulating. A young woman, proud, erect, a bundle on her head, hand on hip, silver and beads about her neck, black robed from head to foot, a child at her knee, stood by the road and gazed arrogantly as we passed.

Small solemn ambling donkeys and undulating camels bearing massive heaps of maize, sugar cane and reeds swayed by and everywhere the blessed burgeoning of the silt, the eddy and evidence and flow of water.

Soon the dirt road bred strips of potholed tarmac. The mud-brick gave place to occasional concrete in the little villages along the way. The sun was well behind us and the shadows of our vehicles cast far ahead. White egrets flapped lazily to roost.

At last we came upon the main road from Giza to Cairo. Across it the rays of a dying sun shone pink on the Edwardian splendours of the Mena House Hotel.

Gratefully we turned south towards the city. Lights were beginning to twinkle along the way.

Once the convoy was safely on its way to base Carol and I made our way to Mena House, intent at last on Comfort Day. Ragged, bedraggled and bearded, our appearance attracted astonished and disapproving glances in the foyer. So much so that, having booked a room, we ignored the lifts and headed for some unobtrusive stairs. Round the corner came a rather smart-looking woman. She suppressed a scream, clapped a hand over her mouth and backed against the wall, clearly expecting to be despatched on the spot or worse. This was no time for pleasantries. We sped on, found our room, ordered champagne, dinner and the barber – we had no razor. A long and increasingly confused discussion followed about what ought to come next on our Comfort Day schedule – during which we fell asleep.

The project so lovingly devised and long awaited faded into oblivion.

————|————

5

DOINGS IN BEIRUT AND BENGHAZI

After our return from operations I was sent on extended leave to Beirut. It was hoped my indisposition would disappear.

The short month I spent there was full of incident. I discovered that the first British Army ski school had been set up at the Cedars of Lebanon, ostensibly to train mountain troops. It was directed by a well known pre-war British racing skier, James Riddell. His instructors were mostly middle European refugees. There were few British qualified. This didn't stop my friend Frank Waldron, then stationed with the Regiment in Palestine, who thought he was. I went up with him hoping to learn to ski.

Riddell collected his aspirant staff on the mountain and told them to schüss down to a ridge, clearly visible in the middle distance and stop. All obliged except for Frank, who continued out of sight heading apparently for the Mediterranean. He was deemed to have failed. To my surprise the only students seemed to be submarine crew. I'm sure it did them a world of good, although the connection with their calling was obscure.

My own attempt at a free skiing holiday was more or less abortive, and after two or three days I hitched a lift back to Beirut with Andy Lassen, the now legendary Danish Officer who was training with the Special Boat Section near Beirut. He later won a Military Cross with two bars and a posthumous VC. He was killed in an heroic raid on the German positions in Lake Comacchio during the Italian campaign. The road was a precipitous track round hairpin bends. I have never been more terrified and well understood later how Andy got so many medals. We hurtled down to sea level on two wheels. Fear was simply left out of his disposition and alas, he paid for it.

Wartime Beirut was as entertaining as it was beautiful. Unlike the British who created clubs for themselves all over the Empire in which they imposed the standards and conventions of Aldershot or Cheltenham, the French had a way of combining their incomparable view of civilisation with the local mores. Life in Beirut reflected this happy melange in spite of Wavell's bitter five week campaign against the Vichy garrison in '42 and the prickly state of Anglo French relations which followed.

Divertissements were many. Arab racing flourished, more or less in the hands of some enterprising officers in the RAVC who were nominally in charge of a large draft of mules. I believe the mules came in to their own later in Italy, but at that time they were unemployed. So were their guardians who made a good thing out of training race horses for the rich Lebanese sportsmen. With the aid of two English ex-jockeys who were also on the strength, they won practically everything. Good tips were nevertheless hard to come by.

We made friends with a number of Lebanese families. My battalion was by that time resting in Palestine and many friends visited us. Grand young Lebanese ladies seemed happy enough to come out with us. They were pretty but inclined to be prim. I got into trouble, together with Hugh Rose from the Battalion, for taking two of them to what we thought was a fairly respectable nightclub. In fact it was run by a notorious "Madame" d'Esterley who had previously managed a house of ill fame in Paris. We had found her intensely amusing on previous visits and she certainly could sing. The fact that her songs were excessively bawdy was more or less lost on us, so we invited her to begin. With a wicked glance at our young ladies she did. After about three verses, Hugh's companion hit him across the face and swept out. I can still see his expression of furious bewilderment.

Our stay was much enlivened by the presence of Nigel Davidson, one of the more unusual of my brother officers, then attached to 9th Army Headquarters in Syria as liaison officer to the Free French. Nigel had been part educated on the continent and spoke fluent French.

His presence was often enhanced by his constant companion, a remarkably pretty Egyptian girl called Amina Baroudi, granddaughter of Baroudi Pasha, leader of the Wafd revolt against the British in 1919. Amina's closest companion in Cairo and subsequently in Beirut was Amal Atrash, divorced wife of the Emir of the Jebel Druse. The connection led to an unusual adventure.

Amal, a distant cousin of the ruling Atrash dynasty, had been married aged 16 to the Emir, who fell helplessly in love with her. For four years she led a dutiful married life and produced a daughter. Then, bored by her existence in provincial Soueida, the Druse stronghold in Syria, she fled with her mother to Cairo. The mother, of comparatively lowly birth, had been a singer and Amal set out to emulate her. She was an immediate success and under the stage name of "As Mahan" she became the toast of Cairo. Melancholy one moment, exploding with uncontrollable high spirits the next, her wild good looks stormed many hearts and later, in the words of

General Louis Spears who commanded the mission to the Free French in Lebanon, she "bowled over British Officers with the speed and accuracy of a machine gun."

Her career from her arrival in Cairo, until her untimely death aged only 27, would and should fill a book.

In 1941 the Luftwaffe, with Vichy French connivance, were using French airfields in Syria, in particular Aleppo. Churchill was determined to stop this dangerous infiltration towards the Canal Zone and ordered Wavell to occupy Syria. Beleaguered as he was in the desert, in Greece and with a German inspired revolt in Iraq, Wavell nevertheless managed to assemble a polyglot force of Indian, Australian, Free French and British units under command of General Jumbo Wilson for the purpose.

Across the route to Damascus lay the Jebel Druse. The Druse are a warlike people. Should they decide to resist the British advance things would be difficult. British Intelligence succeeded in recruiting Amal. She agreed to return to her ex-husband the Emir and try to persuade him at least to remain neutral. She was smuggled across the frontier to Soueida clutching a goat-skin bag full of sovereigns with which to help the discussion. She succeeded dramatically. The Emir stayed staunchly pro-British and remarried her into the bargain. Amal hung onto most of the gold.

On 8 June, 1941, the British force crossed the frontier and after a bitter campaign the Vichy command surrendered.

In recognition of what he had done for us, her Emir was appointed Defence Minister in the provisional Syrian Government and Amal decided to mark this promotion in spectacular fashion. Clad in Arab dress, she rode into Damascus escorted by a troop of Druse horsemen, clattering through the streets to the Grand Serail.

General Jack Evetts, then commanding the 9th British Division in Syria, witnessed her arrival with admiration.

In addition to her other attainments, Amal was a good Druse girl. Her Emir disliked the French occupation and between them they did their best to promote the idea of an independent Druse nation, or alternatively some form of merger with Jordan. The British Authorities, anxious not to upset the French whose mandate they had just invaded, refused to entertain these ideas. Amal was furiously disappointed.

Some time later she was contacted in Beirut by an Abwehr agent and persuaded to travel to Ankara to find out what the German Ambassador, Von Papen, might have to offer. Her failure to get further funds from either the British or the French undoubtedly contributed to this endeavour. Both money and adventure meant a lot to Amal.

Her clandestine departure from Beirut was spotted by security and

Nigel Davidson, who knew her well, was ordered to detain her. With his soldier servant, Guardsman Will, a field security sergeant and his driver he sped to the last rail stop before the Turkish frontier where engines had to be changed. There, by a combination of persuasion and threat, he managed to extract Amal and her murderous looking Druse bodyguard from the train.

Their return to Beirut was interrupted at Aleppo by a despatch rider from General Evetts. Nigel was ordered to book rooms at the Baren Hotel for himself and the Princess, and to dine with them that evening. Evetts' ADC, Harold Morrison (Scots Guards), also appeared.

Amal rapidly recovered her good humour at this turn of events and in spite of attracting a large and suspicious crowd of Arabs (she was well known) they enjoyed a hilarious evening together.

Next day, now under firm Field Security escort, Amal continued her journey to Beirut where she was brought in her wrath before General Spears.

Poor Jack Evetts had been escorting the fatal Princess for some time and his abrupt departure to alternative employment soon after this incident is otherwise unexplained.

After a stormy interview with Spears, Amal was handed over to the French and placed under "*residence surveillée*" which in no way cramped her style. It seems the French Officer from the Deuxième Bureau, deputed to look after her was also captivated.

I saw her only once in the bar of the Normandie Hotel. The place was full. At that time I did not know who she was, but I was riveted by her imperious and challenging look. For a second, time stood still! Louis Spears, who had to conduct more than one furious argument with her, not only over her defection, but also because of repeated demands for money – the goatskin bag having failed her – described her thus:

"She was one of the most beautiful women I have ever seen. Her eyes were immense, green as the colour of the sea you have to cross on the way to Paradise. They were turned up at the ends like the extremities of a gull's wing."

He added that "she spent money as a rain cloud scatters water" and that he found her "terrifying in her rage".

Eventually, because of her unsettling influence she was sent to Jerusalem where she continued to live it up at the King David Hotel.

Her farewell party in Beirut was a sensation. Charles Mott-Radclyffe, also a liaison officer with the Free French and later a close friend of mine in the House of Commons describes it in his admirable memoirs,* albeit at second

* *Foreign Body in the Eye*

hand. Disappointed not to be invited, he had asked a French Air Force officer friend how the party went. The Frenchman thought for a bit:

"*Eh bien, oui,*" he said. "*J'ai visité son appartement hier soir. En entrant j'ai eu une impression tout à fait curieuse: sous le lit se trouve Evetts: dans le lit se trouve* Busk [a British Intelligence Officer] *et suspendu au lustre, Spears. Enfin, on ne se sentait pas seul chez elle!*"

Presently rumours of orgies at the King David Hotel reached the Emir who decided things had gone far enough. The proud name of Atrash in particular and of the Druse in general was disgraced. Courteously he asked General Spears to inform the High Commissioner for Palestine, Sir Harold MacMichael, that he intended to send to Jerusalem and have Amal put down. The message was duly transmitted. MacMichael replied to the effect that under British law murder was generally discouraged and indeed could lead to hanging. The Emir settled for another divorce.

In due course Amal returned to Cairo, took up her stage career again and married an Egyptian called Achmed Salem, an ex-husband of her friend Amina, and a dubious character who had been jailed for defaulting on Government contracts (he contracted to produce tin helmets for the Egyptian Army which were found to be made of cardboard).

Sometime in 1944 a shooting affray took place near the Pyramids. Salem was involved and slightly wounded. It is likely the dispute concerned Amal. Next day, with her constant companion, an Egyptian woman Georgette Kfoury, she left in a chauffeur-driven car for Alexandria. The reason for the journey is unknown but presumably she wished to distance herself from the consequences of a violent lover's quarrel.

About 30 miles south of the city near Ras El Bar the road runs alongside a deep sweetwater canal. The verge slopes to the water. The car left the road and plunged into the canal. When it was eventually recovered the two women were found drowned. The doors were said to be locked. There was no sign of the driver.

Amal was notorious for several reasons and there was a presumption of murder. Speculation and accusation were rife in the Cairo press. One theory was that the British had had her killed since she knew too much and they had no further use for her. I think this can safely be discounted. The mystery of the death of this extraordinary young woman has never been solved.

My leave came to an abrupt end. A signal recalled me to Cairo. I was to fly forthwith to Kufra Oasis in the southern Libyan Desert to join the bulk of an enlarged SAS force already arrived there. A major operation was projected.

Kufra, some 500 miles from Cairo, turned out to be every child's idea of an oasis, waving palms, extensive cultivation, a Bedouin settlement around pools of fresh water. Above on a ridge stood a fort, straight from the pages of Beau Geste. It had been built by the Italians and served as base for their Saharan Companies. It had been captured by a clever French confidence trick in 1941.

Between December '40 and February '41 two patrols of the Long Range Desert Group, the Guards, under Michael Crichton-Stuart of the Scots Guards, and the New Zealanders, under Pat Clayton, had crossed the vast Sahara to make contact with the French garrison in Chad. Their journey of some 5000 miles began at the end of December and they did not see Cairo again until February. The French had responded with enthusiasm and after several successful raids on Italian outposts and bases they returned via Kufra. The Saharan Company had fled the oasis at their approach, leaving a strong Italian garrison in the fort. The Free French column under Colonel Leclerc had only one 75mm field gun but by moving this rapidly about the oasis they succeeded in giving the impression of a battery or more. At night they drove their vehicles quietly some distance into the desert and returned at speed with headlights blazing. After several nights of this entertainment the British and French commanders approached the fortress under a white flag and requested audience. The Italians opened up. It was explained to their commander that, as he had doubtless observed, great reinforcements had arrived each night and that the Anglo-French force was about to attack. Since the outcome was inevitable perhaps the Italian garrison might prefer to surrender rather than suffer heavy and useless casualties. They did.

It turned out that our SAS target was no less than the capture of Benghazi and the destruction of its port. Benghazi lay some 600 miles behind the German/Italian lines and 800 miles north of Kufra. There was to be a simultaneous assault on Tobruk by a force of commandos which included some German Jews in German uniforms. A seaborne landing was also planned and the LRDG under Jake Easonsmith were to attack the airfield and barracks at Barce. This was a massive undertaking compared to anything previously attempted by the SAS. One hundred and twenty new recruits had been drafted into the unit and were quite untrained in its habits or methods. A force of 200 men was now assembled in the oasis with 40 supply trucks, 40 jeeps and it was even rumoured two Honey tanks to come. They did indeed start but both got bogged down in soft sand and never made the operation. There was some scepticism in the unit about the wisdom of this enormous enterprise and it was not surprising to learn later that David had been firmly against it from the outset but had to submit to the dictates of the staff at GHQ. The SAS had been hugely successful. This had at last been acknowledged and the great minds grinding behind their desks at GHQ had devised this plan for us. The concept denied all previous experience and principle on which David's success had been built but nevertheless it was decreed. Even then it might have succeeded had those responsible in Cairo not chattered their heads off in the bars of Shepheard's Hotel. Italian agents were everywhere.

The 800-mile journey from Kufra to the Jebel Akhdar, the hills around Benghazi, involved crossing a neck of the great sand sea, which stretches from the edge of the Tibesti Mountains in the Southern Sahara 500 miles north to Jalo and Jarabub, a passage seldom attempted, except by the LRDG and certainly never by 80 heavily laden vehicles. Because of the need for secrecy our detailed objectives were not to be disclosed until we should arrive in the Jebel. A vain precaution since the whole enterprise had already been widely discussed in Cairo and Alexandria. Gossip was rife.

The sand sea was an experience: great dunes up to 500 feet high of fine grained sand so white and dazzling it could have been snow; the horizon hard against a blue/black sky tended to obscure the tops of the intervening dunes. Each driver had to accelerate hard to reach the top without sinking in, and there was always the danger of a sudden drop from the knife edge of the dune. My friend Alistair Timpson commanding the Guards Patrol of the LRDG, suffered a catastrophic crash over a dune edge. He has carried a distorted arm ever since and his companion Guardsman Wann broke his back.

For two long days, with the aid of sand mats and steel channels, we heaved, shoved and towed our way through, until we reached the better going and could turn north for Benghazi. After eight days the first jeeps reached the Jebel and gradually the huge convoy was dispersed and camouflaged in the wadis and small ravines along the fringe of the mountains.

We hoped we were invisible from the air. We needed to be, for on the very first evening a German Fieseler Storch light aircraft patrolled the Jebel. It was impossible to know whether the pilot had seen us but he returned more than once during the four days we spent there loading our jeeps and waiting for the appointed hour.

Meantime, Fitzroy MacLean, then our resourceful Intelligence Officer, drove off to contact an extraordinary Belgian called Bob Melot, who was living with the Bedouin and sending back intelligence reports by radio to Cairo. Melot was a cotton merchant from Alexandria who had gallantly offered his services and been commissioned. He was well over fifty years old.

Fitzroy, who had already carried out one hair-raising reconnaissance a few weeks earlier into Benghazi with David and Gordon Alston and who has immortalized this operation in his *Eastern Approaches* duly found Melot and together they consulted various Bedouin. The advice was inconclusive so they despatched a shifty looking Arab deserter from the Italian Army into Benghazi some twenty miles away to find out what he could. After two days the man returned with a deeply discouraging report. It seemed the Germans and Italians had reinforced the garrison and strengthened the defences.

Fitzroy, Melot and the spy returned and we awaited their news with eagerness.

"What happened?"

"Well," said Fitzroy with a look of deep distaste at his villainous looking Arab companion, "my – colleague – here went into the town where I understand he contacted his friends. He says our intentions are already being talked about in the bazaar and they even know the date of the attack. The Germans are reported to have moved a regiment into Benghazi. The gist of the advice is that we should go away and think about all this very carefully."

The spy said nothing. He looked even shiftier than before and we were not exactly encouraged to learn that he was to guide us through the Jebel and into the town.

The operation, due 13 September, 1942, was supposed to be synchronized with the attacks at Tobruk and Barce, but the appearance of this German reconnaissance plane and now Fitzroy's report was alarming to say the least and David radioed Cairo to ask for a change in the timing. His request was refused. The reply from GHQ was unhelpful – "ignore bazaar rumour".

David summoned the officers in turn to explain our orders. There were maps and photographs in plenty. I was to make my way to the harbour, capture the Giuliana Mole, a long quay on which it was thought there were several heavy anti-aircraft machine gun posts. When I had dealt with these I was to blow up an oil depot near the base of the mole. I had fourteen men.

I returned to the small camp I shared with Geoff Gordon-Cread, who had recently joined us from Greece, and recounted my orders to him.

"You think that's difficult" he said. "Now I'll tell you what I've got to do. I have to carry a rubber boat into the harbour, there's a large ship alongside or there was when they took the photograph but it may have moved out into the roads. If it has I must blow up this rubber boat with a bicycle pump, row out, throw a shackle over the side, climb up, shut the crew up somewhere on board, escort the Captain to the bridge, get him to arrange his ship in a position to block the harbour mouth and then sink it with limpet mines. And how many men do you think I've got?"

I had no idea.

"Two," he said. "Me and a sailor. You can't get more in the rubber boat."

13. M3 Stuart tanks, known as 'Honeys': "We had watched them picked off like driven partridges" (p.37).

14. The Carrier Platoon, 2nd Battalion, Scots Guards: trouble in the distance.

15. Kabrit: jumping through the hole in a Bombay bomber. The static line is clearly visible (see p.47).

16. "... I did my parachute training, which at that time consisted of jumping off the back of a moving lorry" (p.47).

17. "David Stirling radiated
energy and confidence"
(p.45).

18. "Paddy Mayne, a huge
soft-spoken Ulsterman
whose tally of enemy aircraft
was already legendary"
(p.46).

19. "David Lloyd Owen
[later, Major General CB
DSO OBE MC] ...
persuaded Stirling it was
both safer and more practical
to go by truck" (p.47).

20. "Planes were going up on both sides" (p.64) German aircraft destroyed by the SAS.

21. The Western Desert.

Luckily for most of us we never got into Benghazi at all. We set off the following evening towards sunset, captured a small Italian outpost on the way where one of our officers, Chris Bailey, and Bob Melot who had insisted on being included, were wounded, then descended the Jebel by a precipitous and uncertain route which did nothing to encourage our faith in the guide and fetched up driving slowly along a sunken road with the pinpoint lights of the town clearly visible ahead.

We came to a road block, a bar across the road. The convoy halted while David and Bill Cumper, our indomitable 40 year old engineer officer, got out.

"I suppose we've got to open it, Bill."

"Let battle commence," said Cumper, pushing up the bar. It did!

As soon as the first two jeeps went through we were fired on from both sides of the road. It was an ambush and we were clearly expected. All along the line our jeep crews opened up such a murderous fusillade that the ambush soon quietened down. Clearly there was no longer any hope of surprise and David gave the order to pull out. Somehow we turned the convoy round and drove away with the loss of two jeeps and a handful of casualties. Sadly they included Sergeant-Major Dongin of the Scots Guards, one of the toughest and bravest NCOs in the SAS.

The trouble came next evening. All day we had lain hidden in a wadi in the Jebel while German and Italian aircraft flew around looking for us. There was a particularly persistent Italian bomber which seemed to circle our wadi repeatedly. One of our French comrades (there was a Free French squadron by this time) lost his Gallic patience and shot at it. That did it.

Called up by the bomber the planes roared in and we were bombed and strafed until dark. Most of us managed to scramble away into the scrub and suffered few casualties, but we lost about 15 jeeps and 25 trucks. Tragically Chris Bailey who had been wounded in the stomach on the approach to Benghazi was hit again.

Malcolm Pleydell, our medical officer, decided that both he and Sergeant Major Dongin were too bad to be moved. His orderly volunteered to stay with them. We had several Italian prisoners who were ordered to remain also, while one of their number went back to Benghazi for help.

We had to abandon them. A party remained behind to check and they were eventually picked up. Much later we heard they had died in Benghazi. I can never forget our having to leave them lying wounded there. "Death Valley" the lads called the place.

We loaded the men into the surviving vehicles and fled south into the night. There were up to 30 men on each 3-tonner and 5 or 6 on each jeep. My party was led by Paddy Mayne. We were all to join up at Jalo Oasis which was supposed to have been captured by the Sudan Defence Force in the meantime.

The next few days were among the most unpleasant in my experience: we had no clear idea of our position and for the first and only time in all my months in the desert I began to feel the unsettling effect of chronic thirst. I remember two odd happenings. We were halted. Several of us were standing away from the vehicles, facing roughly west. Towards the far horizon I distinctly saw 3 or 4 vehicles climb slowly over a ridge and disappear. I could not make them out. One of my companions also thought he saw them. We turned eagerly to the others who were facing the same way, searching the desert as we had been. They had seen nothing at all. In my mind's eye, even now, I can see those trucks.

Later the same day, or the next, we watched an aerial battle. No Messerschmitts or Spitfires, just two birds. A raptor of some sort was repeatedly stooping at a small migrant. Eventually the little bird was driven, exhausted, to give up the struggle and fell on to the sand nearby. As one man we all jumped from our vehicles and ran to it. The hawk flew away and we spent some five minutes trying to revive the little creature with the precious water from our bottles. In vain. It died in our hands. We laid it gently on the sand and turned away in silence. I can still feel that moment of helpless sorrow. God's creatures turn to one another when the wilderness threatens.

There were different ideas among us about the bearing we should follow for Jalo. Paddy seemed to be heading due south, but none of us had a true reference point to work from. The more bewildering our plight seemed the quieter Paddy became. "Well, I think we'll just carry on," he would say in his slight North Irish brogue. Somehow, by God knows what guesswork, he got us to the Oasis. I shall never forget the excitement and relief when we saw the first camel tracks criss-crossing the sand and then the outline of the palms. The SDF had failed to take the fort but were encamped in fair comfort in the Oasis. I found one of their Bimbashis (Bimbashi equalled a major's rank) seated in a camp chair attended by a Sudanese mess waiter.

"My dear chap, will you have a whisky and soda?" he said.

It seemed the Italian garrison had also been expecting attack and had made things pretty difficult. Sporadic shelling was still going on. A day or two later a signal arrived instructing the SDF to withdraw and we limped back to Kufra with them. It was a hard journey. We had been near exhaustion and must travel by night to avoid both air and ground attack. After two nights it was thought safe to continue by day but then we had again to contend with the gruelling sand sea crossing. No romantic fiction of the desert could ever equal the relief we felt when the palms and mud huts of Kufra finally hove into view. Haggard, bearded, filthy, many of us in rags, at last we could wash and swim, eat fresh eggs as well as army rations and above all, drink – and drink.

It turned out that nearly all those sent into Tobruk had been killed. Two destroyers were lost and the only real success achieved by the LRDG patrols at Barce who had destroyed some twenty aircraft and caused mighty alarm among the garrison. But the sense of failure and betrayal at the lack of security which had completely comromised the whole operation was mitigated to some extent by a message from Cairo to say that we had succeeded in diverting considerable Axis forces and aircraft from the front and thus in some unexplained way, helped the 8th Army build up. The battle of Alamein was not long delayed.

David, Fitzroy Maclean and some others flew back to Cairo leaving Carol and me in charge of the rear party and the French squadron. We were to cross the desert to Wadi Halfa and thence return to Cairo by river steamer.

The journey was not without incident. The SDF officers, Ombashis and Bimbashis did their best to make us welcome in their smart mess at Wadi Halfa but our tatty appearance and the hilarious conduct of the French tried their patience sorely.

Two days down the Nile at Assiut there was a hospital ship moored. News of our arrival reached the nurses who promptly sent a corporal over in a boat to invite the officers to a dance on board that evening. Probably the poor dears had had nobody to dance with for months. We went and I shall never forget the expressions of shocked alarm as one bearded Frenchman followed another up the ladder, their uniforms in tatters, their heads swathed in Arab Keffiyehs. The girls must have feared their virtue spent. But in spite of this rough introduction the evening warmed up well. The French are like that.

Finally we were delivered to Abbassia Barracks outside Cairo to be kitted out. The men lined up while a busy Quartermaster-Sergeant and Clerk listed their names, numbers and needs. The party came to a halt in front of our remaining Italian prisoner taken near Benghazi. Toni had proved very useful cleaning mess tins and doing odd jobs. He was accepted as part of the unit and I had forgotten about him. Naturally he lined up with the others.

"What's your name and number?"

"Toni."

"I don't care what you call yourself, what's yer name and number?"

I intervened.

"He's a prisoner."

"Prisoner Sir! We'll have to lock him up."

"He's quite harmless" I said. "He's really very useful."

The garrison at Abbassia was not used to prisoners. We had nowhere to put him so to speak now we were back in civilization and so poor Toni was marched off looking deeply crestfallen. It took days to get him back but after much negotiation I succeeded in doing so and he spent the rest of the war happily as a waiter in the SAS Officers' Mess at Kabrit.

This was the end of my nine months service with the SAS. My illness had recurred intermittently and I was sent before a medical board. They told me I had chronic bronchitis and should be boarded "B" for six months. This meant I was considered unfit for active service.

I shall always feel proud and lucky to have served with David. I do not think I was a particularly good SAS Officer. More than a year with an infantry battalion had tended to blunt one's daring. I knew the risks, perhaps too well. Those engaged in special operations, certainly in the desert SAS, lived through times of intense excitement and danger, generally with surprise on their side and free to use their imagination. In between operations were merciful periods of travel or training.

With a regular unit it was the long grind, the circumscription of command, the blind obedience to orders from above, the purpose of which was not or probably could not be properly explained. The inadequacy of much of our equipment, the constraints of a rigid and necessary discipline week after week, month after month. It was these factors as much as the onset of fear and danger which tended to wear a young man down.

I think history shows the British to be outstandingly good at special operations. General Moore's riflemen in the Peninsula are surely direct ancestors of the Commandos. If I had my time again I think that for reasons of temperament and interest I would opt at the outset for Special Operations but equally I know that, for all the extraordinary achievement of the SAS Regiment and the other raiding forces, it was the ordinary infantryman, the tank crew, the gunner and the sapper who won our war in the desert.

Since the war of course the SAS Regiment has evolved. It is no exaggeration to say they have become an essential arm of defence in this wretched age of cowardly terrorism. Their expertise is legendary and their operational range immense. Probably there is no other unit in the Western world which possesses this combination of exhaustive training, daring and ubiquitous resource. From the siege of the Iranian Embassy in London and their presence in Northern Ireland, through the Falklands, Oman and the Gulf to Bosnia the record is there, and SAS officers like Peter de la Billière and Michael Rose have risen to the highest operational command. By comparison with their present competence the early desert operations must seem strangely amateur. They were. But the principles were already established and without David Stirling's imagination and inspiration this essential and extraordinary regiment would never have existed.

Postwar, David's life was not so successful. He started some remarkable initiatives, some political and idealistic, some geared to the demands of what he referred to as "the Sporran". Most ran into the sand. David was never one for the patient follow up, or indeed for patience as a virtue at all.

But nothing can detract from the blazing triumph of those 18 months in the desert from the inception of L Detachment to his capture in Tripolitania. For this he is immortalized.

His memorial service will not be easily forgotten and it was perhaps not entirely inappropriate, both as a warning and a symbol, that the IRA lobbed a mortar bomb into the garden of 10 Downing Street down the road, just before the service began in the Guards Chapel.

In July, 1991, I attended the Jubilee dinner for officers of the Regiment past and present. The company included two field marshals and General Sir Peter de la Billière who commanded British Forces in the Gulf.

I was lucky enough to accompany David Lloyd Owen, now in a wheel chair as a result of wounds suffered with the LRDG. He had witnessed the return of what was left of L Detachment after their first disastrous parachute operation and it was he who persuaded Stirling to use the LRDG patrols as a means of transport instead. Thus began the long partnership between the two units which laid the groundwork for the SAS success so well described in David Lloyd Owen's memoirs.*

Margaret Thatcher, as guest of honour, gave one of the finest speeches I ever heard her make. She concluded, as I remember it, with these words: "Achievement is generally, if not indeed always, the work of the few. Gentlemen, you are the few – and I salute you."

It was a special evening; marred only, for me, by David's absence. He died just four months too soon. He hated ceremony but he should have been there, for he, above all, qualified for her salute.

Extract from a letter of sympathy on David's death to his sister Irene Stirling, who of her choice, now lies buried by his side:
"This letter is not just in homage to David but to you, for goodness knows what his last years would have been like without his devoted sister.

"I wish he could have lived long enough to have enjoyed the dinner we had planned for him this week, but perhaps it is a selfish wish. The strain would have told on his poor frame but at least it may have given him something to look forward to these last days.

"For those of us who served and loved him a light has gone out. Even though it may have burned dimly towards the end we knew it when it shone

* *The Desert My Dwelling Place*, Cassell & Co, 1957

so bright it set life itself alight. Of how many of the so called great and famous can that be said?

"A flame so strong must flicker and burn itself away – and perhaps in a way that is what happened. But so long as bravery and integrity hold place in history his name and that of his creation will live on for he is already a legend – the legend of a true and gallant knight.

"When all the fanfares have echoed away and the sound of the piper fades in the distance what I shall remember is the gentle soul we were sometimes allowed to see within; who cared so much for those near him when they were hurt or frightened, who shunned the limelight and refused to tread the centre of the stage.

"However saddened he may have been towards the end he will know now of the love which surrounded him. For such spirits are beloved of the gods."

———|———

6

CAIRO

This temporary incapacity meant a job on the staff. But who would employ me on their staff? I had no qualification whatsoever as a staff officer. I went off to Headquarters BTE and placed myself at the mercy of the Military Secretary. I was extraordinarily lucky. Richard Casey, Minister of State in the Middle East and a member of the War Cabinet, needed an ADC. No one could think of any particular reason why I should not be an ADC. I went for an interview and, of his charity, Dick Casey gave me the job.

The Caseys lived in the cotton millionaire Chester Beatty's magnificent villa at Mena, near the Pyramids, generously lent for the duration. Apart from private secretaries, the personal staff consisted of a charming Australian girl, Margaret Gilruth, Mae Casey's secretary, and me. I formed the view that I should be just as effective and less of a nuisance if I lived in Cairo and commuted. This caused no problems and I moved into a flat in Sharia Nabatat on Zamalek Island which I shared with a friend, John Walker of the Rifle Brigade, who was recovering from a wound.

It was a seven-month stint to remember. On the one hand I became a tiny cog near the hub of control in the Middle East. On the other I could plunge into what seemed to me the glittering life of wartime Cairo.

Practically everyone who ran the war came to, or through, Cairo for some purpose or other and most stayed or dined with us: Eden, Alexander, Mountbatten, Montgomery, Cunningham; I missed Churchill; even Nöel Coward and the lovely Vivien Leigh, both there to entertain the troops. Coward, a friend of the Caseys, was a wild success playing the piano on makeshift stages in the open desert and singing his ultra-sophisticated satire on society life. I attended once. The troops fell about laughing at his advice to Mrs Worthington and his lyrics on the Stately Homes of England.

I have to confess I recall very little of what the great men said to one another and they naturally said nothing to me.

Towards the end of my time Margaret and I conducted a two-person poll on who of the VIP visitors, regardless of their other values, had seemed kindest and most friendly towards us, the smallest fry around. By mutual consent the prize, by a fairly wide margin, went to General Smuts. It would be invidious and almost certainly unfair to say who came bottom.

By the time I got this job the Battle of Alamein was over and Rommel in full retreat. But Cairo still shuddered with stories of the panic which beset GHQ while the Africa Korps stood at the gates of Alexandria poised, so it seemed, to thrust into the Delta. Montgomery changed all that.

The rot had started after the botched Battle of Knightsbridge. I had left the Battalion there building a strong defensive line behind massive mine-fields. Tobruk was still ours. Rommel attacked frontally and suffered heavy casualties. The German armour and assault troops lay in wounded confusion in front of the British position. Now was the moment to counter-attack both from Tobruk and with our armoured formations which had not then been engaged. General Lumsden, who commanded 7th Armoured Division, besought General Ritchie to give the order. Ritchie, who commanded 8th Army, seemed paralysed and nothing happened.

Rommel collected himself and, now familiar with the British defences, swept round to the south, took Bir Hacheim where the Free French put up a tremendous fight, and then dealt piecemeal with the inferior British armour.

What could have been a stunning victory turned into a rout. The broken 8th Army fell back in headlong disorder to the East.

In overall command at GHQ in Cairo was General Auchinleck. Daily, as reports of the disaster reached them, Dick Casey told me how "the Auk" came to his office. The appalling danger was clear to both. Contingency plans for the evacuation of the Nile Delta were activated and the British position in the Middle East seemed fatally threatened. Yet Auchinleck, pacing back and forth in front of Casey's desk in grim and tense silence, seemed incapable of any reaction.

Finally Casey, a soldier himself with an MC from the first war, felt bound to press the General. Did he seriously believe Ritchie was still in control? Ritchie was Auchinleck's appointment. He had been reluctant to accept and had subsequently suffered considerable back-seat driving from his Com-mander-in-Chief. Auchinleck rounded on the Minister of State. "Are you suggesting I don't trust him? Of course I trust him, I put him there. Do you expect me to sack him?"

The tension lasted several days while the desperate retreat continued. Finally, to Casey's relief the Auk decided to relieve the unfortunate General Ritchie, go down to the desert himself and take command. With the help of an Indian Brigade he managed to stop the rout and stabilized the defence at El Alamein. The Afrika Korps was already stretched to the limit and the front held. The 8th Army was never to retreat again in Africa, but, not surprisingly, General Auchinleck's days of command were numbered. Churchill replaced him with Alexander while Montgomery took command of 8th Army.

Later in the year (1943), Montgomery came to the villa for a weekend's leave from "my army". His ADC, Johnny Henderson of the 12th Lancers, was allowed leave also and I had to attend the General. Casey was away so I saw quite a lot of him. I learnt very little and cannot say I took to him, though his air of devastating confidence was infectious.

"Where are my pills boy? Everyone in my Army takes pills at this time of day. Can't afford to be sick."

I can't remember what his pills were for but I recall the anxious search.

When my three days duty were ended I accompanied Montgomery to Al Maza airport where his personal Flying Fortress with its American crew waited on the tarmac. At the end of the line stood Johnny, complete in every sartorial respect except for the cap. This constituted an inspection however cursory.

"Johnny, where's your cap?" barked the General. Johnny winced visibly. He was clearly beyond subterfuge.

"I'm very sorry General, the elephant ate my cap." This startling revelation silenced even Montgomery.

"Get in the plane, you bloody fool."

Afterwards, long afterwards, I discovered what had happened. Johnny's Regiment was back from the desert. He and his friends had been living it up all weekend and had finished at the Gezira Club where, much encouraged by lunch, they decided to take their girls to the zoo. Someone removed Johnny's cap and gave it to the elephant who immediately entered into the spirit of the thing.

I did not envy Johnny his job but he managed his General with much skill, cap or no cap.

Towards the end of my time in Cairo Mountbatten was appointed C-in-C Far East. He and his hand-picked and somewhat over-gilded staff stopped off in Cairo on their way to Kuala Lumpur. There was a grand dinner at Mena to which all the mighty came including, naturally, Admiral Cunningham, C-in-C Mediterranean, who had to come up specially from Alexandria, and didn't seem too pleased about it.

In days gone by Mountbatten had served as a midshipman aboard a destroyer commanded by Cunningham, years his senior. Rumour had it that he had ordered Mountbatten beaten for some misdemeanour, but, however that may have been, here he was called upon to attend his former midshipman, now his senior officer. Mountbatten had been hoisted in one remove from Captain to full Admiral by Churchill.

After dinner, when the women had left, Mountbatten sat at the head of the table, Cunningham on his right. All Mountbatten's staff including himself were arrayed in a natty new naval tropical ensemble designed, so it turned out, by Mountbatten himself. Conversation was stilted, to put it mildly, but Mountbatten was not easily discountenanced. He talked confidently on.

Suddenly old Cunningham could stand it no longer.

"Why the hell are you all dressed up like Americans?"

The mask slipped.

"Well Sir, you see Sir, my idea was . . . it was felt, you see Sir . . ." I do not recall the reasoning but the tone was unmistakably that of the midshipman to his Captain.

Admiral Cunningham, elbows on the table, with his back half turned to the C-in-C Far East, was not impressed, but those of us who were not on the Mountbatten staff hugely enjoyed it.

Focal and fashionable point for the British *monde* in Cairo was Shepheard's Hotel. Dating from the earliest days of British tourism it had an air of Imperial and Edwardian splendour, from the long mahogany bar, through the great dining room, to the lofty palmed and panelled hall, out onto the Terrace, where tables were set and where one could sit, watch arrivals and departures, spot the girls and generally keep the score.

Some twenty yards across the terrace, between more massive potted palms, steps descended to the level of the street, crowded both day and night.

The servants at Shepheard's were invariably discreet and efficient but perhaps the most impressive was Arslan, the Commissionaire, who dominated this entrance, an Albanian of magnificent aspect, clad in a livery which would have graced a minor chamberlain of the Sublime Porte: claret-coloured tarbush, *pantalons buffons* and white leggings, a splendid *salta* with wide slashed sleeves and double-breasted gold waistcoat. He it was who glided to the staff car door, terrorized the taxi drivers, summoned gharris, quelled the drunken Australian soldiers leering at the terrace and held general sway in the street.

On the pavement, at a safe distance if Arslan was about, crowded the dragomans and touts. They ranged from dirty squint-eyed pimps, wheezing pathetically "Captin' Captin', you want meet my black sister?" to the immensely dignified figure of Moses, six foot three in his red Arab sandals, with the hook-nosed profile of a vizier in an 18th dynasty relief. He would advance on his victims, bowing low:

"Would you like Moses as a guide, Sah?"

If there was no immediate reaction he bowed lower still.

"I highly recommend Moses, Sah."

This schizophrenic assessment frequently succeeded as well it might, for Moses commanded a limitless if expensive range of *divertissements* and, within the somewhat elastic conventions of his profession, was held to be reliable.

As I walked up the steps on one particular evening the velvet Egyptian night was falling fast. Yellow street lamps went on and from the terrace the irregular outlines of Cairo set hard against a cobalt sky. The all-pervading clamour of the city, honking horns, braying donkeys and Arabic altercation gave way to the laughter and multi-lingual conversation of the evening's drinkers. British uniforms abounded. Staff officers, from GHQ, sometimes unkindly referred to as "the Short Range Shepheard's Group", sat with their regular dates; officers on leave from the desert limbering up for a night out, still smart in blue patrols or skin-tight cavalry overalls, for, in spite of the nearness of the desert war, Egypt was nominally a neutral country. No blackout, no shortages and the lingering habits of pre-war.

I was alone and looked round for any familiar face. I found one. Slumped in a wicker chair so placed that he could see everyone and everything was a large rotund figure. I had met Archie Lyall once before at some party, but one did not forget Archie. I was conscious of a gimlet-like inspection from two small shrewd and rather bloodshot eyes peering at me through the cigar smoke. Above the cigar was a small bristly moustache. His great bulk was arrayed in a shabby and shapeless approximation to a uniform and there were crowns on the shoulder straps of what had begun as a bush shirt. He was alone.

Archie removed the cigar and cleared his throat with a noise like a burst from a machine gun. A girl at the next table jumped in startled surprise.

"Have a mint julep," said Archie. I joined him.

"Why does everyone here drink mint juleps?" I asked.

"It was Nelson's favourite drink. It's been going on since the Battle of the Nile." No reply seemed safe to this.

"Tell me my boy, what did you do before all this inconvenience broke upon us?"

"I was at Sandhurst actually," I said. "I suppose I am one of the last regular officers. What did you do?"

"Me, oh a number of things, varied career, don't you know."

You could not fail to be intrigued by Archie and at the risk of seeming impudent I asked:

"What?"

He took a pull at his cigar and a gulp of mint julep.

"What did I do? Well, I was a reporter in the Spanish War until my friends were all put in gaol or shot. Then I was third officer aboard a Greek tramp steamer for a bit."

"Good Lord," I said. "That must have been interesting. Why aren't you in the Navy?"

"Precisely because of my experiences in the Greek Merchant Marine my boy. I had never been to sea before except in an unofficial capacity, across the channel, and I never wish to again. It was simply a means of locomotion, dirty, uncertain and excessively uncomfortable but more or less obligatory at the time." Archie paused for more mint julep.

"But my most successful enterprise to date was the founding of a hospital for sick donkeys in Fez."

"Of course," I said.

"Oh yes my boy. You see I was supposed to be writing a travel book but somehow the retaining fee slipped through my fingers in Tangier. You know how these things happen. So I passed on to Morocco. Things were really tough there, until I remembered Cousin Emily."

"Cousin Emily?"

"Yes, my boy. Every good man deserves a Cousin Emily. I hope you have one. They are more than useful, particularly when resident in the United States as elderly spinsters. They invariably have kind hearts and are full of concern."

"What could she do for you in Fez?"

"Fez, my boy, as any casual traveller will observe, is full of donkeys. The donkey population is high by any standards. Moreover the state of many of these donkeys is deplorable. The more I looked at those pitiable donkeys the more ashamed I became of the human race. And so I conceived my great veterinary project and wrote to Cousin Emily."

"But are you a vet?"

"No, but neither was I a qualified seaman before joining the Greek Merchant Marine. It is a question of temporary vocation."

"So what?"

"Well, Cousin Emily came up trumps; a straight hand of trumps in fact. She was so moved that she not only agreed to finance the project but introduced a large number of similarly placed American ladies all of whom were equally concerned. The lolly fairly rolled in. I engaged an assistant and founded the donkey hospital."

"What did you do for the donkeys?"

"Alas, my boy, there was little we could do for the donkeys. We put them out of their misery as quickly as possible. The corpses were a problem to begin with but my assistant had a friend who ran the local salami factory. That solved it."

"Good God," I said. "Did they all go into the salami?"

"Every little bit my boy, except the hooves. I never did discover what they did with the hooves. But no matter, we were providing a useful service, re-establishing the food chain, so to speak, and Cousin Emily was delighted with my descriptions of our progress. I got quite rich. I even opened a bank account – in Timbuctoo. Do you know anyone else with a bank account in Timbuctoo?"

"No," I said.

"I thought not. Most useful. It took my London bank manager at least six months to catch up with the pace of events in Timbuctoo by which time I had always moved on."

Archie clapped his hands for a waiter and ordered us two more drinks.

"What are you doing now? In Cairo I mean?" I asked.

He looked about him and assumed an air of elaborate conspiracy.

"P.W. my boy," he said in a gravel-like whisper.

"What's that?"

The vast figure glanced about again. "Psychological Warfare."

"Is it very secret?"

"Not particularly but discussion always leads to questions and I wish to avoid questions. I have an office and a charming secretary whom I have sent temporarily on leave. There is no need for questions."

"So you don't know what you are supposed to be doing?" I said laughing.

"There is a large number of people in exactly that condition in this city my boy. There is nothing whatever unusual about it. Most of the Generals we have had in command here were clearly in that category. Now we have this fellow Montgomery who shows every sign of knowing what he is doing. It may yet prove fatal. Do you know what you are supposed to be doing?"

"Well I am supposed to look after the Minister of State. But before that I was with David Stirling in the SAS. That was sometimes confusing."

"Exactly. They never know what they will do next and I am told they are extremely successful. You must leave room for intuition. The British are very good at it. The Germans do not understand it. That is why in the end we shall win this war. Have you a plan this evening or is it intuitive?"

"Well actually, I have to meet a girl here later. I've booked a felucca."

"Ah, that can lead to trouble my boy. You cannot escape very easily from a felucca. Personally I find all women equally dangerous if they are in a position to pursue. So far as love is concerned command of movement is essential. In Madrid I had a number of entirely satisfactory relationships, all of which developed, flourished and eventually expired in the same place."

"Where was that?"

"The Bordello my boy. The ladies in question were confined to barracks,

99

so to speak. You had an equally effective escape route into the desert. But no longer, it seems. Take my advice. Make no binding agreements in a felucca."

I saw quite a lot of Archie during my time in Cairo. I never really discovered what he was supposed to be doing or what P.W. amounted to but his contribution to morale in general was unsurpassed.

After the war he returned to his travel books and sadly for me our paths seldom crossed. The last time was in Paris in 1958. He was wandering down the Faubourg St Honoré, apparently without any fixed plan. It was plain he had lunched well.

Overjoyed to see him, I invited him for a drink that evening at our house in Boulogne-sur-Seine. We had a small party arranged. To my surprise and delight he turned up and as was his wont became an immediate centre of attention. His stories were going down as well as ever when suddenly without warning, like a great oak tree in a storm, he swayed and fell. He did not collapse or crumple, he crashed. Several of us – it needed several – hoisted him upright.

"Funny thing," he said, "it has something to do with the little canals of the ear." Which of course it had. Then completely unabashed he continued the conversation where he had left off. No one who had not witnessed the crash would have guessed that the whisky, and God knows what else before that, had just overcome the little canals of his ears.

Archie died some years later alone in a clinic in Switzerland, mourned by all who knew him. The finest of several tributes was provided by his friend and mine, Peter Kemp, in a memorable and extremely funny contribution to a symposium produced in memoriam by a number of his friends. They met originally during the Spanish War where Peter was serving with the Spanish Foreign Legion. Peter ends his piece with words from *Henry V*.

"Would I were with him, where so e'er he be
either in Heaven or in Hell,
Nay, sure he's not in Hell."

There are people whose tragi-comic lives bring more pleasure and leave a more lasting sense of gratitude among their contemporaries than all manner of successful men. He who laughs at life and lives with laughter is not just a boon to his friends, he is close to the Gods.

We walked together through the palms and eucalyptus of the Tahir Gardens on Zamalek Island, the girl and I, towards the river. The last rays of a brilliant sunset lit her face and threw rippling shadows across her long swaying skirt. I was glad I had discounted Archie's advice.

"Where is he?" she asked.

"Over there at the landing stage: the last one with the little light on."

I led the way down through the gardens to the landing stage. Now we stood at the very point of Zamalek Island, listening to the small lapping noises and watching the great river eddy massively past us.

All along the west bank, dark against the dying day, was the profile of Cairo. Close by, a minaret with the domes of its attendant mosque. Beyond stood the irregular angles of the poor hovels by the waterside. Further again spacious villas and palms; a tall modern hotel. We could hear the faint hum of traffic over the Kasr El Nil bridge. The lights of cars moved across it. Pinpoint lights twinkled everywhere, reds, warm yellows and greens, reflected in the viscous surface of the Nile.

We walked carefully along the floating pontoon, over ropes and gear towards a group of craft moored at the end. Four or five graceful little feluccas, the single tall lateen sails hoisted and motionless on their long spars, a shaded lantern hanging from each masthead. There were mattresses and cushions amidships.

"Achmed," I called.

"Iewa, effendi Captin." Several felucca proprietors rose hopefully from the shadows.

"Achmed," I called again.

"Iewa, Ta'ala, plees, plees madam."

We made our way over the gunwale and thence to the cushions. The girl settled into them with the fastidious precision of a cat, shaking the wrap loose about her bare shoulders.

"Come on," she said. "Have you got the wine?"

I put down the basket I was carrying, took out a bottle and tumblers.

"Yalla Achmed."

"Iewa, Mr Captin."

Deftly with a single oar Achmed manoeuvred the felucca away from the mooring and into midstream. The sail filled almost imperceptibly above us in the darkness and we could tell from the urgent whispering ripple round the bow that we were heading upstream. The lights and sounds of the city moved along with us, yet there was a feeling of complete detachment. We seemed nearer to the canopy of night with its first faint stars than to the teeming shadowed world along the river banks. Our pilot sat above us by the long tiller, a model of wooden discretion.

I poured the wine and in silence we watched the night unfold above us with its myriad reflections. There was the strong reek of the river, mingled with the smells of the nightbound city, a pôt-pourri of dust, dried dung and Arab cooking.

"Find me some stars," she said.

"Well there's the Milky Way, so clear out here; and there's Cassiopeia, the Seven Sisters; and Orion with his belt and sword. I never can find his head. And there's the best friend to sailors and desert navigators, the Pole Star."

"Where?"

"Do you see the Plough, low down on the horizon? Take the last two markers of the ploughshare then extend the line upwards and there he is. He never moves."

"Yes, I see," she whispered as though the existence of the Pole Star were a miracle exclusive to the two of us.

This voyage promised well . . .

Later: quite a lot later, Achmed called quietly, "Yalla".

He was putting about. With a creaking and straining of ropes the spar swung lazily round the mast. Achmed steered across the stream then towards Zamalek. Once on course downstream the passage of the felucca was noiseless.

The girl sat up, smoothed her skirt and searched for her bag. Presently she started to brush her hair. It is a gesture of arrogant female confidence. Her face half turned away the slow sensuous hissing stroke of the brush stretched her long hair until it seemed to flow like a dark waterfall glinting in the lantern light, breaking at last and springing back into ever widening waves. She shook her head and looked at me smiling.

Behind her was the outline of a high square building on the bank. I recognized it. I had been there with Margaret Gilruth to the 15th Scottish General Hospital by the Nile, not long before, to visit Ward 10 with cigarettes for the boys and to take them for a walk in the gardens. Books were useless for they had not yet attempted braille. They were not used to the darkness yet. Polite to their visitors; we were not of their world; their new and terrifying blind world. They called anxiously to each other, clung to each other.

"Taffy, Taffy, where are ye Taffy? Are ye all right: I'm over here Taffy."

They were all sappers, mutilated lifting mines in front of the advancing tanks during the Battle of El Alamein, just two months before, all blind for life.

The felucca glided now among masts and the tall dark silhouettes of palm and tamarisk whispering together in the breeze. We were back at the Island.

"Wahad hour Mr Captin! You want more?"

"No Achmed, how much?"

The girl collected her bag and wrap, slid under the sail and slipped ashore as the bargaining rose to its inevitable crescendo. Money passed. Achmed assumed an attitude of helpless but dignified resignation.

"Good night Captin, good night lady. You come again. Make it two hour."

But a spell had been broken. Somehow the felucca didn't seem relevant any more.

The magical attraction of wartime Cairo lay in its contrasts. From an uncertain existence in a desolate, hostile wilderness, just two days in whatever transport happened to be available led to a life of soft seductive Levantine luxury, or so it seemed to a young soldier, eyes wide with wonder, a few days leave to spare. From Shepheard's to the roof of the Continental where the celebrated Hehmet Fahmy swivelled her sinuous limbs until in due course, and quite properly, she was arrested as a Nazi spy.

No one who has not seen it performed in the Middle East by a professional at the top of her class can ever appreciate the wonder of the Raa'sa, which we so inadequately describe as the "tummy dance". This is the ultimate sexual exposition of the female form, expressed with passion, yet just held within bounds by a disciplined veneer of modesty.

It was at the Dugout Club she reigned, Carioca, queen of them all. They said she was Farouk's mistress, but they said that about a lot of women. We knew her well. Slowly she would gyrate across the floor until she danced by our table, two feet away, every square inch of golden brown flesh vibrating, and above the swaying torrent of ebony black hair. Amber gold eyes unblinking, seemingly half conscious, so consumed was she with her body's possession. Now slowly the coffee-coloured frame spins on its axis. Long lacquered fingers stretched and spread before eyes downcast, buttocks and breasts shaken to destruction. The dance reaches a final paroxysm. Cymbals and drums signal an orgasmic finale. Head flung back, her body locks, she looks gracefully drained – and subsides into a chair.

"Hello darling, have you whisky for me?"

Nowhere was the contrast more emphatic than at the Gezira Sporting Club, a typical British Institution, exclusive, though in no sense only to the British. To those of us returning from the desert, it was like a time capsule, immune from the events whch flowed around it. Duty as well as pleasure took me often to Gezira. You could sit on the terrace beside the large swimming pool with a John Collins before you and eliminate reality.

British officers with their wives or girls were everywhere but one heard snatches of talk in Arabic, French and Italian. There were members of the Diplomatic Corps, politicians, a good many Anglophile Egyptians, rich merchants from Alexandria and the Levant, and a sprinkling of American Officers lately arrived, sitting uncertainly in their stiff uncomfortable looking tropical uniforms. The women were smart, sunburnt, and often extremely good looking.

Apart from the Europeans here were the faces of immemorial Egypt, the mixed blood of the Levant, traces of victor and vanquished since the Assyrian chariots first glinted in the dust to the East; of Pharaoh and Phoenician; Greek and Roman; Muslim and Copt. The waves of conquest and religion which have rolled over the Delta while the Pyramids grew old, since the dawn of language, had formed these features. Here in Cairo, one felt, the pretensions of alien armies and administrations passed as the seasons, became tempered and absorbed by the gentle cynicism of an ancient and civilised people.

Beyond the swimming pool, never empty until after sunset, were the racecourse and polo grounds. In the distance a few white-clad figures cantered lazily about practising shots. The drum of hooves and the faint click of a polo ball well struck merged with the talk, the cries and splashing in the pool. It was hard to remember that only five miles away all fertility ceased, that the dark burgeoning soil of the Delta, the lines of palm fringed canals and teeming impoverished villages gave way in a few scrubby yards to the emptiness of the Western Desert. Hard to recall that over a stretch of a hundred miles west two armies were locked in battle, a battle for this ancient city. Before El Alamein and only an hour's drive to the north, down the road to Alexandria you could have seen by night a dim flickering as of distant lightning beyond the horizon and heard the rumble of the guns, while here at Gezira life went lazily on, or so it seemed.

I went back to Gezira a few years ago. The once impressive entrance to the Club House looks forlorn now, a respectable elderly relic of another age, dwarfed by hideous modern developments on every hand. Across the polo grounds rise huge tower blocks of steel and concrete. I walked again down to the stem of Zamalek Island where the Western or Blind Nile flows and there I found a few sad yards of white chipped running rail where once the racehorses thundered by.

Field sports were limited around Cairo except for those lucky enough to be invited to the great duck shoots. One of the best in the delta belonged to the Embassy. Enormous bags were possible. Cartridges were difficult to come by and I was astonished to learn that officers on leave who were asked to shoot had to buy their ammunition from the Ambassador.

John Walker and I had a shikar friend, a Bedouin named Ahmed, who dwelt on the fringes of the desert. Well over six foot tall, his leathery face creased in a permanent wolfish grin, he would appear outside our block of flats whenever there was a fall of snipe. The delta is a vast haven for migrant fowl and waders in winter. Ahmed harbured a deep and voluble contempt for all Egyptians. He was a man of the desert and regarded these dwellers in cities and cultivation as soft, cowardly and worthless. I believe that in ancient

Egypt the people of the desert such as Ahmed were called the Mesh-Wesh and generally held to be a dangerous nuisance. It seemed nothing much had changed.

As befits men of the open air Ahmed used to arrive before dawn.

"Snips, Mr Captin!" he would bellow, brushing aside the Boabs or watchmen asleep on the doorsteps who tried to restrain him lest he wake the street.

"Snips, plenty snips!"

Unless there was some overriding objection we would grab our guns, collect a picnic and go. An hour's drive by waterways and marsh brought us to the apppointed place, where, as if by magic, Ahmed summoned a large number of Walads or small boys who acted as beaters and retrievers. For several happy hours we stalked the marsh. The "Snips" flew in all directions and whenever we were lucky enough to hit one every Walad within sight ran after it. They ran in worse than spaniels and represented a considerable hazard.

When the sun was high and the day grew hot we would go back to share our picnic with Ahmed. This was always preceded by a shrill and frightful altercation with the Walads who insisted they had been shot and demonstrated all manner of small scratches and holes in their galabiehs to prove it. I do not believe any of them had ever been shot. On some previous cocasion one probably had been and the resulting blood money had inspired all his successors.

After the pay off Ahmed, whose faith in the Prophet's instructions was decidely shaky, drank large quantities of beer, and recounted long and incomprehensible stories of the chase.

On our way back to Cairo we passed through several teeming villages. Ahmed, full to the brim with Stella beer, would lean out of the back window, shout insults at the passers-by and, if he was near enough, take a swipe at their tarboushes or whatever else they had on their heads, subsiding onto the back seat with a fearsome cackle.

"'Gyptians, bloody fool!" was his war cry.

It was lucky for us our old car never broke down during these assaults.

We were much attached to Ahmed but I do understand how it must have been with the Mesh-Wesh.

A never-failing entertainment was the Muski. Here was the true breath of the Levant, the sounds and smells unaltered surely since Ptolemy's soldiers wandered in. I would go there sometimes on Sunday evenings, pay off my taxi outside the El Azhar University, stroll among the crowds along Sharia Gohar el Qaid and turn down one of the small streets to the right into Khan el Khalili. On either hand now jostling crowds milled up and down the narrow alleys of this amazingly diverse market. There were merchants of every produce of the orient, Pachas' servants, ponces and peddlers of hashish, legless beggars squatting on little wooden carts, tall men of the desert and veiled black-robed women.

Groups of soldiers on leave from the 8th Army wandered up and down, bewildered and fascinated by the colour, bustle and the wares on every side. The cocked bush hats of the Australians were much in evidence, men of the New Zealand Division also, tall Sikhs in immaculate turbans, their bearded faces set and inscrutable. Here were the badges of many British regiments; the side caps of the cavalry, the bonnets of the Highlanders, and the stiff straight forage caps and ramrod tramp of the guardsmen.

Few knew for what they had come, except to see the sights; all were potential prey to the touts who flitted among them constantly pulling at their sleeves. This for me was Cairo, the very fraudulence fascinated and there was much that was not fraudulent if you knew where to look.

Now I was among the merchants of spices. The fragrance of their wares eddied about me and the sacks of seeds neatly arranged in tiers arose on every side. Long brown arms like tentacles grabbed at me as I passed.

"Hinna, hinna!" they hissed.

Here was attar, saffron and peppers of many kinds, aniseed, ginger and salamen, daphne, tahina and caraway, coriander and myrrh. There too were chickens, live in slatted baskets and the quacking of ducks. I turned a corner into the street of the sellers of perfume. Ancient apothecary's bottles filled with deep coloured essence stood crowded on the shelves of small booths and glinted in the lamplight inside dark open-fronted shops. Eyes followed me. A pause, a look of intent, and instantly a palm or wrist is dabbed with scent.

"Perfume Sah? 'Gyptian perfume, scents of Araby."

There was essence of the lotus fit for a Pharaoh's queen, the intoxicating fragrance of musk, the subtlety of amber, naphthali and full, the sweetness of jasmine and violet, of the rose and the tuberose.

Not all was sweet. One repellent concoction was called "Secrets of the Desert". The secretary of a friend of mine spilled it all over the secret files in her office in GHQ. She was not allowed to forget it, nor indeed could anybody else.

I turned left into another crowded little thoroughfare. Here were sellers of silver and leather, of pottery and antiquities, jewellery, baubles, junk and trash of every description. It was full of soldiers. I am temporarily pinned by the crowd. At my feet in a dusty little shopfront there squats cross-legged a maker of prayer beads. With a bow and thong in his left hand he turns a spindle on which is mounted the little cylinder of false green amber. In his right he flourishes the sharp tool with which he fashions the intricate shapes of his beads. As he worked he kept up a flow of talk to two customers who sat opposite listening with reverence.

Half way down the street was a comparatively large and open shop garishly lit and labelled "Mohammed Moussa, Jewels, Souveners, Gold, Silver, Marvels". It was packed with laughing arguing soldiers accompanied by gaudy looking girls.

Levantine bargaining adds an intellectual dimension to economic satisfaction – or even dissatisfaction. It is properly conducted over small cups of mazbout. I was never good at it but the process justified itself. How boring and barbarous the supermarket and all the instant computerised means of modern exchange seems by comparison. Only among horsemen is the bargain still struck as it should be.

In the middle of the Muski was a *Maison Particulier*, a rarity in itself. There lived the "Sheika" Zaheya, a pederast of indeterminate age and roguish look. Robed as a woman, he claimed to be the reincarnation of the Sheika and enjoyed a considerable reputation as a seer and fortune teller. The Sheika held court in front of his house among foraging chickens and a patient queue of shrouded women waiting to solicit his powers. My friend Victor Simaika used to take people to visit the Sheika. The poor women would be brushed aside as soon as the Sheika spotted more important business. I never chanced my luck with him but many testified to his accuracy.

Victor, one of the most imperturbably cheerful people I have ever met, and incidentally a high goal polo player in his day, had considerable experience of the occult in Egypt. Once, much troubled by a law suit, he consulted the Sheika. When he finished explaining his troubles the seer reached below his galabieh and produced a small folded piece of paper on which were lines in an unknown cabalistic script, written in red ink. Victor was instructed to place this in a bowl of water under his bed at the next full moon. He did so. Two days later he won his case. I never knew how the Sheika managed to establish this influence over the judiciary but he certainly added to the delights of the Muski.

There was plenty of entertainment during my six months in Cairo, but perhaps the most memorable party happened towards the end of my time when the Battalion was back on leave. John Walker and I, with the help of our neighbours from the flat beneath, Patricia Russell and Rosemary Adams, both of whom worked at GHQ, prepared a reception. Our Sudanese sufragi borrowed a mass of cutlery and glasses from his friends who worked for people who lived in the flats round about, and practically everyone we knew in Cairo was invited. The revelry went on throughout the night; the last to leave as dawn broke were some Egyptian friends and several of my brother officers, Brian Mayfield who commanded the Battalion included. The Egyptians offered to lift them home to Peter Stirling's flat, sometime SAS HQ, where they were all staying, but on second thoughts wisely abandoned the idea. Thus our guests were left on the pavement with a long walk across Zamalek Island and the Boulak to Garden City. Half-way through the Boulak, crowded by night as well as day, they were tiring rapidly. No taxis were available or likely so they stopped an Egyptian with a donkey and after some brisk bargaining bought the animal. Taking it in turns to ride they wove their way towards the more fashionable parts of Cairo. Happily no Military Police patrols spotted them. Beyond the Boulak quarter they finally hailed a taxi. By this time they had become naturally and correctly attached to the donkey. There could be no question of abandoning it and there was very little market for donkeys in Mohammed Ali Square. So they pushed the donkey into the taxi and made their way slowly back to Garden City. Peter lived on the second floor, so it was a considerable achievement to entice and shove the donkey up two flights of stairs, but it was done. Complaints from the neighbours about the noise and indeed the mess did not deter them. Having let themselves into the flat, they made their unsteady way to the large dormitory room which Peter kept for officers in the 2nd Battalion on leave, collapsed on their camp beds and passed out. The donkey was left to his own devices.

Around seven in the morning, Mohammed, or "Mo" as he was known, Peter's long-suffering sufragi, arrived to make the breakfast. Horrified to discover this unexpected guest he ran into Peter's room and woke him up. A rash course of action at the best of times.

"Mr Peter, Mr Peter. This too much! No pay for three weeks. Now donkey in flat."

Peter naturally thought that Mo had at last taken leave of his senses, told him to go away and went back to sleep. Mo grumbled off to his lair in the pantry. When next Peter woke and turned over he was confronted with a long lugubrious face, a pair of waving ears and pieces of straw from one of the mattresses dangling from its mouth. The shock was considerable. Mo was evidently still sane.

Some of us had been invited to go round for a drink before lunch at Peter's. When I arrived two Egyptian policemen were hanging about outside the flat and I noticed one of the stained glass panels by the front door was broken. Even by Stirling standards this was unusual. Mo opened the door, giggling helplessly.

"What's the matter, Mo?'

Mo relapsed into a fresh paroxysm and led the way to the drawing room. Inside was a number of somewhat jaded people who had been at the party. Behind the sofa stood the donkey, ears going like a semaphore, its back end on the balcony in case of accidents. A girl on the sofa was proffering a large bowl of something. I never discovered what it was but Mo later hinted darkly that there was gin in it. Whether it was the gin or some other stimulus the donkey's considerable manhood was suddenly displayed for all to see. The gramophone was playing a popular tune called "Hold Tight". The girl on the sofa looked deeply embarrassed.

"It's all right," Peter said to her. "It's nothing to do with you, he does it whenever we play 'Hold Tight'."

"Peter," I said "there are two Egyptian policemen outside!" After all he was Second Secretary at the Embassy across the road and I was uncertain what the diplomatic rules might be concerning donkeys.

"It's OK," said Peter. "The neighbours sent for them because of the noise. They don't mind. They're trying to buy the donkey for 12 quid but we're sticking out for 20."

Later in the afternoon Peter got Mo to invite all the Boabs (doorkeepers-cum-watchmen) from the neighbouring buildings and interest was considerable. They played "Hold Tight" as loud as they could and the donkey was eventually knocked down for £25.

All too soon my six months were up and I was passed fit. The Battalion, last heard of in Tunis, had left to take part in the Salerno landing. After the SAS experience and encouraged by several friends, whose adventures in the Balkans sounded more than intriguing, I decided to apply to Special Operations.

Rustum Buidlings in Kasr el Aini housed the HQ of the Special Operations Executive (SOE) Cairo. Its purpose was pretty well known. Indeed the Cairo taxi drivers used to refer to the place as "Secret Building". I knew a number of its denizens and got myself recruited without difficulty. The first idea was to send me into Yugoslavia but in the end I was posted to the Algiers HQ with a view to being sent into Southern France.

I sailed from Alexandria in a Greek troop ship full of Free French military prisoners bound for the nearest French Army lock up. They were an uninspiring bunch.

I joined the Algiers station, code named "Massingham" at a pleasant place by the sea near the city. They were flying agents into the South of France in preparation for Operation Anvil, the invasion of the Côte d'Azur by the Americans. It turned out that my job was to go in with the landing, join the maquis somewhere in the Basses Alpes and report on their needs.

It was a pretty farcical interlude. To begin with the invasion itself was probably unnecessary. Churchill's alternative, a landing in the Balkans, if it had succeeded in getting through the mountains, could have saved half Eastern Europe from the communist tyranny. Operation Anvil was not seriously opposed and the American advance through Provence could have done little to help their main thrust from Normandy to the Rhine.

My little party, consisting of an artist, Ralph Banbury, a radio operator and myself invaded St Tropez, as pleasant a place for an invasion as you could wish, and, apart from a few snipers being hunted down in a desultory way by an American infantry company, the place seemed open to tourists.

We contacted a powerful Maquis in the Valleé de St Jean de Maurienne. They had all they needed. There was a German formation opposite backed up against the Swiss frontier which had no chance of escape and was showing signs of incipient surrender.

Joined by Brooks Richards (later Ambassador in Athens and Deputy Secretary of the Cabinet Office) from Algiers, we decided to abandon our superfluous assignment and drive north.

It was quite a drive. In some villages we were welcomed by the local resistance. In others along the way the Germans were still in residence. After various detours we got to Dijon where liberation was in full swing. The streets were jammed with people, near hysterical with relief. There was an air of carnival and the chief entertainment consisted of rounding up the "*putains*", girls known or believed to have slept with the Germans. They were marched through the streets by the resistance fighters to some central barracks where they were ceremoniously stripped, had their hair shaved and turned loose, followed by jeering crowds, some with swastikas daubed on their bodies. It was not a pretty performance but at least their lives were spared and their humiliation was the only act of revenge we witnessed at Dijon.

Outside the city, to our considerable surprise, we were hailed on the road by a tall, weatherbeaten, blonde American woman. She turned out to be Martha Gellhorn, wife of Ernest Hemingway and a freelance journalist, who had contrived by some subterfuge to land on D-Day in spite of her husband having removed her accreditation. She seemed relieved at the prospect of an escort, as well she might be, the situation being what it was.

We reached Paris in the early morning without further incident, sought a restaurant and ordered an approximation to an English breakfast. There seemed to be no shortage of food. Martha surprised us by mixing jam with her bacon. When one of us remarked she must be very hungry to mess up the first chance of a decent breakfast she overheated badly and told us this was an entirely acceptable American custom not to be despised by a bunch of arrogant British officers. Our brief role as knights errant seemed to be over and our ways parted soon after.

Martha Gellhorn had a distinguished career as a journalist and author but in our experience that morning she was a bit short on jokes.

———————|———————

7

LIBERAZIONE

I contacted the recently established Headquarters of the Special Operations Executive in Paris and waited for orders. I was increasingly afflicted with guilt. I had chosen the unorthodox extra-regimental path for the second time and made nothing of it. The Battalion had been thrown in to the Italian Campaign and suffered casualties. My friend Ian Weston-Smith, recovered from his wound, had returned and been captured. What was I doing fiddling about in France? Either I must return to them and confess that my foray had been a failure, or I must find something useful to do within this amorphous and ubiquitous half-secret organization. The chance came. A signal arrived from Bari. Volunteers were urgently needed to go "into the field" in North Italy. A burgeoning resistance movement had established itself in the Apennines since the Italian surrender, made up of Italian soldiers and civilians, escaped allied prisoners from the camps which had been opened long enough for many to get out before the Germans closed in. There were deserters from the pressed ranks of the Wehrmacht, including Russian minorities who had readily transferred allegiance or had been forced into service against the Red Army and who had subsequently become disenchanted with their German masters. Some had shot their German officers and NCOs before taking to the hills. There were even a few German deserters.

The mountains were thus crawling with partisan bands who lived by the generosity and often great courage of the mountain people, poor by any standards and virtually beggared by the war. There was much disorganization and some treachery but at the core were groups of genuine partisans armed mostly with captured or purloined Axis weapons, Italian-led and able to deny large tracts of the mountains and their lines of communication to the enemy. Much needed to be done to help them, arm and prepare them effectively while the 8th Army and the American 5th Army pushed north against the Gothic Line and thence into the Po plain for their final confrontation with Kesselring's divisions.

A number of British Liaison Officers (BLOs) had been dropped in to help. More were needed. I was loaded into a DC10 and flown to Brindisi, where I met the man selected to go in with me as interpeter and second in command. Giorgio Insom was half Russian/half Italian, in his early 20's. He had been conscripted and commissioned into the Italian Army but quit immediately after the surrender and volunteered to join the British. Someone had been shrewd enough to assess his qualities. His English was impeccable and he spoke fair German. He was commissioned forthwith in the rank of lieutenant, and posted to No. 1 Special Force, the branch of SOE controlling operations in Italy. The headquarters were in Bari. Giorgio was despatched to meet me, accompanied by our conducting officer, a tall willowy, carefully groomed officer whose task was to see to our equipment, our welfare and generally soothe us if necessary.

I liked Giorgio Insom from the outset. He was a splendid companion, possessed a shrewd and balanced judgement, was tough and could laugh.

We were kitted out at Brindisi airport with our parachutes and operational equipment, then taken to No. 1 Special Force HQ in a large holding camp near Bari where our radio operator was already waiting. At the first moon we were to be dropped into the winter mountains. All seemed set fair. It was not.

The nearer we got to the centre of operations the more frustrating things became. Nobody could tell us where or exactly when we should be needed. Among the large staff at the base there was an atmosphere of polite evasion. The place was full of other BLOs destined to be dropped about central and southern Europe, in the Balkans, the Alps and the Apennines, even into Poland. Several were my friends from Cairo days. Most were well matched and eager, other groups ill-assorted and already at odds with one another.

Time dragged by. Conditions in the camp were bad. Occasional expeditions into Bari and the presence of some bright and very pretty secretaries helped. They belonged to the First Aid Nursing Yeomanry (FANY), an exclusive women's unit dating from the first war, the qualifications for which seemed to include good looks as well as reliability and intelligence. Off duty they sometimes favoured us with an evening out. Eventually three of us, John Stott, due for the Italian Alps, Peter Kemp, recently returned from a gruelling time with Mihailovitch's Chetniks and now destined for a stint in Poland which ended with protracted Russian imprisonment, and myself, decided to move out and set up as living-in tenants with a fisherman's family in a village nearby, Monopoli. To our surprise no one objected. The fisherman was never there; either he was dead, had deserted or been removed by the war. His wife, our landlady, was as fat and as jolly as could be. She mothered us all and fed us, more or less. There was another tenant, a thin pallid and wistful Italian lieutenant who seldom smiled but owned a violin which he played whenever circumstances permitted. He did not seem exactly cut out for military duty and was almost certainly a deserter. Who could blame him? Then there was the bambina, a dangerously precocious and very pretty 12 year old who made enormous eyes at us all. We slept in a small room with one double and one single bed for which we tossed up each evening. Breakfast consisted of bread and very small almost raw fish floating in olive oil washed down with draughts of an abrasive red wine. Paddy Sproule, who was working with the FANY at the time, has since told me that our billet was out of bounds to the girls, "because it was a brothel". That neither Peter Kemp, John Stott nor I ever discovered this must be one of the major mysteries of the war. But we did not. I protested to Paddy that our bambina, well forward though she was, could not have been employed in such a capacity. "Oh no," said Paddy "Downstairs was respectable, but I think there was an elder sister upstairs."

Once a day we tramped up to the headquarters to find out about the weather reports, otherwise we laughed a great deal and hoped for the best. But time weighed heavy.

One day someone reported having seen a fox. We spun into action, collected four or five scrawny horses, a mule, about three couple of assorted mongrels, which we encouraged with bully-beef, and, together with some like-minded among our brother BLOs, we set forth for the chase.

The Brindisi Vale hounds only met twice and, as their Huntsman, I could not claim much success. Several cats were given a nasty turn but escaped. Much abrasive red wine was drunk; we scampered about among the scrub oak, olive and carob trees by the shore, but of the foxes there was no sign.

Gradually things took shape. My mission, codenamed Clover II, was to be preceded by another, Clover I, which consisted of Colonel Peter McMullen and Major Basil Davidson who had both been in Greece. They were to take over responsibility in the mountains dominating Genoa, known as the third zone. Peter, scion of the Hertfordshire brewing family, was an extremely capable commander, decisive, determined and experienced. He had a real knowledge of the oddities and limitations of guerilla war and no illusions at all. Basil, an ex-journalist, had a remarkable and invaluable gift with simple people, and also the not so simple for that matter. I took to them both. They told us much about partisan life and the principles of survival in the mountains. The lessons they had learned in Greece turned out to apply equally in the Ligurian Apennines.

My mission was to be dropped by parachute near San Stephano d'Aveto, into their area and placed under their command. Thence we were to move

north and take over the 13th Partisan Zone, a large area of the mountains dominating Piacenza, where the Partisans had suffered badly from enemy drives, or "*Rastrellamenti*", and morale had reportedly degenerated.

Peter came of a conventional, conservative, county family and his political views were entirely consistent. Basil was an intellectual and a Marxist – albeit a romantic one. This would not have mattered except for the fact that all partisan life is governed by politics and the mountains were full of well organized communist bands. It was much to the credit of Peter and Basil that their political disagreements were never bitter and their mission an unqualified success. My own grasp of politics at that stage was tenuous to say the least and the advice I got was inevitably conflicting but there is no sharper political school than the guerrilla.

Our radio operator turned out to be a Sergeant White in the Signal Corps, unsurprisingly nicknamed "Chalky". He was a gem, small, cocky, bold as brass, a former instructor and a brilliant operator. Working the 'sched.' in nominally occupied territory was a nervous business and reception in the mountains uncertain. The tension which attended this slender link with base was unavoidable; yet Chalky, crouched beneath an inadequate torch, conscious of the need to get off the air as soon as he could, sometimes cursing sulphurously beneath his breath, practically never failed to get through. He could even identify his correspondent by the distant touch on the key.

"That bloody idiot so and so on the end again," he would say as he hurried to us with his signal pad. Chalky did not suffer fools and in his estimation there were quite a few about. Also he had a healthy liking and capacity for the beer.

Peter and Basil departed and we were told their drop was successful. A fortnight later we were taken to a pleasant, if decaying, manor house near Livorno, to await our turn. The moon was right, the weather wrong, the weather right, something amiss with the aeroplane. Finally after a week of this jerky existence we were told to be ready for certain takeoff at 9 pm on the evening of 2 February, 1945.

I wrote a last letter to my mother and another to some, alas, no longer identifiable girlfriend and spent the early evening trying to compose myself and reading some dog-eared novel. At about 6 pm our elegant conducting officer came to the Mess – the flight was again cancelled. I can't remember why. Giorgio and I were desperate.

"Have you told Sergeant White?"

'Yes."

"Where is he?"

"I think he's gone to the Sergeants' Mess."

And so he had, determined to drown his frustration. About one hour later back comes our advisor wreathed in smiles.

"You are going after all; there's a break in the weather."

We threw ourselves into gear again, collected our kit and got into the jeep which was to take us to the airstrip. Where was Sergeant White? Our conductor appeared again looking distinctly set down.

"He's drunk," he said.

I had a terrible grey vision, yet another perhaps irreversible postponement and this time our fault.

"Get him into the jeep if you have to carry him," I said. Mercifully it was dark. Presently Chalky and his escort appeared, travelling at speed on a very unsteady bearing. Somehow we got him and his kit on to the aircraft without the NCO dispatcher noticing anything, or if he did he kept quiet. The American crew knew nothing about it anyway; they had other things to occupy them. We waved goodbye to our much relieved conducting officer. Chalky collapsed, mumbling threateningly into a heap of packages, containing boots and warm clothing for the partisans and went to sleep. The rear door slammed shut. The DC4 shuddered into life. We were off.

It was no more than half an hour's flight up the Italian western littoral and thence into the mountains. Presently we felt the DC4 bank steeply and wheel. After several turns one of the crew clambered down to me. The Captain wanted to speak to me. From the cockpit the moonlit and snow-clad ribs and walls of the mountains looked alarmingly close.

"Do you see that?" said the pilot, pointing into the valley on our port side. Some two thousand feet below us flickered a pattern of bonfires. Nearby someone was flashing an Aldis lamp at us.

"What do you say soldier?" asked the pilot.

Now, our briefing had been unforgettably clear. The reception committee would burn fires in the shape of an 'H' and flash the letter 'B' for identification. These fires were in a rough 'T' and the letter flashing below us appeared to be an 'M', or was it an 'N'? Anyway it certainly was not a 'B'.

"It's the wrong one," I said.

"OK, that's what I think; we'll have another look."

I groped my way back to my place by the rear door as the plane soared above the surrounding peaks. After about 20 minutes we started to circle again and the messenger reappeared. I returned to the cockpit.

"All I can find buddy. Do you want to go?"

Far below the same fires flickered and winked at us. I thought pretty desperately, but not for long. They might be anybody these people lurking in the dark valley – Germans or the dreaded fascist black brigades. On the other hand, we faced an ignominious return to the frustrations of the base and that was not to be borne.

"We'll go."

Giorgio's relief was palpable. Chalky seemed subdued but undoubtedly conscious. I dared not interrogate him closely in front of the Sergeant Dispatcher lest even now he should be banned. The plane banked steeply.

"Are you OK, Sergeant White?"

'Yiss, Sir," said Chalky sitting down abruptly on a bootbale.

The dispatcher called me up and first made me watch while my static line was firmly attached to a hawser runing fore and aft. I took my stand by the open door. The pilot began his run. The small red stand-by light came on. I watched it, mesmerized. Green – go! Jump!

The roar of the aircraft engines gave way to rushing wind, then a wild tumbling sensation, a jerk and I was swinging serenely beneath the canopy of my parachute. I watched the plane heading away and to my intense relief two more small dark blobs floated above me.

Below, Liguria was approaching fast. Ominously there was no sign of the fires. I was heading for a forest and could see no open ground to aim at. Not that there was much point in trying. Wartime parachutes were not equipped with brakes. I swung dizzily in among the trees. There was a crash of branches and I was stuck in a pine, which stood not more than 15 feet or so from the face of a precipitous slope disappearing into the gloom. I banged the release drum on the front of the harness. Eventually it gave way and I clambered and fell down to earth. A few scratches but no damage. The silence was profound. No wind, not a sound but the throb of distant engines as the plane began another run over the dropping zone. The parachute which I should have hidden was inextricably snarled. I picked myself up and struggled uphill. After a few minutes the trees gave way to more open scrub. The aircraft was overhead again. There was a sudden loud thump and a free falling package of boots landed a few yards away. Not, it seemed to me, very near its target. On through the moonlit forest.

After some minutes I made out three figures in front. I drew my revolver. My Italian at that stage was basic to put it mildly, but there seemed no disposition on their part to shoot me. Indeed they seemed astonished and delighted to find me.

"All this and parachutists too," was the gist of their welcome. They were clearly partisans.

They led me to the fires around which was a group of some twenty of their comrades. In the middle stood Georgio who had already established the bonafides of our reception committee. We were somewhere near the tiny hamlet of Priosa under the Rocca Bruna, and as the crow flew some 20 kms away from where Peter and Basil must have been waiting for us. Of Chalky there was no sign.

We searched. Chalky had jumped last and the three of us were scattered. At the first grey streaks of dawn we saw a group of gesticulating figures under some trees. It was Chalky all right. He was in a tree. Or to be more accurate he had been in a tree from which he had eventually extricated himself and was struggling to hide his parachute when a number of people appeared out of the night. Chalky, uncertain of their allegiance, had gone back up his tree in order to negotiate. He was much relieved to see us – and dead sober.

We spent the day sorting out our kit. There seemed to be an awful lot of it. We managed to procure three mules and after a few hours' sleep in a cottage we set out with an escort and guides to join up with Peter whose whereabouts we knew to be near Alpepiana.

It was bitterly cold. We marched all that night along the snowclad and icy ridges of the Rocca Bruna, eventually descending to the little village of Alpepiana, crouched under Monte Oramara in the late morning, tired but

22. Crossing a dune in the Sand Sea.

23. "...on each of which were mounted a twin Vickers K machine gun on a steel upright on the front, with another in the back" (p.58).

24. Jeep armed with Browning machine gun.

25. "Andy Lassen…the now legendary Danish Officer…won a Military Cross with two bars and a posthumous VC" (p.79).

26. Amal Atrash "became the toast of Cairo" (p.80).

27. "Focal and fashionable point for the British *monde* in Cairo was Shepheard's Hotel" (p.96) — the long bar.

28. "Out on the Terrace… one could watch arrivals, spot the girls and generally keep the score" (p.96).

29. "Our landlady was as fat and as jolly as could be" (p.113).

30. The author as Master and Huntsman of the Brindisi Vale Hounds (see p.114)

31. Peter Kemp after much "abrasive red wine". He got the doll. (p.114).

overjoyed to find Peter and Basil. They had waited in vain by their fires all night and were more than a little contemptuous of our American pilot.

Peter told us their news and what they had picked up about the Piacentino. They had arrived in the closing stages of the worst enemy *rastrellamento* of that long winter and had to take immediate evasive action. The partisans had suffered; villages had been burned and the usual category of horrors perpetrated by the Germans and their mercenary troops. But the third zone was strongly held by several divisions of "Garibaldini", the title chosen by the communists, and they had survived.

When Peter and Basil first arrived they had appeared to be far from welcome. The Garibaldini command had despatched a courier to Genoa to request instructions on how to deal with these supposedly capitalist officers. After a week the courier returned and the atmosphere changed immediately. All was now harmony and collaboration.

We re-divided our kit, abandoned the mules and with Peter's help recruited a small band of partisans to act as our bodyguards, porters and couriers. We were eleven strong in all. After another convivial night in Peter's village, we left for the Piacentino not a little apprehensive as to the state of affairs we should find there. Clearly the Garibaldini di Genova harboured no great respect for their comrades to the north. Indeed in some valleys it was rumoured that their spirit was broken and that some groups had even resorted to banditry.

We made our way down to the Val Trebbia, crossed Highway 45 and up over the mountains to Val Nure which marked the rough boundary between the 3rd and 13th zones. All the bridges had long been blown this high up in Val Trebbia and Val Nure. The country was nominally controlled by partisans, although there was a risk of enemy foot patrols on the main roads. We crossed the Nure River, skirting round Ferriere and climbed steadily into a less stark and forbidding land than we had left around Monte Antola and the Mountain of the Three Crosses, the snowcapped heads of which we could still make out across two valleys.

Headquarters of the 13th Zone was reported to be in the small mountain village of Groppallo. After two days' march we reached it: a single street some quarter of a mile long lined with stone houses, two trattorias, with little or nothing to offer, and much evidence of a partisan presence. To the east the slopes of Monte Menegosa, still deep in snow, held a few isolated crofts and farms. To the west a narrow road snaked down to the Val Nure where it joined the broken highway leading north down the valley some 10 kms to Bettola, a frontier village on the way to Piacenza. This place had changed hands more than once and was currently occupied by a fascist outpost.

We found the commander of 13th Zone at his headquarters in one of the trattorias. Il Colonello Marziolo welcomed us with every mark of satisfaction, indeed relief. A professional soldier with strong anti-fascist convictions, he had taken to the mountains from a sense of patriotic duty. Aged about 50 with thick beetling eyebrows over mild eyes and a ready smile, he looked like a particularly friendly and unaggressive owl. Indeed his authority, such as it was, seemed to lie mainly in the fact that it was impossible to dislike him. In a situation fraught with political antagonism this was no disadvantage.

His staff consisted of a second in command, Major "Gioffre", a Chief of Staff, "Francesco", and a Commissario called "Venturi'. Neither the duties nor indeed the allegiance of this Commissario were clear to us. He appeared at all our meetings and seemed to regard himself as a political consultant cum intelligence officer, or in other words a general snooper, collector and purveyor of gossip and rumour, most of it alarmist and much of it inaccurate. The institution of the political commissario had been universally adopted by the partisan units of all persuasions mainly as a counter to the communists.

The atmosphere in Groppallo was one of suspicion and uncertainty. The zone had been badly shaken by the *rastrellamento*. Routes from the plain into the Piacentino were easier for the Germans than those into the mountains of the 3rd Zone. Partisan resistance had more or less collapsed during midwinter. All units had suffered heavily and morale was indeed low.

Marziolo had only recently been appointed and his position seemed far from secure. We suspected this in Groppallo and our subsequent journeys among the partisan units confirmed it. A main cause lay in the machinations of a man called "Franchi", his predecessor in command it turned out. I had been warned about Franchi; he was reported to be useless as a military commander but a dangerous intriguer and far from honest.

He and a small band of cronies were still about in the Piacentino trying to gain support by stirring up trouble for poor Marziolo. There was a strong suspicion that Franchi had condoned what amounted to banditry, the harsh treatment and bullying of the local mountain people on whom some of the defeated partisans had battened for food and shelter. Moreover it was even rumoured he had made a deal with the fascists by which his partisans agreed to cause no trouble if left alone. It was impossible to establish the facts.

Nevertheless, Franchi and his friends had some influence with the shadowy regional resistance authority known as the Comitato di Liberazione (CL) Nord Emilia, whose representatives operated in the city or the plain and who appeared to support him.

Marziolo and his staff spoke at length of the devastation wrought by the Germans during the winter; of lack of arms, ammunition and food, of worn-out boots and burned villages. I was shown a photograph of 20 or 30 grinning

German soldiers grouped around the body of a woman they held naked and spatchcocked between them, while a NCO posed above her body with a long dagger ready to strike; another of a girl, her hands tied behind her, hanging on a meat hook like the carcase of a pig. They had died in the *rastrellamento*. When, they repeatedly asked, would we be able to bring the aeroplanes?

In our turn we sought information about the partisan units, their leaders and their whereabouts. Clearly the next step was to discover them.

There turned out to be three "Divisions", plus a few unattached and more or less independent groups. The Divisions had been decimated during the German and fascist attacks and now consisted of no more than 100 or 200 at most, divided into various brigades.

Around Groppallo and in the hamlets and farms strung along Val Nure was the Division "Justitia e Libertà", commanded by a rather lugubrious officer called Renato. His second in command was introduced as "Salaami" and there was a Commissario called "Dan". Their political allegiance was to the Action Party, left wing, anti-Monarchist but bitterly suspicious of the communists. They distinguished themselves by wearing blue rags or scarves around their necks.

To the north towards Morfasso, in the Val d'Arda, was the Division Prati, Christian Democrats. Like the others they had suffered badly, but their commander, Prati, refused to be downhearted. A soft-spoken skinny little man, with his pointed beard and pointed hat, he could have sprung straight from a renaissance canvas. Prati's allegiance, and thus that of his men, lay firmly with the Pope. He had a Christian Democrat Commissario called Arnaldo and was intermittently supported by itinerant partisan priests. In earlier days he would have been a Guelph, as opposed to a Ghibelline. I liked him.

To the west in Val Trebbia was located the First Division Piacenza. These were communist Garibaldini. The Commander was an authoritative figure called "Fausto". There was a second-in-command, a jovial fellow called "Sandro", with whom I found it easy to make friends.

The Garibaldini were the best disciplined and, it has to be admitted, the most effective of the three Divisions. I knew nothing then of the historical confidence trick upon which the Marxist dialectic is founded, nor, I suspect, with the exception perhaps of their leaders, did most of the Garibaldini. Yet one could not miss the spirit of revolutionary hope and comradeship. Unlike Peter McMullen's experience, Fausto and Sandro were instantly co-operative; since their main objective was to get their hands on as many weapons as possible, this was not surprising. Their business would not end with liberation. They took the long view.

Our main task was to try to weld these disparate groups into a coherent force, arm them and prepare them for eventual descent "*alla battaglia*" for Piacenza, once the allies broke through the mountains into the valley of the Po.

The welding was far from easy. If anything was to be achieved it seemed essential to support and enhance the somewhat theoretical authority of the Central Command. In effect this could only be done by telling the Partisan Commanders that deliveries of arms, ammunition, boots, blankets, food and other requirements could only be afforded to those who were loyal to Groppallo. At the same time we tried to eliminate Franchi and his gang, by a combination of threat and negotiation, conducted mostly hy courier (he refused to meet us and was too elusive to be cornered) or over the radio link to base and thus to the Comitato di Liberazione Nationale Alta Italia (CLNAI) in Milan.

In the end it worked and at the beginning of April I was able to signal: "The Command of 13 Zone has finally been decided following a very strong letter from CLNAI to CL Nord Emilia. The new appointments are satisfactory and it can be said the Piacentino is at last on its feet. Nord Emilia have ordered the detention of Franchi and Aceti (ex Vice Commander of Nord Emilia) and with the disappearance of these two the intrigue, weakness and suspicion which had eaten into the partisan formations of this zone will disappear."

Much had intervened before this and by the time the call came for urgent action all the Divisions played their part more or less effectively.

But like everywhere else politics was the breath of the resistance and political discussion among the Communists in particular was perpetual and to me mostly incomrephensible. The dogma even took root in my own little party. Two of my bodyguard were Communists. After several weeks with us they came to me shamefaced and full of regret to say they had to leave.

"Why?"

They squirmed under Georgio's interrogation.

It was because we, the British Officers, mostly ate separately from them and this was not good Communism. We certainly did mess separately and for good reason. I was not prepared to make this ideological leap so they departed much saddened. We replaced them with two of Prati's boys.

The pattern of partisan life soon took shape. Our march over the mountains would average 5–6 hours in the day. We never entered a village we did not know until after dark and after sending an emissary to sound out feeling and find shelter. Generally he applied to the priest. Most of them were actively helpful to the partisans, at least to the non-communists – anyway to us. As time went on we built a network of safe houses where we knew we were welcome. The courage and generosity of those mountain people were inexpressibly moving. They were poor. What they had they gave us, and they knew the risks. The pathetic blackened ruins in their villages spoke for themselves and stories of recent rape and murder by the Germans and their "mongol" mercenaries were all too common.

These German anti-Partisan units comprised ex-Russian prisoners recruited or drafted from the prison camps and used exclusively under German officers and NCOs against the Resistance. Most of them came from the Central Asian republics, hated the Russians and had good cause to turn their coats. In the Piacentino they were mostly Kazaks rather than Mongols. Of their brutality under German command there was ample evidence, but not all were prepared to accept these degrading duties. One complete Kazak Company had deserted to the Partisans in 13 Zone, having murdered their German Officers and NCOs. They were ably commanded by "Gino", an Italian and a butcher by trade. This lot was more than willing to turn its guns again on the Germans. Sadly I learned that after the liberation they were all returned to the Russian authorities and summarily shot.

Our second task was to provide intelligence. Partisan information was tendentious, highly coloured and often inaccurate. Gradually we built our own network. Our agents moved freely in fascist territory and we compiled an accurate record of the German and fascist units in our area, even down to the names and habits of their officers. All this seemed to be well received at base, although I was doubtful whether any of it was likely to make much difference to the course of the war.

Near Groppallo was the Partisan prison camp. About ten German NCOs and soldiers were held there and the number increased slightly as time went on. They lived on a deserted farm under a surprisingly loose guard, yet none tried to escape.

For security as well as effect we had them marched blindfold to another house to be interrogated. I am sure they thought they were going to be shot. Georgio had some German and between us we got everything they could give us. There was one exception, a Feldwebel, and a brave man. To my repeated questions he answered in a low shaky voice that he was only compelled to give his name, rank and number. He was right. We sent him back to the prison unharmed and with honour.

As the snow retreated we journeyed faster and further. The time had come to organize supply drops. With air superiority the Allies were now flying in by day and accuracy was therefore likely. Our dropping zone was near Selva in a fold of the mountain. Instead of fires we were to spread blankets in the shape of our code letter. All was agreed with base and we gathered anxiously each evening round the radio to listen to the "personal messages" on the BBC. At last it came "Gli hirondelli sono qui" – "The swallows are here".

Soon after dawn we were on the DZ, with a large gang of partisans from Groppallo. Bang on time we heard the faint hum of engines, rising to a roar as the first Dakota banked round the shoulder of Monte Menegosa to make its dummy run. The excitement was palpable and probably audible for miles. Three planes came that first time, containers and packages swinging and thumping around us, free-fall packs of boots and blankets following in their wake. They were needed. *Dio Mio!* They were needed. The chorus of one of the best of many good partisan songs told of boots: –

"Scarpe Rotte, pur bisogn'andar"

Our boots are broken but march we must.

Our small team was hard put to supervise distribution but it was a bit better than every man for himself.

In mid-March, not long after our first drop, I got a message that I was needed for urgent discussions in Groppallo. Politics again, but this time from an unexpected quarter. It was a deputation of priests. We received them as soon as we could. To my surprise their manner was positively menacing:

"Did I and my friends understand whom I was arming? What did I and the Allies mean by dealing with *"questi brigati rossi"*?"

I said I thought they were better than the black brigades and that, anyway, I was there to fight the Germans. The Vatican deputation left grumbling and far from satisfied.

I had an assignation with Basil shortly after and crossed Highway 45 to meet him. It was a joy to see him and I spent a happy 24 hours exchanging intelligence and gossip. I hoped the priestly delegation might have visited the 3rd Zone and was agog to learn how they fared. No such luck. They had not cared to venture into exclusively red territory.

It was clear from what Basil told me that, despite their mutual and personal empathy, he and Peter were finding their relationship increasingly strained. The life of a BLO tended to be nervy and introspective anyway. Basil's evident and enthusiastic sympathy for the communist cause and Peter's deep suspicion of their motives was beginning to tell. Both had the Greek experience behind them; both were well steeped in the mixed motives of the Resistance. I said goodbye to Basil with a growing sense that we swam in deeper waters than I, a 23-year-old soldier with no political experience, had ever imagined.

On the way back at Fontana Rossa, a hamlet clustered round its fountain, I met an Italian doctor serving with the partisans. We dined together, well; there was pasta, salami, grappa and even quite good *petillant* red wine to drink, a welcome change from the normal diet of chestnuts. The doctor was clearly a character. His comrades were chiding him for belonging to a safe non-combatant profession.

"Ah," he said to me, eyes atwinkle, "they are ignorant these people; they do not understand. I am not simply a doctor, I am a hero. Yes, a hero. Io solo, I killed a mongol!"

The partisans grinned and nodded.

"Only a small mongol granted, *un piccolino*, but still a mongol, *è vero?*"

They assented, watching my reaction.

"How?" I asked.

"*Dunque*," said Il Dottore. "There was this girl. A nice girl, lived near Santo Stephano. The mongols came; she was raped. *Madonna Mia, e stato violentata dei mongoli, forse alcuni* – several mongols. Disgraceful. And later there was, *mi spiego*, a little mongol on the way. I alone, I killed that little mongol."

Wild applause greeted this revelation. Never was abortion more popular, and in the shadow of the Vatican at that. I wondered which way my priestly deputation would have argued it.

Gradually as the weeks passed confidence and the chain of command tightened. Morale was immensely helped by the air drops of arms and supplies and we got down to planning with the 13 Zone staff for the day we should be ordered to go into serious action as the Allies launched their final thrust into the Po plain.

The idea was to attack all the communications we could get at south and north of the Via Emilia. Then there were the local garrisons particularly in Bettola, Groppallo and Monte Chino to deal with. Ultimately, as a second phase, we were to await the order to attack Piacenza itself.

On 23 March mission "Insulin" dropped by parachute to a DZ controlled by the American OSS group south and east of San Stephano. It consisted of Captain Charles Brown of the Intelligence Corps, Flight Lieutenant Ripping-dale and a Radio Operator, Corporal Bradley. They were to come under my command in 13 Zone. On the 24th they arrived at Peter Mac's headquarters at Alpe, and on the 25th set out with him across the mountain for Val Nure. We met in Ferriere on the 28th. I decided that the most profitable division would be for "Insulin" to go over to Val d'Arda to support Prati who was somewhat out on a limb, while I retained contact with Renato and Fausto in Val Trebbia and Val Nure. The partisan units were far too scattered for us to ensure adequate contact as things hotted up and we were all much relieved to get this extra help.

On 5 April the signal came to mount our all-out effort. At the same time we learned that a mixed German and Italian force of company strength was advancing on Castell Arquato. In days gone by this would have been enough to send the partisans scampering for the mountains. No more: two brigades, one from Renato and one from Fausto, went on the attack. If we were to move effectively on Piacenza we needed the bridge at Castell Arquato and the enemy, now clearly bent on defence, were out to destroy it. Our partisans drove them off and held it for us.

Much encouraged by this success and with the help of Prati's brigade, they moved to attack both Groparallo and the post at Monte Chino. This proved a tougher nut. Both positions were strongly held, particularly the castle on the hill at Monte Chino. Air support was needed and I signalled Base repeatedly for it. None came. We were furious, but by this time 5th and 8th Armies were fully committed over the Gothic Line and I suppose our little battle might have been considered rather less important than it seemed to us. I felt we had let the partisans down and it was a relief when the enemy evacuated both of these strong points on 19 April. By this time the rest of the Piacenza Division and the Justicia e Libertà had been in action in Monte Chilli, on the road near Cortemaggiore, at Pontenure and Firenzuola. The Via Emilia was more or less free of enemy from Pontenure to Fidenza, although we were driven out of Fidenza again by German units trying to defend Parma against the American thrust up the Via Emilia.

On 27 April our mission had reached a safe house near Villa Nova, returning from a visit to the Garibaldini forward position, when the message came on the evening sched. Reception always unpredictable in the mountains, was for once clear. Chalky brought a clean set of groups and we set out to decode with our precious one-time pad on the dim-lit table top. The code word was unmistakeable, its import long anticipated although we had not expected it as quick as this.

8th and 5th Armies had broken through. Attack and hold Piacenza.

Our couriers sped off that night to Groppallo and to the Divisions. We had agreed a simple plan for them to descend and envelop the town and if possible to establish a bridgehead over the Po. We were uncertain of the exact position in the city, but, provided enough well-armed partisans got there and were able to cut the Via Emilia each side of the town, it could be they might at least make things hot for any Axis troops trying to run for it. That was the idea anyway but there was still a strong garrison including some SS troops.

We set off at dawn for Groppallo. Little control was possible once the descent to the plain began; all we could do was follow up and encourage where we could.

Next day, on a mountain track near Bettola, a communist Distaccamento passed us, in fine spirits, singing. Speed was important but this lot was halted frequently to wait for the Commissariat consisting of two sledges; on the first were their meagre rations, on the second ammunition, this last pulled by one rather elderly partisan and a mule. The load was too heavy; moreover, it included 3 large 75mm shells as well as the ammo boxes.

"*Salute Signor Maggiore!*" Clenched fist salute.

"*Salute compagno.* What is this?"

"*Abasso Gli Fascisti! Viva la liberazione!*"

"*Eviva.* What is this?"

"*Munizioni, Signor Maggiore. Che bello.*"

"But where is the gun for these?"

"*Eh! non so. Pietro lo sa.*" Pietro knows.

Pietro is produced from the column.

"*Salute Signor Maggiore. Scenderemo alla battaglia.* We will capture Piacenza tomorrow. We will hang every Fascist in the Piazza dei Cavalli."

"Yes Pietro, but where is the gun for these?"

A look of pained surprise, a gesture of helpless protest, then: –

"*Non lo so, io.* I don't know exactly," but, brightening up, "*fa niente, Signor Maggiore.* When we get down there we'll find a gun to fit."

Gino, father of the ill-fated Kazaks, is apprised of the order of the day by courier.

"Will they march?"

Gino didn't know but would do his best. He summons the Company, stands on a rock and embarks on a spirited exhortation in flowing Italian, not one sentence of which could the Kazaks possibly have understood. When he reached his peroration the dark heads drew together in earnest conclave. After some minutes their spokesman advanced and nodded vigorously.

"*Da!*" he said. "OK."

What enterprise they imagined they were in for would have been hard to guess but march they did and to some effect.

At Groppallo we had a German open staff car, captured and given to us by the partisans. We loaded Il Colonello and the general staff into it and sped down the valley to the bridge over the Nure at Bettola. The village was clear. On to Ponte d'Olio where we caught up with a *Distaccamento* at the crossroads. There was some sporadic shooting. A man arrived in a high state of excitement on a bicycle from the direction of Piacenza.

"*Auto blinda, auto blinda!*" he shouted, gesticulating wildly down the road. Through my glasses no armoured cars were visible but when I turned round to consult there was no one but Georgio, Chalky and I in the vehicle. The general staff had fled across a ploughed field. We recovered them. Happily no armour appeared.

It was here that Georgio and I parted company, he to contact Charles Brown and Prati's Division while I continued towards Piacenza. He found the partisans in action against a determined outpost on the Eastern Approaches and was wounded by a mortar shell near San Lazzaro on the 27th. By the time I found out, he had already been evacuated by the Americans. I learned that his wound was not serious but to my lasting sadness I never saw him again, such was the confusion of liberation and its aftermath. No one in my shoes could have been granted a better or more loyal comrade.

We drove on towards Piacenza and around midday on the 25th came into Grazzano Visconti, a model village built perhaps in Victorian days to house the estate and stable staff attached to some great mansion. Facing the small piazza were imposing wrought iron gates and a drive disappearing among the trees. Draped and sprawled outside the cottages was a brigade of Garibaldini, bleary eyed, bearded, red scarves round their necks, armed to the teeth. They had marched from the mountains overnight and were plainly exhausted. But morale was high and to anyone who didn't know them they must have looked as dangerous a bunch of sans culottes as could be imagined. I trembled for the inhabitants of this apparently aristocratic establishment.

Sandro was with them. "*Eviva!*": clenched fist and wide grin.

"Who lives here?" I asked.

"Il Duca di Grazzano," Sandro said, in reverential tones. Clearly there was no disposition on the part of these particular revolutionaries to dispossess His Grace.

"Perhaps you should call on him," suggested Sandro with no trace of class struggle in his voice. I made my way up the drive to the front door of a truly imposing reconstruction of a Renaissance castle set in lovely gardens. I rang.

To the door direct came the immensely tall, thin and elegant figure of the Duke. I introduced myself and apologised for the invasion.

"It is nothing," he replied in impeccable English. "I am delighted to see them. You see it has been very difficult here. The Germans requisitioned one wing and I had the partisans from time to time in the other. Will you have tea or coffeee?"*

---

* Grazzano Visconti. Originally the property of the Auguissola family who obtained the investiture in 1414, Grazzano was sold to another branch, Auguissola di Volgone in 1576. It

The battle for the city lasted from the 25th to the 29th. On the 26th an SOE Liaison Officer, Hugh McDermot, made his way by scout car through the lines to join us near Ponte Nure. He had news of the American 135th Infantry Regiment in the area and I set out with the General Staff in our German car to meet them. It was a stupid thing to do. We bumped into one of their forward patrols some miles down the road. They leapt out of their trucks and sprang into the ditches on either side. I think we were in greater danger at that moment than at any time since our arrival in the mountains. But the several flags flying from our car and the general air of hilarity exhibited by the General Staff saved us from being gunned down. I was escorted to the headquarters of the 135th US Infantry where I was treated with some incredulity. No one seemed to know that the mountains, and indeed all the approaches to Piacenza, belonged to the Partisans. I briefed the American Colonel as best I could and was glad to be released. We managed to maintain a liaison with them from then on and after liberation I got a very handsome letter of thanks from the Colonel for all that the Partisans and our missions had been able to do.

By now Charles Brown had joined us at Pontenure. Our Partisan patrols were already in the city itself and they reported the remnants of an SS Battalion with some ten armoured cars mounting 20mm guns. This was rather more than we could cope with and I sought American aid to deal with them. The Americans refused. They needed their tanks elsewhere they said and made clear they were content to leave Piacenza to the Partisans.

The Via Emilia had been cut both east and west and the Garibaldini had established their small bridgehead over the Po at San Vittorio, west of the city. But we could make little headway within the walls. On the 28th the Americans relented and sent us three Sherman tanks. At seven o'clock in the morning we and our Partisans went in with their support. There was not much resistance. The armoured cars disappeared after a few ineffective shots and by the morning of the 29th the SS and their Fascist friends had fled. Piacenza was ours. Moreover the Partisans had saved the power and water supply. Both were working when the city was liberated.

A fragment of my signal reporting the fall of the town read as follows:

"It must be realized that German morale was extremely low at this juncture and that their orders, if received, were certainly confused, but nevertheless there is no doubt the Partisans fought better than ever during these last three days and surprised us all with their determination and fighting spirit."

---

later passed to Visconti di Modrone. My host, Guiseppe V rebuilt the original castle and the model village in 1937. Sadly he was the last of his line.

And so it was.

The official SOE report on this action concluded:

"In the Piacenza area the Italian Partisans were undoubtedly allotted as difficult a task as any given to patriot forces in the Italian campaign. Although they were unable to take and hold the city itself which was a vital centre of enemy communication, they succeeded in holding down a large hostile force, and in destroying transport and material of vital importance to the enemy."

The battle over, we had to find lodgings. The partisan command installed us in the Palazzo Scotti di Sarmato, via San Siro, where we were delighted to learn Napoleon had lodged when he captured Piacenza. The accommodation was on a fair scale. The radio operators had one wing, the officers another.

Life in the town reached new heights of hectic and joyful anarchy., *Partigiani*, many of whom I suspect had only joined up at the last moment, careered about in captured or looted cars. At night the streets echoed to fusillades from automatic weapons. Scores were being paid off. Life was, to say the least, uncertain for suspected fascists. We did our largely ineffective best to calm this down.

We heard that Mussolini, shot by the Partisans somewhere near the Swiss Frontier, had been strung upside down in Milan with his mistress Clara Petacci. This became a popular tourist attraction and in due course postcards sold well.

AMGOT arrived. This was the Allied Military Government in the shape of an American Major. He had an indisputably Italian name and that seemed to be the basis on which he had been selected for his complicated mission, for he knew neither Italy nor its language. Amiable and understandably nervous, he produced a set of standard instructions for governing. His first task was to fill a number of administrative posts with reliable people.

What was to be done? The official report on my mission states most generously that "Major Hastings' control of the military and political elements of the Resistance Movements in his area was admirable . . . and the AMG Officers relied implicitly on his advice."

It wasn't quite like that. Control was strictly a matter of chance in our situation.

Conferences broke out, between AMGOT, the partisan commanders and the people from the Comitato di Liberazione who had emerged from the woodwork and were becoming more important by the hour.

"We ought to have an election," said AMGOT, looking earnestly at his regulations. I have to confess I vetoed the election. It would have to be contrived. This was no time for a sudden outbreak of democracy.

So far as I was concerned the only people with any claim to authority were the Partisan Commanders because they had done the work, because they were my friends and anyway they had the guns. I would try to arrange a selection of those who seemed most deserving and AMGOT could work it out for himself. We commandeered an office in the Palazzo del Commune, a splendid gothic edifice from which the Farnese family had once ruled the town. Word spread and a large crowd filled the anterooms. I had warned our partisan chiefs to position themselves as near to the door as possible. Once we had AMGOT in position behind an imposing desk, we opened the doors enough to let one in at a time. The rush was sensational. When we had roughly the requisite number of dignitaries we heaved them shut. A line of grinning panting heavily armed aspirant Mayors and Questure stood facing AMGOT. Somehow he sorted it out without too much ill feeling and some firm advice from us. That was the election.

Then came the victory parade and a proud sight it proved to be. The idea was that each division would march round the Piazza dei Cavalli and dump their arms on a pile before parading in front of the Palazzo for the speeches. Our NCOs were in charge of the dump. AMGOT took the salute, reinforced by several American officers whose significance I never really sorted out.

The parade was to some extent confused by the unexpected arrival of several large trucks belonging to a Brazilian division which had just relieved the Americans. They seemed mostly to be full of live chickens, presumably flown in from Brazil, and the drivers, understandably frustrated at having to join in this unscheduled victory, hooted continuously.

But nothing could mar the euphoria and pride of our marching Partigiani. Prati, diminutive and stiff as a ramrod, led his Division, Fausto with the Garibaldini next, decked with red banners and proudly carrying large photos of the fallen. Renato, Salaami, Dan, the Division "Justicia a Libertà" followed, clearly advertising their political opposition.

I had never seen them all together and was amazed at how many there were, a great many more, I suspected, than had been around when we arrived. But no matter.

We collected quite an arsenal, even though it was certain that many more weapons had been stashed away in the mountains or hidden elsewhere. Indeed the volume of firing at night betrayed it.

Our time had nearly come. Hugh McDermot left us to return to Modena. But there was still one notable event to come. We learned by signal that we were to be visited by no less a personage than General Gubbins, commanding SOE. He was to arrive with a small staff on his way up the Via Emilia to visit the various missions. We tidied up our Palazzo and prepared a feast for the occasion. Alas, he was nearly 2 hours late and I regret to say that we had eaten quite a lot of it by the time he arrived. Moreover, Chalky and Corporal Bradley who had been ordered to stand by had done themselves rather too well on spumante.

The General was charming to us and the only nervous moment was when our NCOs stood unsteadily to attention before him. He thanked them most handsomely for what they had done and then aksed if either of them had any complaints about the service provided by Base. I saw the danger but failed to intervene quickly enough.

"Ah bloody 'ave, an' all," began Corporal Bradley with the directness and broad vowels of the North Riding. Chalky hiccuped menacingly.

Somehow I brought the interview to an abrupt end. The General took it in good part. There was nothing else he could do.

We spent a last evening with our Partigiani friends. There was much to celebrate. The songs of the mountains echoed through the night, nostalgic songs of rebellion, privation and hope.

> *"Per I nostri morti scaverem' la fossa . . .*
> *Sulle superbe cime sara posta*
> *Per lor' risorgera la nuov' Italia*
> *Con la guerriglia!"*

> "We dig the graves of our dead
> on the highest peaks
> Through them will rise again
> a new Italy
> with the Guerriglia!"

After 50 years the words still ring in my head.

Weeks before, when visiting one of the outlying *Brigate* I had stood on the watershed of our Ligurian mountains in a burned-out village somewhere near Maggiorasca, above Santo Stephano, and looked south to a shimmering sea far below. Dimly but unmistakably in the blue haze I could make out the peninsula of Portofino Mare. I vowed that if I survived I would go there.

Still in possession of our German staff car we drove round the mountains to Genoa and then straight to the little port. Apart from reams of barbed wire stretched across the harbour mouth, it looked much as it does today. Happily no one had yet thought of liberating it. So we did.

Joined by my friend Jim Davis from the 12th Zone, Hugh MacDermott and some others, we summoned the Mayor, a shifty individual with, we decided, definite fascist tendencies. After some feeble protests he allocated us a splendid pagoda-like house near the village, with a lift in it. We employed, if that is the word, a chef and arranged regular daily deliveries of quite good wine.

In no time we had collected many well-wishers. Portofino was, I suspect, a haven for dubious characters hoping to shed their fascist or collaborationist skins in discreet surroundings. There was one impressive blonde, who, we were subsequently told, had been the mistress of an SS General. It was quite a week before orders and authority caught up with us.

I went back recently to Piacenza and to those mountains: sombre, lowering and poor by contrast to their great Alpine neighbours. At Groppallo not much is remembered any more but we ate well and drank the same mountain wine in the little trattoria which once served as Command Post for Il Colonello Marziolo and the 13th Zone.

The tall and charming Duca di Grazzano emigrated to Canada where he died. Grazzano Visconti is now open to the public. The village is full of gelaterie and tourist shops. Yet for a fleeting moment I felt I could still sense the shades of the Garibaldini there. The Partigiani are a legend now – as they deserve to be.

> "*Dei monti noi farem un baluardo*
> *Saprem' morir e disprezzar la vita*
> *Per noi risorgera la nuov' Italia*
> *Con la guerriglia!'*

> The mountains formed our barricades
> We learned to die: to scorn to live
> Through us will rise again a new Italy
> With the Guerriglia!"

————|————

8

AUSTRIA AND AFTER

I returned to London from Italy, still on the strength of SOE. The war in Europe was over and I sought a posting to the Far East to which theatre several of my friends among the BLOs, including Peter Kemp and Roland Winn, had already travelled. Too late. No sooner was I told to get ready than they dropped the bomb on Nagasaki; manifestly the journey was unnecessary.

I spent VJ Day in London and among vivid impressions of that memorable night none was more unexpected than what happened in Piccadilly Circus. There was a vast and dense crowd swaying hither and thither in aimless relief and happiness. There was much singing. Suddenly on a high balcony at the top of the Criterion on the corner of Lower Regent Street, a young woman appeared. After a series of dramatic gestures she took off all her clothes. The crowd cheered wildly until some unseen being grabbed her from behind and she disappeared unceremoniously through a window. What connection her demonstration had with victory over Japan was unclear but at the time it seemed entirely appropriate and was certainly popular.

I rejoined my Regiment, fearing admonition for so long a time away, but they were kind to me at Regimental Headquarters and I was sent off to command a Company in training at Hawick and subsequently in North Wales.

After four years of warfare and travel the wanderlust was still strong. One day I bumped into my great friend Jim Davies. We had been neighbours in Italy. He had commanded the mission to the partisan zone next to mine, and with distinction. We had shared much including the hilarious liberation of Portofino Mare and the peninsula of Santa Margarita.

Jim, who was a few years older than I, had secured himself an enviable job in the Control Commission for Austria. He had pre-war experience of business administration and was well qualified to help sort out the manifold problems of the inhabitants of Lower Austria. He spoke German, was a first class skier, an ex-member of the Oxford University Team, and a keen field sportsman. Austria looked like suiting his tastes well. Mine too. I had long wanted to learn to ski. How to get to Austria?

Jim told me the Controller of the Economic Division of the Control Commission for Austria, no less, was at that very hour searching for a personal assistant. Indeed he was probably conducting interviews. No time to be lost. I located Mr Berthoud in a Whitehall office and approached his current PA, a friendly Gunner officer about to be demobbed.

"Had I a degree?" Alas, no!

"Ah, well," he said, "you never know your luck. Turn up tomorrow at 10 o'clock."

I was there, buttons polished and Sam Browne belt gleaming.

I was impelled into the great man's presence, stood to attention and saluted smartly. Berthoud greeted me courteously.

"Ah, Captain Hastings. You have an Economic Degree?"

"No Sir."

"You have business experience perhaps?"

"No Sir."

"You have office experience though."

"Not very much, Sir."

"Captain Hastings, have you ever worked in an office?"

"No Sir."

"Thank you for coming to see me."

Perhaps it had been worth a try but I felt deeply conscious of my inadequacy in general and my inability to dissemble in particular.

To my astonishment I got a message next morning to say I'd got the job. By what process of elimination I could only guess but in case anyone had second thoughts I lost no time in settling my meagre affairs, secured a movement order and a place in an RAF Dakota bound for Vienna.

The Economic Division was located in Hiezing, in what had been a reasonably prosperous suburb. My quarters were nearby. I had an office to myself next to the Controller. There was a chair and a desk with two large trays labelled "in" and "out". I had never felt more utterly lost. A girl came in laden with large files and dumped them in my in-tray. When she had gone I made a random inspection. They might have been in Chinese for all the sense I could make of them. What to do? There seemed only one possible course: I put them gingerly in the "out". Presently to my delight another girl came in, gave me a friendly smile and whisked them all away. So far so good, but there must be more to my duties than providing a temporary resting place for official papers.

I never really solved the mystery but I had been an ADC and knew all about that. Mr Berthoud's programme was meticulously arranged. His car was always ready on time, and polished. So was I. I accompanied him on all prestigious occasions and saluted whenever it seemed even distantly appropriate.

The C-in-C British Troops Austria was General Dick McCreery, the last Commander of the 8th Army. He was a dominant figure, generally surrounded by a glittering entourage. He had no less than three burnished cavalry officers as ADCs. I think Mr Berthoud felt that in this severely military environment my solicitous presence helped at least to keep him in sight of the "Jones's". At any rate he was a very kindly and charming chief.

Vienna that winter was a grim and tragic place, much bombed, cold, clad in dirty snow, streets and parks unswept. The forlorn splendours of the Hofburg, the Stephan's Dom and Schönbrunn stood as ghostly symbols of a past glory so foolishly dismantled by the Allies in 1918.

A defeated people shuffled about the streets, scraping their way back to normal life. They were terrified of the Russians, who had subjected them to days of terror, indiscriminate shooting and rapine after the city fell, and whose soldiers and patrols were still arresting people without warning on the streets.

Relations between the occupying powers in Vienna were distant and occasionally violent. There was a large dance hall for other ranks in the British Sector, not far from Schönbrunn, and a popular rendezvous for off-duty troops on a Saturday evening. On one such a group of Russian officers appeared; they were clearly having less luck with the local girls than were the British soldiers. Several forced Austrian girls to leave with them at the point of their revolvers. At the time the lads in the dance hall, many of whom were from a Scottish regiment, were taken by surprise, but their fury afterwards knew no bounds. Some days later these barbarians unwisely returned with the same intent. This time the Jocks were ready. Punishment learnt in the Gorbals can be swift and capital. I do not know what they did with the bodies, but I learnt there were no more such visits – and no complaints either from the Russians.

Der Kopf ohne Körpe – the head without the body – was the sad verdict on their city by the Viennese. Of all Hitler's audacious grabs the lukewarm resistance to the Anschluss was surely the most understandable. While qualified doctors and scientists were reduced to menial jobs, the longing to belong to some greater entity again must have been strong for these heirs to what had once been the Holy Roman Empire.

Grim though life was for them, there were corners of the city where the natural gaiety of the Viennese still flickered: dingy nightclubs, existing doubtless on the black market, where Allied officers were sometimes welcome, particularly when loaded with tins of pilchards. It was the world of *The Third Man*, a film which for once stuck close to reality.

The problem of our integration with Austrian life was always hampered by lack of currency. Swiss Francs were at a premium but commodities were the usual clandestine method of exchange for those of us who wished to forget the enmities of war and the rules of non-fraternization, mercifully lifted about the time of my arrival.

Under the terms of Yalta the Russians had agreed to retreat from their penetration of Styria and Carinthia. The British were thus welcomed as liberators. For some time contact with the Austrian people was inhibited by the fraternization rule but, even in spite of this, "fratting" flourished.

"I will never forget," one ravishing ex-enemy said to me, "the day it was allowed to speak!"

The boldest blackmarketeer of my acquaintance was Otto Thwaites, a Captain in the 9th Lancers and a most unusual character. He had a Prussian mother and spoke German fluently. During the advance up Italy with his armoured regiment he had distinguished himself and there was a story of him standing in the turret of his tank after the Arno battle haranguing a bedraggled group of German prisoners.

"You cowards," cried Otto, in German, eyes bulging. "My grandfather would have had you shot."

With his command of the language Otto had little difficulty in securing a job in the occupation. His normal expression was one of impenetrable conspiracy, but he had a wicked sense of humour, his face would suddenly split from car to car into a leering grin. The transformation was a considerable shock unless one was used to it.

One day Otto brought off a coup. By some stratagem he obtained two cows from a mountain farmer, loaded them into an Army lorry and ran them into Vienna where he sold them on the black market for untold sums in Austrian currency. Generous to a fault, he decided to spend part of this loot on a tremendous reception at an enchanting if still woebegone inn on the little peninsula of Maria Worth on the Wörthersee. His guest list not only included his British friends, but the Austrian nobility from far and near, to several of whom I believe he was related. Gracefully he also included the Commander-in-Chief, then General John Combe. Not surprisingly the General had another engagement, but nothing happened to Otto and I shall remember that party to my dying day.

Tragically Otto's life was short; he was posted back to his regiment then on duty in the Middle East. Iraq was, as so often, in turmoil and Otto was killed on a border patrol.

After three months of my sojourn in the Economic Division Mr Berthoud told me he was to return to some senior post in Whitehall. Moreover, he warned me kindly, his successor and second in command, a somewhat grim individual, might not take the same view of my duties as he did. I agreed without hesitation and said I thought it was time I retrieved my military career. This caused no surprise. I shall always be deeply grateful to him for providing me with Austria and for indulging me for so long.

My next objective was the British Occupied Zone consisting of the provinces of Styria and Carinthia. Such were the vagaries of the occupation that I was soon offered another job. Styria was garrisoned by the 46th Division. There was a strong cavalry element and they played polo. I had some sort of reputation as a horseman and had certainly schooled polo ponies. It was enough. I became a staff officer at Divisional Headquarters. On the door was a notice – GSO 3 Transport. This time no papers came, either in or out. There was no transport, unless one regarded the polo ponies as such. My sole duty was to look after them and occasionally to play. There were also two racecourses at Graz and Klagenfurt constructed by the Displaced People or DPs from the camps, who seemed to have nothing better to do. I rode at these meetings whenever I got the chance and at one stage had a liberated Hanoverian horse in training for the equivalent of 2s 6d a week. This idyllic existence lasted all summer until 46th Division was posted. But my luck held. I was sent as Chief Instructor to a mountain training school on the Schmeltz above Judenburg in Styria. This had been a Wehrmacht training centre. When the winter came Schmeltz was transformed into a glorified ski school for the troops. We had over 20 Austrian instructors led by an ex-Wehrmacht Officer called Friedl Wolfgang who had captained the Austrian international team before the war. My ambition to learn to ski was well catered for and I worked hard at it, studied snow conditions and avalanches and fell in love with the mountains.

The Styrian Alps are not giants but they can be testing enough and they teemed with game: chamois, red deer, roe, capercailzie, and black game. There were two jaegers or keepers on this vast estate. I spent many happy hours with them and there I learned to call the stags.

It was early October and I had climbed to one of the Jagdhütten with Ernst. We were to spend the night there before clambering higher at dawn for a gamsbok (chamois). We had finished supper – strips of smoked bacon, bread and cheese flooded with Jaegertee, a fearsome brew of bitter Indian tea and Austrian brandy – and went out to look at the night. The hut stood on the edge of a bluff. There was a near full moon and the forest fell away steeply below us wreathed in slowly shifting mist. Across the valley the hump backs of the Seetaler range seemed to hang in midair. There was a hint of frost. It was very still.

The rut of the red deer had not begun but conditions seemed right. *"Die werden vieleicht ankommen,"* grinned Ernst. He led me down to a thicket of alder and reeds among the first twisted outcrop of firs, stuck his Alpenstock into the ground, cupped his hands, threw his head back and roared. His summons ended with a series of grunts, then another roar, as he slowly lifted his head.

Silence. We waited. Twice more he called. Then, magically, from far away below the mist, faint in the distant forest, came the first answering challenge. Soon, to my wonder and delight three stags were calling. Time stood still. They were coming closer. Presently there were only two, but they sounded no more than a few hundred feet below us.

That one is *"ein kleine"* (a small one) said Ernst. "We'll send him away." Subtly, his next roar must have signalled a stag of warrant. Did I hear sound of movement? I could not tell, but we heard no more from the *"kleine"*. But the other beast came on, closer and closer, until we could hear him moving, hear him grunting as he quested about for the rival he should yet could not see. He was no more than yards from us but we were well hidden. I caught the rank smell of him.

Suddenly Ernst grabbed his stick and started thrashing the alder. I thought he was trying to frighten the stag. But no, an instant later the bushes below us were rent and cracked in response as the great beast swung his antlers in furious frustration. Slowly we heard him move round us, suspicious now, for where was this audacious rival? Then he got our wind. There was one mighty bound, a shivering of the alder – and he was gone.

In the spring and summer of '47 I spent many hours alone in the mountains hunting or watching the wild things. I have seldom been happier. A much-travelled friend once told me that Austria was a country only to be indulged in in one's early years, when a sense of romance was at its strongest. It may be so, but for me the charm has never cloyed.

I was well catered for. I had my own chalet, two ex-German soldiers as servants and two pigs called Castor and Pollux. These were originally procured for the table but I became fond of them. Pigs are never given a chance. These two were highly intelligent. They followed me on walks in the mountains and throughout my time at least they were safe from all carnivorous threat.

On the tree line above the camp stood the Adler's Ruhe, a small gasthof patronized in summer by sturdy people from the valley. I had once sought shelter there after a winter descent of the Zirbitz, our local peak, in an unscheduled blizzard. I had first degree frostbite in one foot and these kindly folk dressed it for me. Afterwards I took to climbing up there of an evening. There was Lisl, daughter of the house, an enchantingly pretty fifteen year old who played the zither and there I learned the haunting songs of Steiermark, simple ballads of mountain life, among them the Erz Herzog Johann Lied, unforgettable lilting yodler and tribute to Austria's hero Archduke, younger brother of the last Holy Roman Emperor and nephew of Marie Antoinette. Johann, aged 18, led an army against Napoleon, governed the Alpine provinces and maried morganatically the daughter of a postmaster. Much beloved of the Styrian people, his legend lives on. His song is a challenge to the most flexible epiglottis, but properly rendered it can pull at the hardest heartstring.

The mountains gave me many things including a precious moment I still treasure and have sometimes sought to live again. It was an overture, so to speak, to understanding. Such a lifting of the spirit's veil may come more easily to young eyes and minds uncluttered with conviction.

It was a summer day. I had climbed half way up the Zirbitz, our local peak, and was sitting above the tree line looking down across the forest of larch, spruce and birch, into the valley. Nothing stirred. Smoke rose lazily and straight from some cottage far below. Sunshine and shadow crept across the grass, the linn, the rocks and dappled the trees. No creature moved.

Gradually the quietness possessed me. It was like some sweet symphony half heard in the distance, gradually swelling with a rhythm to which all belonged: the sky, the forest, the mountain and its creatures – and even I. Here in this secret quietness lay the meaning of all things. Here was the joy of creation, the transcendent rightness of life. Here was a gentle all-embracing power the surrender to which was surely the true purpose of existence. Joy – joy is the nearest word in our vast yet inadequate vocabulary with which to attempt an expression of the power of love; the resolution of the opposites, the presence of God. But He is not to be found in the city, at least not by me. Least of all has He much to do with the frenzied ambitions of men. He comes gently and small, softly enveloping, out of the silence, opening the way to our belonging. Goethe knew Him in similar circumstances:-

> "Über allen Gipfeln ist Ruh;
> Über allen Wipfeln, spürest Du
> Kaum einen Hauch.
> Die Vögelein schweigen im Walde
> Warte nur: Balde, ruhigst du auch.*

* See translation on facing page.

This experience may come in different ways to each of us, but I do not think it can ever last for long. We lack the strength to sustain such a presence. A glimpse of existence itself is too fragile, or so it was for me that day in Steiermark.

In this moment I am trying to describe I knew humility. Not the self-deprecating cringing representation so often found in Judao-Christian teaching, but the humility bred of acceptance; to be small in the silence, for an instant a part of nature, is to realize the futility of much that we do, that this does not matter and yet that we must try.

I came down from the mountain with a light step that day.

I have a dear and intrepid friend, Penelope Tremayne, who once encountered the Virgin Mary during a lonely and hazardous descent of the Samaria Gorge in West Crete, which she should certainly never have attempted without a guide and which might well have finished with a fatal fall. She described her experience in her delightful book *A Writer or Something*.

I have been trained to analyse and interpret information, how to assess its source, his motive and access, and have thus learned to doubt much that is reported to me, nearly everything I hear or watch on TV current affairs programmes, and all economic forecasts. I do not for one single second doubt that Penelope met the Virgin Mary. These things happen in the mountains.

My debt to Austria and to my occupied friends is deep indeed. I became a reasonably proficient skier for a late learner and was appointed captain of the British Troops Austria ski racing team. This grandiloquent title meant that we could travel to different resorts to train. We had enormous fun but our ambitions overtook our ability. Some idiot decreed we should challenge the French. The downhill course was set on the Kanzel in Carinthia and thither came the Chasseurs Alpins. I think the best English time was some two minutes slower than the last Frenchman. I broke a leg.

The Army doctor shot morphia into me and I was carried to the cable car in a state of general euphoria. I suppose I was on what is now called "a trip". They installed me in a hotel on the Wörthersee near Velden, taken over as an Officers' Convalescent Home, and there they plastered me up. I was one of several similar casualties. We amused ourselves by hobbling the quarter mile across the lake, over the ice, on our plaster legs to the village of Krumpendorf, where things brightened up of an evening. All went well until the thaw set in. Our well-worn track became distinctly damp and one night

---

Over all the mountain tops is peace;
Over the treetops scarcely a whisper.
The birds are silent in the forest.
Wait, only wait: you too will be quiet.

when I and a friend were returning in good cheer and a touch over the limit a series of booms, cracks and shivers sobered us up sharp. We finished the journey on hands and knees and it was difficult next day to explain why our plaster legs had dissolved.

In the course of this enforced incarceration I developed a genuine wish for further learning. My education at Eton had been of the best and, in spite of my preoccupation with extra-curricular activites such as race riding, enough of the Classics and history had taken root so that when the winter of war gave way a few tentative shoots appeared. I tried for university. I wrote to people I thought might help. My old housemaster Cyrus Kerry was ailing and far from sanguine. I did not possess the qualifications. It seemed my sudden spurt through the school certificate barrier was not enough. In the end I even tried Upsala University in Sweden. They did not reply. What to do?

One evening I was complaining to a friendly West Indian doctor who was recovering from some illness or other about my lack of academic progress.

"Further education!" said he. "Don't waste your time, I'll write down what you need."

And so he did on the back of a menu card. It was a catholic and perceptive list looking back on it. I do not recall all it contained, but remember Gibbon, Arnold Toynbee, James Burnham and Carl Jung. Then there was a dreadful thing called *Science for the Citizen* by Lancelot Hogben.* I never quite made it through Gibbon and I fell at about the third scientific fence, but the stimulus my friend provided led off in various unexpected directions and I suppose did serve to increase knowledge and to develop the beginnings of a concept about politics and the human condition.

But the leg mended. I could ski again, ride again, generally live it up around the lake again. Further education advanced slowly.

In the spring of '48 I was posted, this time to a comparatively elevated position at headquarters, British Troops Austria, with the title of G.S.O. 2, Staff Duties. This involved undeniable responsibilities, the most significant of which was control over the distribution of all captured or liberated cars, of which there were a good many in the Command. People were suddenly and extraordinarily nice to me. A liberated car more or less doubled one's capacity for fun and travel. I was always well motorized myself.

The headquarters were near Klagenfurt and I had the great good luck to be invited to board at Schloss Tentschach a few miles distant. "Tentsch" belonged to the Goschen family and Sandy, younger of two brothers, had a

* A prominent Marxist. Perhaps I had a premonition.

job in military government for which he was singularly well equipped. He had served in the 60th Rifles during the war, but had an Austrian background, spoke the language and the dialect fluently and knew everyone around from the Hochgeboren, struggling to keep their castles going, to the best ski instructors.

Sandy's grandfather, sometime British Ambassador in Vienna, had struck up a friendship with a distant Austrian connection, also a Goschen, who in due course bequeathed this enchanting schloss to the English branch of the family. Sandy and his brother Teddy*, who visited Tentschach whenever he could, were immensely kind to us casual boarders.

We became close friends, Sandy and I. We explored almost every remote valley and village in Carinthia together, skied and hunted to our heart's content. Tentschach was open house and its denizens were visited by a colourful series of itinerant characters including Fitzroy MacLean, whom I had not seen since desert days in the SAS, and who passed on his way to stay with his former comrade, Tito, and Catherine Macmillan, lovely daughter of a future Prime Minister, and later married to my friend Julian Amery. British wives began to arrive from England to the satisfaction of most married officers – though not, I fear, of all.

Staying at Tentschach was a splendid Gunner Major, Bill Martin. Bill had lost an arm somewhere but despite this was an accomplished horseman, possessed a bubbling sense of fun and spread his affections liberally. We all loved Bill but he had one bad habit and one great fear – he would go to sleep dangling a lighted cigarette and then set fire to his bed. This led to a panic-stricken awakening in fire and smoke. Handicapped as a firefighter by his one arm he would throw his blazing bed out of the window and go back to sleep in what was left. Next morning the disaster would slip his memory until Frau Richter, Sandy's beloved and long-suffering housekeeper, would appear at breakfast laden with blackened sheets and clucking indulgently at Bill.

"*Schade, Herr Major! Noch mal feuer, Herr Major!*"

Bill's great fear was the arrival of Mrs Martin. For months he postponed this dire event by a series of ruses which beggared the imagination. Illness, overwork, lack of accommodation, rumours of an imminent posting to the Far East, all were tried and for a time succeeded. Poor Bill's moods soared and sank according to the current odds on her descent. Meanwhile, such was his description of this dread being that we felt bound to sympathize, although in charity we thought she couldn't be as awful as she was painted. We were wrong; she arrived; she was! Bill's varied and virile activities were immedi-

* Sir Edward Goschen Bt, DSO.

ately and drastically curtailed. Happily, some years later she disappeared, or he escaped, to marry a charming girl he had known in Austria.

Sandy, in his position as a local laird, brought many of us in touch with the Carinthian grandees and as the tension eased courtesy visits grew into friendships, some of which last to this day. The Göess family of Schloss Ebenthal near Klagenfurt: Hans Marish of Hollenburg, a splendid fortress guarding the Slovene March and the Drava Valley; and perhaps most spectacular of all Hoch Osterwitz, set upon its pinnacle near St Veit, home of the Kevenhueller family.

Kevenhueller had been among the most powerful families in the Alpine provinces of the Holy Roman Empire with lands in Tirol and Salzburg as well as Carinthia. They were Protestants and war with the Bishops of Salzburg had gradually reduced them. But Osterwitz remained and it was here that one of the most spectacular entertainments in my experience took place. The family lived modestly in a dower house at the foot of the Burg, but, encouraged by their new-found British friends, they determined to open the castle for one splendid night; at least that was the original intention. Like everyone else in occupied Austria they were without resources so the occupiers provided both drink and transport. To reach Burg it was necessary to follow a winding path round the mountain and to pass through half a dozen or more keeps. The family had retained their own armour in spite of the Bishop of Salzburg. British Army jeeps waited at the foot to convey the guests upward. At each keep, on either hand, stood a man in armour, lighted torch in one hand, a halberd in the other. On the narrow steps leading to the castle door stood more of them, whilst Melie Kevenheuller, in her dirndl, waited smiling in the torchlight to welcome her guests.

I believe many distinguished people came from as far as Italy. We had a banquet. The festivities lasted through the next day and on into the night. Most guests were a bit unsteady towards the end but I have never since seen an unsteadiness to comapre with those clattering armoured men.

By the Wörthersee, in the summer of '48, I met a young widow Sally Jephson, of surpassing beauty with a small two-year-old son at foot. Her husband, Tony Jephson, already wounded and decorated, had returned to his regiment against medical orders and been killed in the Reichswald forest within weeks of the war's ending.

We were married and she shared many years of my life. In due course Neil and Carola arrived. That we did not live happily ever after was largely my fault but at least the little boy I met by the lake remains one of my closest friends. Sally died in 1979.

By now I had completed ten years in the army. Peacetime soldiering seemed to hold little attraction, so I returned to England and resigned my commission.

I have returned to Austria. God grant I shall do so again. The beauty and romance of her cities, her castles, her mountains, and their people filled a part of my life and my heart. Such things are sometimes granted even from the ashes of defeat and the animosities of war.

What remains so long after those years of war and turmoil? What deep impressions planted in what was still a young mind? What scars reopen? What nightmares recur? Practically none at all, it must be said. Old comrades, those that are still with us, gather with increasing frequency from battalion, regiment, the SAS, the Italian Resistance, even Sandhurst. Memory becomes foggier as the years pass but there is comfort in familiar faces and old loyalties. The only serious mistake is to include wives in these reunions. The women have few shared experiences, are more than used to hearing about their husbands', and do not necessarily like each other anyway. The last time I was persuaded to take Elisabeth Anne to one such, she sat between two stone-deaf comrades who fought booming battles across her throughout dinner. "Do you think," she said faintly to me as the coffee appeared, "you could remove me from no-man's land".

We are all heroes now, the fear, the inadequacy, the discomfort, the occasional horror and above all the boredom mostly forgotten; the memory of some who fell still vivid, more so indeed than friends I have since lost. Of course reactions depend on the degree of exposure. I was lucky. My experiences could never begin to compare with the sufferings, for instance, of those incarcerated in Japanese prison camps, nor with those of our fathers on the Western Front in 14–18. Ours was a war of mobility and comparatively light casualties. Moreover, if you have to fight, the desert is surely the best place for it. Infinitely to be preferred to jungle, the blind enclosures of Normandy or the streets.

Indeed in a rational world (as if such a phenomenon were ever likely) the UN should run a War Department. Any two nations minded to take each other on should bring their dispute to the UN and if peaceful resolution proved impossible they should be offered the Sahara at a suitable rental for as long as they could afford or thought necessary.

Yet there was a bond forged in those years, when all were united in a common cause and everyone was relatively and some amazingly unselfish.

Young minds heal surprisingly quick. I was astonished to read of plans to "counsel" those due to return after the four-day war in the Gulf as though they were expected to have suffered some traumatic mental breakdown. Such intention says a deal more about the delusions of the would-be counsellors than it does about the likely health of the returning warrior. Psychiatric treatment offered as an alternative to rational common sense may be a disease of our time and can surely be the cause of distress rather than its cure. "Pull yourself together" is an admonition which seems to have gone out of fashion. It is a pity.

———|———

9

AND SO TO FINLAND

I left the army without any notion as to what I should do instead. At 27 the world still seemed an oyster. I was offered a job with Gillette. A charming manager said I must begin by learning how razor blades were made, in Sheffield I think. Somehow I felt there should be more to life. I applied for a place with the BBC. I cannot remember why, but I did not take to the man who interviewed me, nor he to me.

"This is a highly strung, artistic, emotional profession," he said. "Do you think you would fit in?"

"No," I said.

Then the father of a close friend suggested some form of foreign service. He was not particularly explicit but it seemed to have to do with keeping an eye on the Queen's enemies. The dialogue had a familiar ring. After due process I was accepted as an officer in the Secret Intelligence Service and began my new career in London. I am precluded from writing much about it, and of this I make no complaint. But as part of my preparation I was required to do an intensive course in Marxism/Leninism. I think it added to my small store of further education and it was an eye opener.

Now that Soviet Russia, the guarantor and fortress of socialism and Marxist-Leninist orthodoxy, lies in ruin it would seem perverse to consider the matter further but I think anyone who has been subjected to the Marxist doctrine will admit that it widens horizons.

The very scale and sweep of it is persuasive. One needed to count ten and puzzle hard to understand what a mountainous concoction of deceit and fortune telling it really is. Moreover although the theory is now mercifully dead the practice of destruction which accompanied it lives on like some evil virus, indeed has become a way of life for assorted terrorists and trouble makers, and is still prevalent in some backwaters of the extreme left here in Britain.

Apart from dialectical and historical materialism my studies seemed to open a small window into that dark and impenetrable paradox of human nature, the Russian character.

It had been a rough road for the comrades before the revolution in 1917 and equally bumpy afterwards. The convoluted row between Slavophiles and Euro-Russians, Mensheviks and Bolsheviks, anarchists and nihilists, their hatreds, rivalries, constant defections and betrayals, led to the definition of numberless dialectical crimes; narodnism; legal Marxism; opportunism; spontaneity; khvostism, or following in the tail; insufficiently Leninist iskrasim; Manilovism, or smug complacency, and many more. Indeed this category of abuse inspired Archie Lyall to re-write the words of the Red Flag:

> "The petit bourgeois philistine,
> He didn't know the party line.
> Persistent left wing deviation
> Caused him much mental perturbation.
> Until at last bewildered quite
> He became a bloody Trotskyite.
> The moral of this tale is when in
> Doubt consult the works of Lenin".

Anyway it was clear to me this was an evil thing. Manifestly a new war had begun. Whatever their other attributes, the Russian genius for intrigue and subversion was never in doubt and this talent was now devoted to the destruction of western civilization. The tentacles of the conspiracy lay everywhere, its methods subtle and ruthless. Moreover it was powerfully supported by western revolutionaries prepared to betray, deceive or kill in order to further the interests of Slavdom masquerading under the Marxist banner and claiming to be its only true interpreter.

To discuss any serious subject with an intelligent communist was to realize that his values were not as ours, his moral sense utterly alien, his reactions predictable only in terms of this twisted philosophy. His mind in fact was that of another kind of human being. It never ceased to surprise me later that men of good will and some knowledge, even dedicated anti-communists, failed to recognize this gulf and often stepped over the edge.

Thus for the next twelve years, like many others, my efforts were dedicated to this hidden combat with Marxism/Leninism and its executive arm, the KGB.

Secret service is necessarily something of a strain if only because of the necessity to live a double life. The rewards are rare and can only be acknowledged among close colleagues but the hunt can certainly stimulate the adrenalin and an insight into the ruthless nature of international politics is a safe guarantee against many illusions. I am grateful for this.

Years after I left the service, when I was already a Member of Parliament, Sandy Glen, then a director of what was still British European Airways, kindly invited me to join their inaugural flight to Leningrad. Visas duly arrived for all his guests – except for me. Enquiry at the Foreign Office disclosed that I had been declared persona non grata in the Soviet Union. I consoled myself with the thought that this was, after all, some sort of accolade.

In 1950 I was sent to Finland as a minor military attaché. My wife who had hoped for Paris or Rome wept when she heard about the posting. I left alone by car to cross Sweden and thence to Åbo by the ferry. Finland seemed remote. I knew of the Finns' heroic resistance against the might of Soviet Russia right through the winter of 1939. That was all I knew. The language proved a barrier. But I picked up Swedish without too much difficulty. It is spoken by most educated Finns and there is of course a large Swedish-speaking minority, particularly along the coast, a legacy of the days when Finland was a Swedish province.

In the early 50's the Red Army still occupied the Porkala Peninsula, a few miles to the west of Helsinki, and its looming presence provided a constant source of tension in the city, where it maintained a large staff of military attachés. This was my first sustained contact with the Russians and their suspicious, narrow-eyed and aggressive truculence confirmed my worst suspicions. The Finnish officers who became my friends regarded them with a mixture of hatred and contempt, and, despite their overwelming strength and bullying attitude, I believe the Russians still feared the Finns. You could sense it. I had a friend, Captain Errki Poroila, a linguist from the Foreign Desk who spoke Russian fluently as well as English. He was not above quietly translating to me what the Russian officers were saying at the occasional diplomatic function. At one such entertainment, a national day I think it was, we identified a particularly repulsive young Russian Colonel called Cherepov, an officer of the GRU (Military Intelligence) who was often drunk, and this day excessively so. He stood swaying among a group of silent smiling Finnish officers.

"We know you cursed Finns. We know you are only waiting for a chance to take to the forest again with your Pukko (a straight-bladed dagger carried by almost every Finn). We know what you are planning!"

The Finns showed no reaction whatever. They just smiled and stared.

Our existence was geared to this threat of a take over by the Red Army.

They could of course have achieved it in hours. The Finnish Army was reduced by treaty to an ill equipped minimum at the end of the war. Yet the Russians never moved against them and eventually evacuated Porkhala in 1955.

Kekkonen, the Finnish Prime Minister, trod his tightrope with consummate skill. He balanced a special relationship with Moscow, which inevitably involved restrictions on trade and foreign policy, against real internal liberty. Despite a strong Finnish Communist Party the Finns never surrendered their democratic practices, freedom of speech and opinion. Tact was officially necessary, but the Russian experience of Finnish arms was enough to ward off the fate of the Eastern European countries already trodden so ruthlessly into the Soviet Empire, and this despite the fact that the Finns had sided with Germany in order to liberate their country after the Winter War and Hitler's invasion of Russia.

It is a remarkable fact that this small northern land, then of only some four million people, fought three separate wars against the might of Soviet Russia; in 1918 to secure their independence; in 1939 to resist invasion and finally with their German allies in 1941. In this last campaign the Finnish Army finally surrounded Leningrad. Why they never closed in is something of a mystery. There were rumours of a secret correspondence between Churchill and Mannerheim in which Churchill besought the Finnish Commander not to push further. The Allies were certain to win the war and it would be harder for them to defend the Finnish position – which was well understood – if the Finns inflicted further damage on the Soviets. However that may be, I was shown photographs of the retreating Russians on the ice of Lake Ladoga after the winter battle of '41, in the approaches to the city: of dead men and horses, among guns, carts and trucks, frozen upright into grim still life.

The outcome of their efforts after the German defeat was the state of qualified independence which became known as "Finlandisation". The word unfairly came to imply a degree of subservience which Finland never in fact conceded.

Then in his 80's and in retirement Marshall Mannerheim, former Regent, later Finnish wartime President and Commander in Chief, was still to be seen occasionally in Helsinki. Born to a Swedish/Finnish family of Baltic barons whose lands lay in Karelia to the east of what was then the Russian province of Finland, he began his Army career before the First War as a Tsarist cavalry officer of the Garde à Cheval, served until the collapse of the White Russian resistance in 1918 and thereafter in the Finnish War of Independence. He had thus fought in all three of Finland's wars and commanded her armies in two of them. A remarkably erect and stylish

32. I was luckier, I got the bambina (see p.114).

33. "The small mountain village of Groppallo" HQ of the Partigiani of 13 Zone.

34. The author (in beret) with partisan escort in the mountains. Sgt. 'Chalky' White on right, Giorgio Insom (see p.113) is seated left.

35. The author with Giorgio Insom, "half Russian/half Italian" (p.113).

36. My bodyguard of Partigiani after the liberation of Piacenza.

37. "Then came the victory parade and a proud sight it proved to be" (p.131).

38. "At each keep... stood a man in armour, lighted torch in one hand, a halberd in the other" (p.144).

39. The author in Austria, 1947.

military figure he still made, with a discerning eye for the girls. In 1952 he died, midst this small nation's grief and gratitude. His coffin was borne on a gun carriage through the streets of his capital in the dead of winter, followed by his Generals in their distinctive white fur shakos. Behind in turn marched the Foreign Attachés, American, British and French. Of the Russians there was no sign.

There had been confident predictions of a strong communist demonstration against this assertion of Finnish patriotism: there was none. The pavements were packed with silent people, the only sound the rumbling of the gun carriage wheels and the creak of our boots in the snow.

My duties involved getting to know the country. There is a lot of it – from the Baltic to the Arctic, 500 miles of trackless primeval forest and lonely lake. At the top: the forest dwindles to a fringe of twisted birch and alder, and finally surrenders to the tundra and the barren fells. At the bottom a jigsaw of inlets and wooded islets border a brackish sea.

I travelled alone by car along roads and tracks, even the best of which were pitted by the merciless winter conditions. Tarmac and concrete buckled in the frost and the surfaces consisted of gravel in summer, beaten snow in winter. Main roads in winter were often easier once the heavy snows had fallen but the routes were inevitably restricted and lodgings often non-existent.

In summer I camped at night in the forest, wherever possible by a lake. The land has a melancholy beauty. The light changes constantly on rock face and still water, while the lone twilight of summer has a strange timeless quality. It has been said of Sibelius, composer of Finland's haunting anthem, that his music lacks any hint of people. His symphonies are full of the wind, the forest, the storm, the lakes and the wild creatures that live there. Never are they demeaned by any sense of human voice or presence. They are the true music of Finland.

I journeyed to Lapland in both summer and winter. In February, 1952, I left Helsinki with my colleague, Colonel Gerald Bowser of the Sussex Regiment, the Military Attaché. We flew to Rovaniemi, capital of Lapland, thence by car well north of the Arctic Circle. At the end of this road we set off to travel some hundred miles on skis, accompanied by two Finnish Officer friends as guides, together with two Lapps and two reindeer. The deer pulled small boat-like sledges called Akkias on which our tent and provisions were carried.

The Arctic night was relieved by about two hours' hint of twilight around what should have been midday. You could see well enough by the stars to ski.

We pitched camp when we were tired and, when the time approached, one of our Lapps searched for a dead pine, our fuel for the night. They drove their axes into every likely trunk. The timber must not be rotted. When they found one that fitted the purpose we halted. The moment we ceased to move the cold closed upon us like a shroud. It was over 30C below.

We dug; two metres of snow and more to the earth's surface, a circular pit for the tent. This was a simple single skin canvas contraption with a hole in the top from which rose a metal flue from our stove placed in the middle. Pine branches formed our communal bed and logs were wedged around the stove to stop us burning our feet. We stayed awake by turns to feed the fire, for if it should fail death would be swift.

But before we slept there was a meal cooked by the Lapps and a deal of Bränvin or Schnapps passed round. We sat there in open shirts, warm both within and without, singing the songs of Finland and, for aught I remember, Scotland too, with nothing but the canvas between us and the Arctic night. When I touched my ski boots stowed behind me they were frozen stiff.

When camp was satisfactorily pitched the two Lapps and their reindeer would leave us to visit their friends in the nearest settlement, for these people are largely nomadic, following and living off their herds of deer. One such evening I watched as they skied away. The Lapps preceded the deer. The first sleigh was pulled by the stag, followed by the hind. As they got underway the hind hopped neatly into the stag's sledge in front of her and rode off into the gloom, pulled along chivalrously and uncomplaining by her mate.

Father Christmas is a reality. He is a Lapp and his image must have reached us via Norse rune and sage.

Too little is understood, or taught, about the origins of the Finnish people. Emanating from the Steppe like every other nomadic tide I have heard of, they are a branch of the Finno-Ugrian group of peoples, one spur of which swept up the Danube. There is a connection between Finnish and the Magyar tongue.

Of the three main Finnish tribes the northern and the southern people made their way in coracles across the Gulf of Finland. The eastern people advanced north via Lake Ladoga, while an offshoot stayed put in what is now Estonia. Of the three tribes, the weakest were thrust steadily northwards until they crossed the Arctic Circle. They are the Lapps. Their territory knows no frontier and, until the coming of Communism, many moved readily between Finland, Russia and Norway following their herds or to mark the run of the salmon. To some extent they still did when I was there.

They are a hardy race. One morning in the fleeting twilight we met a Lapp on the trail dressed in traditional smock of coloured felt and breeches with a floppy tricorne bonnet and deer-hide boots. He rode in his Akkia sleigh behind a reindeer stag. As in all lonely places when people meet, initial greetings were followed by a prolonged silence, while questions were gradually formulated. Since we were the foreigners it was his turn first. How far had we come? Whither did we go? How many days from the south? He eyed us curiously and our Finnish friends volunteered that we two came from England. The Lapp nodded uncomprehendingly; wherever that might be it was certainly of little consequence. Now it was our turn.

Where was he going? A short speech ensued.

"He is going to look for some reindeer lost on the fells," our companions explained. I looked up at the windswept hills, the dark skyline lost in swirling snow and cloud.

"Where will he sleep?"

"He will find a tree."

This seemed an inadequate explanation but we were to learn the technique. The Lapp would fell his tree, chop it in half, wedge one half atop the other, chip the bark between for kindling and set it alight. Properly managed, it would burn for hours. The Lapp and his deer and his dog would curl up on the leeward side.

My summer expeditions were more comfortable and more interesting. The furthest north I penetrated was on a fishing trip accompanied by a stern Finnish General who regarded my small spirit stove as both effete and unnecessary. He used sticks. We drove to the limit of the road well north of the Arctic Circle and thence travelled by canoe driven by outboard up the Tenoyoki, a great river which flows from the Arctic Sea and marks the march with Norway. It took over nine hours before we pitched our two small tents and set to with the rod. Daylight in July lasts 24 hours. The sun simply dips in brief homage to the calendar on cither side of what ought to be midnight. For some time I stuck doggedly to the dictates of my watch. It was midday, therefore time to eat. Midnight, I should be asleep. My Finnish friend paid no attention at all to this superfluous routine – and caught more fish. Happily my watch got wet and stopped. I soon learned to eat when I was hungry and sleep when exhausted. The trouble was I soon forgot the date and had to trudge to the police post at the frontier to find out. Sometimes they knew, sometimes not. Once the whole establishment was drunk. Some Lapps had crossed from Norway and the welcome had been a touch overdone.

Thus I discovered that there is little more peaceful than to lose touch with time and I came to understand what the Swedes call "Lapland Fever". We visited two young Swedish women who ran a medical centre in this harsh wilderness. They confessed they had contracted "Lapland Fever" and never wished to leave. Stranger still was the case of an Austrian doctor who had served in Lapland with the Wehrmacht. After the war he had quit his practice in Vienna and returned. He was living as a Lapp with his own considerable herd of reindeer and reckoned a rich man in consequence. I tried to trace him, but in vain. There was no time.

At the end of my week I left by canoe, thence by car a day's journey distant. I carried with me a 4lb grilse I had caught. The Lapp ghillie showed me how to salt it. This was not difficult. First gut the fish, then rub a generous amount of salt along the backbone. It took me three successive nights camping in the forest before I reached Helsinki and in the process, with the aid of an extra sharp pukko, I sliced and ate that raw fish. It tasted like very delicate smoked salmon.

Apart from my fishing trips, sporting activities were limited, but I was once invited on an elk hunt. The Scandinavian elk is identical with the Canadian moose. The season lasts just three weeks. Casualties among the hunters are not infrequent. I was to discover how.

I spent the night with my Finnish friends at an inn some hundred and fifty miles north of Helsinki near Lahti. Soon after dawn we arrived at the rendezvous, a crossroads on the main route north. What seemed like a hundred or more hunters were milling around, mostly dressed in brightly checked shirts designed to startle the most comatose of elks. Around us lay the trackless forest.

After some discussion, incomprehensible to me, I was handed a 9mm rifle and ten rounds, then led off down a fire lane into the forest, accompanied by many more participants, all armed as I was. Every hundred yards or so one of us was instructed to fall out. When my turn came I was given a wrist compass by our leader, who luckily spoke Swedish.

"It's four kilometres on a bearing of 270 degrees," he said. "You'll be all right. Just keep shouting and you'll hear the others shouting on either side. Try to keep in line."

A most unwelcome suspicion was dawning on me. "What's at the other end?" I asked.

"Well, the others will be waiting," he said.

"What! With 9mm rifles?"

"Of course," he said, hurrying off down the fire lane with a grin which I think was intended to reassure. I checked and double-checked my bearing and waited. Presently a whistle blew. I moved off stealthily into the unknown, shouting busily. The forest was thick, the going rocky and difficult. For about twenty minutes my shouts evoked answering shouts. Whenever I heard a shout I shouted back. I took repeated bearings on trees and rocks. I know how to work a compass and I did not deviate from my bearing by one yard if I could help it. Presently the shouting died away on either side; no one answered me any more. I gave up shouting; I was getting hoarse anyway. I plodded on more slowly but certainly on my bearing. My best hope of suvival clearly lay in strict adherence to 270 degrees and four kilometres, although the risk must be expected to increase the nearer I got to the line of intrepid hunters, waiting for the elks I was supposed to be driving at them.

It was a still day. About me the only sounds were the creak of branches and the dripping trees. Suddenly I heard a rustling ahead of me. I saw the undergrowth move. It had to be the elk – what else? I got behind a tree, steadied the rifle and pushed my safety catch forward. If I had been a Finn I would surely have fired on the off chance.

Out of the bushes shuffled a hunter, gazing intently at his wrist compass. I stepped from behind my tree. The man nearly fell over with shock. When he had recovered, he launched into a torrent of Finnish, pointing at his wrist compass. I declined as politely as I could to follow his advice. Eventually he gave up, clearly taking me for a foreign lunatic who would probably never be seen again. But I was not as mad as he thought. I was on the correct bearing and after half an hour or so several shots rang out in front of me, followed by a crashing in the forest. This time it was the elk, or elks. I never saw the great beasts but soon after the engagement I came up with a group of disconsolate hunters. They had missed their elk. It seemed that luck was in for me as well as the elk that day.

The Olympics came to Helsinki in 1952. In those days we did things properly. A cruiser sailed in with a Royal Marine Band which beat retreat every evening on the quay, watched by a large crowd. Prince Philip arrived and joined the cruiser. The British presence thus upstaged everyone and the Finns were delighted. It was as well, for our athletic performance scarcely matched up. We won only one gold medal and that was in the last event of all – the show jumping. Harry Llewellyn on the famous Foxhunter won a thrilling jump-off. All the long-distance races were won by a Czech called Zatopec. The only bad moment for him was when he was led round the last bend in the 5000 metres by an unknown Englishman called Christopher Chataway. Alas for us, Chataway either tripped or was pushed or fell over. But it was a noble effort. The next time I met him was in the House of Commons.

Prince Philip flew away in a Comet, the world's first commercial jet. More prestige for Britain, short-lived unhappily. Weeks later metal fatigue took its tragic toll.

My term in Finland ended in the summer of 1953. My wife and I travelled home via Norway where we stayed in an isolated hotel at the head of the

Naeröy Fjord. The view down the fjord, when one could see it, was breathtaking. It rained for a week. Poor Sally got little benefit from this holiday. I fished and caught nothing. On the last evening, soaked to the skin, I had reached my half-hopeless decision to try just six more casts. The light was fading. I was fishing a deep pool whence the cliffs rose sheer some thousand feet on the far bank. A storm which had been threatening gathered and broke. Lightning flashed vividly across the breadth of the fjord. The rain hissed on the water. Thunder rolled and echoed along the rock walls. There was a shattering crack above me. I ducked involuntarily – and at the same second felt a tug on the line. Cold and disbelieving, I lifted my rod. The reel screamed and a great salmon leapt twisting and writhing three feet from the water. In a flash of lightning I saw him. He ran again. I tried to hold him but he was too strong. Soon he was over the lip at the tail of the pool and down the rapids. I stumbled and struggled down the bank, caught up with him twice and recovered the backing on my line, to no avail. He ran on downstream again and of a sudden the line went slack. He was gone and the thunder rolled again as if to mark his triumph. I was elated and the vision of that splendid silver leap in the lightning lingers with me yet.

I trudged back to the hotel and found it difficult to explain why I felt so happy.

For some time before that I had become increasingly dissatisfied with myself for smoking. I suppose the feeling was accentuated by the excesses of a series of farewell parties in Helsinki. That evening after dinner I threw away a last cigar and have never smoked since. My escape from this unpleasing habit is in some sense a homage to that glorious, thunderous salmon.

———·|———

10

TO PARIS

In 1954 I was posted to Paris. We settled in a house at Rue Gambetta in Boulogne sur Seine. From the flat roof you could watch the tennis at the Roland Garros stadium, the French equivalent of Wimbledon, but never hear the score. During the French Championships the betting could be intense on our roof.

At the end of the road was the Porte de Boulogne and the Bois. Once through the Bois and the Porte Maillot my ascent was direct up the Avenue Foch to the Arc de Triomphe, down the Champs Elyseés to the Rond Point, into the Faubourg St Honoré and thence to my office. Whatever one's mood, this majestic approach to the day's happenings promised challenge and adventure.

Haussmann's great stellar plan radiating from the Arc is a statement in civilized clarity and logic, like the French language. London implies no such statement. It is an agglomeration of villages, a muddled jungle, great buildings jostled by ugliness, full of unexpected corners, often interesting, sometimes beautiful, but at no stance do you catch your breath, nowhere is the spirit lifted as mine so often was on the way to the Faubourg St Honoré.

London never welcomes the returning commuter on a Monday morning. A weekend away from Paris and one had the sense something might have been missed. The city pulsates, she exercises a powerful centripetal force. She poses as the centre of the world. Of course she is not. She is not even the centre of France.

London, with its air of sombre diligence and financial power by the side of the great river, is still nearer to the hub.

But the appearance and ambience of both cities say much about the respective characters of the peoples who created them, and perhaps explain something of the exasperation which each evokes in the other.

My life in Paris was an adventure in many ways but the most important led, I think, to some understanding of the causes of this everlasting *malentendu* and of the rare harmony which both our peoples are occasionally capable of distilling together. Oldest of the established nation states of Europe, our experiences, whether in conflict or amity, lie too close to be ignored. Our defaults so often balance our respective qualities. We wear our prejudices like comfortable old coats, remove them and at heart we believe in the same values. We are often closer than we know. There are many relationships in Europe which may seem superficially easier and more natural for the British and are thus the more disturbing when the mask slips.

Now, as Europe is gradually moulded or distorted, whether willingly or no, into shapes that no one can predict for reasons that are no longer clear, it will be the fears, the ambitions and the lessons of her history which will bring France closer to us in the end. Fulminate and criticize as we may, we will always find it hard to do without one another, and we shall be ever stronger for trying to understand. But, I grant, a considerable effort is necessary and as a rough guide to the student: when a Frenchman decides to trust you, even suggest you should "*tu toyer*", the barriers are down. If he starts to tell you about his mistresses, he will open his heart. It is a friendship without reserve. We English alway retain a reserve. It is not ill will. It is second nature. We consider it unwise to admit to mistresses. There is a great gulf here.

Paris is a place where the whole range of human emotions are faced openly and realistically. Nothing is hidden. It is a bad place for secrets and a good one for all who are stimulated by contrast, particularly by night, and it is important to appreciate Paris by night. The life of politics, the theatre and the media is laid bare in the Chansoniers with an immediacy which defies the comprehension of any who are not up to the minute with the latest scandal. From such sharp satire one could, in my day, cross the street and listen, for instance, to Suzy Solidor, bejewelled and besequinned, ample in body and sentiment, with her lyrical songs of ships, sadness and the sea. The Diseuses of Paris are a genre I have never discovered elsewhere, these female troubadours with their ballads about life. The incomparable Edith Piaf was still going strong. There were others.

Across the river in Montparnasse there waited a splendid subterranean experience, if you could find it: "*Aux Oubliettes*". Down several flights of precipitious dim-lit stone steps you descended to the dungeons of old Paris, there to sing in 16th Century French the songs of the 100 years war. They were not especially anglophile:

> *Nous vimes venir sur le vent à nous*
> *une Frégate d'Angleterre*
> *qui creusait les mers et les flots*
> *c'était pour aller à Bordeaux*

Buvons un coup – buvons à deux
à la santé des Amoureux
a la santé du Roi de France
et merde pour la Reine d'Angleterre
qui nous a declaré la guerre!

Every tourist knows the splendid floor shows at the Lido or the Crazy Horse, but the nature and setting of the striptease can vary surprisingly. Uphill from the Sacré Coeur towards the Butte de Montmartre there winds a narrow alley. A stone's throw from the great Cathedral there was a gap in a wall and by it, chalked up on the stone, the singular announcement *"Le Bouc"* – "the Goat". Pass through and one was in a miniature farmyard. Chickens ran about. You could be greeted by a pig. Within was the restaurant, crammed generally. If you were lucky enough to get a table you would, as like as not, have your bread neatly removed by a sheep. There was a piano and we sang there too. One day the patron, a commanding figure with an unexplained sympathy for his occasional English clients, announced in stentorian tones:

"Partout à Montmartre il y a des 'strips'. Moi, ce soir, moi aussi, je vous offre mon 'strip!'"

With that the pianist struck up and the "strip", a rather sheepish looking girl, minced into the minute sawdust covered space before the piano.

"Allez. Vas y! Fais ton 'strip'," shouted the patron, beating time on the piano by way of encouragement. The unfortunate stripper had no alternative but to attempt her display, among the tables, followed closely by the sheep which clearly anticipated something to its advantage. Luckily the girl was slim enough to squeeze through, but it was a close thing whether she or the clients did most of the stripping. The ribaldry was intense and, rather sooner than planned, she escaped in fits of giggles and to roars of appreciation.

The act was never repeated but it was the best "strip" I ever witnessed.

I spent many hours in the galleries and painted quite hard while I was in Paris, hurrying back at lunchtime to my easel before the paint dried out. To the English, painting for the amateur is a nice hobby. To the French, amateurs are referred to witheringly as Sunday painters. *"Ill faut s'adonner à la peinture"*. It is true. I nearly did. There was a bar not far from the Deux Magots Café where the patron showed paintings by unknown artists. They hung for a week and there was a note book in which the clients wrote what they thought. My work was accepted. The criticisms varied from a longish interpretation of my supposed character to a cryptic "one liner" – *"Enfin un bistro avec un service qui vaut la peine!"* (At last a bar with a decent service.) Some fair critic had written, *"Bravo pour les toiles, mais oh la taille de leur auteur!"* I never did find out who she was. Another said, *"Vous savez pêutetre peindre, mais vous ne savez pas très bien ou vous allez.*" And that was probably nearer the mark.

Sally and I rented a weekend cottage from a friend in a small village off the Route d'Orleans called Ormoy la Rivière. It was a charming untidy place with the Côte rising sharply behind it, covered in alder, oak and pine. We spent many happy weekends there and developed a new sport. We were occasionally visited by a snail hunter, a ragged, nearly toothless individual full of cunning and good humour. He would appear, *au hasard*, with a sack of his victims over his shoulder. We were good customers but habitually chose too many. The answer lay in snail racing. The most athletic-looking snails were spared the pot and their shells painted different colours. The races took place on a round metal table with a hole in the middle designed for a sunshade. The start was behind a circle round the hole and the finishing line was the edge. The race provided a popular betting medium for Sunday guests but they took a long time and were very frustrating. The odds-on leader would suddenly change its mind within inches of the line, turn round and return to the start.

Racing snails were invariably released.

My four years in Paris were marked by three dramas: the Hungarian Revolt, the Suez Crisis and the return of de Gaulle. All three could be said to have changed the course of history.

It was a tragic accident that the first two coincided. Had they not perhaps the Free World, and in particular the Americans, might have reacted more positively both to the gallant and tragic Hungarian resistance and to the Anglo-French cause in Egypt. However that may be, I never felt greater shame at the impotence of the West than when Hungary was crushed. General Pal Maléter stood then for liberty as few in our time have done. I cannot forget his last dimly heard broadcast message in the face of the Russian tanks, outside Budapest.

"The lights are going out."

This brutal application of the Brezhnev doctrine may have seemed unchallengable at the time. The Americans who voted against us over Suez had not the courage to do the same against Soviet Russia. Yet the spark that glowed so briefly and brightly in Budapest in 1956 surely lit a fuse which in the end served to blow the whole hideous Soviet Empire into kingdom come.

We took in a young Hungarian refugee couple at Rue Gambetta. It was a sadly inadequate gesture in the circumstances.

The Suez operation was always likely to end in confusion, since all three contestants – you can scarcely call them allies – had different objectives. The

French saw Nasser as the main source of support for rebellion in Algeria; the Israelis needed a *casus belli* in order to frustrate Egyptian-led and Soviet-supported Pan-Arabism; the British were interested in safeguarding the canal. Of the 14,666 ships which passed though in 1955 one-third were British.

Although Eden finally and somewhat ridiculously compared Nasser to Hitler, the Egyptian dictator's elimination was not seen as essential to the British. To the French it was. The Israelis were more than ready to do the whole business on their own but lacked both arms and air cover to compete with the Soviet Migs. The French were happy to provide both. The Foreign Office, because of their attachment to the Baghdad Pact, a somewhat shaky organization designed to counter Soviet influence in the oil-rich states, and of which Iraq was then still a member, mistrusted Israeli intentions and even seemed to have persuaded themselves that, if hostilities were opened against Egypt, the Israelis would turn on Jordan, though what motive they could have had in the prevailing circumstances is hard to see.

The dilemma was resolved in London largely through the good offices of the French General Maurice Challe who suggested that if the British regarded both Israel and Nasser as opponents the answer was for an Anglo-French force to strike direct at the canal, thus protecting the canal base, while at the same time appearing to separate the combatants, Israel and Egypt. "Good idea," Eden is alleged to have said.

On this false compromise the expedition was launched and immediately gave rise to ludicrous accusations of collusion with Israel. Of course there was collusion, that is to say the French supported both their allies, one of whom was regarded as an enemy by the other. The British Government knew the true position perfectly well and their protestations were rightly seen in Paris as grossly hypocritical.

It was not our finest hour. Nevertheless, in Paris the enthusiasm for the joint venture was remarkable. You could feel it in the streets as well as the offices. "*Enfin on va les foutre en l'air ensemble*", seemed to express the reaction of most of my French friends and contacts. It was a lifting of the spirit.

In the middle of the action I was ordered to London with a French colleague, Marcel Chalet of the DST (equivalent of our MI5). American antagonism was mounting fast but the landing had gone well enough. The Israeli Army had struck a devastating blow and the French were within hours of securing the canal when, to our amazement, Chalet and I were told of the ceasefire by an apparently relieved Foreign Office official. We could not believe it. The French pleaded for three hours to enable their paras to reach Port Said under cover of the Israeli tanks and artillery. To no avail.

I had not appreciated the depth of political opposition which existed at Westminster, nor the fatal lack of resolve of which Eden and his government were capable. Of course American pressure was a significant factor, but it should never have been critical. Both Eisenhower and Dulles subsequently admitted they had been mistaken (Nixon dixit).

Whether or not we were right to start the operation, the consequences of this fatal loss or nerve by the British Government when their objective had been virtually reached proved baleful indeed. Described by the French Commander General Beaufré as *"un brillant succés militaire et défaite politique"*, the Suez débâcle meant the end of any decisive European influence in the Middle East. Where was the alternative? Having thrown their weight against their most dependable allies, the Americans proceeded to rely on the Shah as their main agent. When Iraq went down in bloody revolution they lacked any alternative policy. Their eventual landing on the Lebanese beaches outside Beirut among the bikinis and the coke drinkers achieved nothing and did little for their reputation. Nor did their disastrous helicopter operation in the Persian desert in April, 1980. Designed to free 53 diplomatic hostages, it culminated in the foul public display of the dismembered bodies of American airmen in Teheran.

The scourges of terrorism and hostage-taking have grown steadily more aggresive and humiliating for the west over the years since then. Finally we have to suffer Saddam Hussein. No one would deny the Americans their technological triumph against Iraq, but they then contrived to throw away the advantages of their victory. The consequences of Saddam's survival seem a poor reward for such a prodigious deployment of men and arms. American efforts to establish stability in the Middle East have met with small success. Perhaps they might do well to study the Roman record in the 1st century. Not so much has changed if it comes to that and Vittellius Lucius, Governor of Syria, who took over from Pontius Pilate, made a rather more effective attempt to control affairs in this cauldron of treacherous chieftains and religious fanatics than the purveyors of the laser bomb.

Little of this was clear to my French colleague or me as we returned in bewilderment to Paris, but that we had assisted in however humble a capacity in what seemed a great enterprise wilfully abandoned by politicians who lacked both courage and foresight was certain. What was the point in struggling to supply people like this with information. And if there was no point perhaps I had better try to do something about it. I did. I went to Conservative Central Office for advice. Dick Casey, then Australian Foreign Minister, kindly consented to sponsor me. I was put on some sort of list and stayed there for so many months that I scarcely took my candidature seriously any more.

11

THE RETURN OF DE GAULLE

"It was not worth my readers' while to occupy himself with the alterations by which bungling practice corrects absurd theory."

Letter from Edmund Burke in answer to some objections to his book on French affairs.

The third drama which enhanced my term in Paris came close to destroying the cohesion of the French polity all together.

Although I believe I was as close to the extraordinary events which unfolded during the last two weeks of May, 1958, as a British official in Paris could be, I have drawn on French sources and particularly heavily on Nerry and Serge Bromberger's splendid narrative *"Les Treize Complots du Treize Mai"* to fill the gaps in my knowledge at the time.

Of all the arbitary experiments in government imposed by the French intellect, the Fourth Republic should surely rate among the most unsuccesful.

After 150 years of constitution-mongering one might have expected by 1945 some advance in practicality. Not so. They devised a system after the war which in the name of equity reduced politics to a parlour game, an introverted calculation nearer to bookmaking than to authority.

In the twelve years since de Gaulle withdrew to Colombey-les-Deux-Eglises there had been no less than 17 Prime Minsters of 24 separate administrations, many of them men of worth but all, in their turn, overcome by the idiotic provisions of the constitution before they could get a grip on events. The ceaseless and unpredictable tides of intrigue and defection in the Palais Bourbon and the Luxembourg had led, by the time I arrived in Paris, to a swelling undercurrent of contempt for Government.

On the surface, much encouraged by the press, interest focused on the manoeuvres by which each new and inevitably powerless administration was contrived. Beneath it both Paris and Algiers seethed with frustration and thence gave way to revolutionary plotting.

There were two further factors which contributed to this general instability. It was nearly 10 years since liberation. The habit of clandestinity dies hard. France's heroes and heroines had lived and died by it. Experience in the Réseaux was a badge of honour and respect. Moreover those who had thus served were still in close touch. The figure around which all this activity had turned was of course de Gaulle.

The second factor might be termed the politicizing of the Armed Forces. Since the collapse in 1940, officers in the Army, Navy and Air Force had been faced continuously with the need to make political choices. These decisions, of an agonizing nature, often involved consideration of career against patriotic duty, of the authority of one general against another, even of one government against another. Politics had been imposed on the Army, in cadet school, in the prison camps, in London with the Free French, in Dakar with Boisson, in Syria between Dentz and Catroux, in Tchad with Leclerc, or at Algiers with Darlan and then again between Giraud and de Gaulle.

Added to this was the frustration, mounting to despair, at the inability of successive French governments post-war to cope with the end of the imperial era. After Dien Bien Phu, the evacuation of Tunisia and Morocco, the sudden volte-face within sight of victory at Suez, and now the intractable and bloody struggle in Algeria the French soldier perceived only too clearly that political solutions were inevitable. Yet in Paris the eternal squabbling rendered ministers incapable of negotiating them. The only likely outcome was inertia leading to defeat.

Thus the Army constituted a political time bomb. In 1956 a fuse was already burning, although the purpose of the explosion was as yet uncalculated. Events took charge of this.

Soon after my arrival in Paris I had been lucky enough to make friends with Tommy Yeo-Thomas*, the legendary *"Lapin Blanc"* hero of the Resistance in Paris and beyond. A stocky pugnacious little Welshman born in 1901, Tommy was educated in England and France where his family had been in business for several generations. He served, under age, at the end of the First World War and subsequently fought for the Poles against the Russians in 1919/20. Captured and condemned to death by the Bolsheviks, he escaped the night before he was due to be shot and returned to France. On the outbreak of war in 1939 he was working in Paris as manager of Molyneux the couturier. He immediately sought to volunteer and after some difficulty succeeded in joining the RAF. Too old to fly, he eventually managed to transfer to the French section of SOE in November, 1942. Dropped twice into occupied France, he was finally arrested by the Gestapo in Paris in March, 1944. Tortured mercilessly and entirely unproductively

* Wing Commander F. F. E. Yeo-Thomas, GC, MC & Bar

by the Gestapo, he and some other prisoners were finally dispatched to Buchenwald concentration camp, destined for almost certain death. After suffering and witnessing unspeakable cruelties at Buchenwald and subsequently at Rehmsdorf, Tommy was loaded into a train with other inmates and dispatched eastward towards Bohemia. During the many stops he and those of his companions who were still strong enough were ordered to carry the bodies of prisoners who had died or been murdered by the SS on the train and throw them into hastily dug holes. From one of these grim fatigues Tommy and some others ran for the woods under heavy fire. Not all made it. He was lucky.

The story of his exploits, of his escape and unbelievable struggle towards the Allied line, of his rearrest, his second escape and final deliverance, emaciated and half-conscious, to the Americans, has been graphically and movingly told by Bruce Marshall in his book *The White Rabbit*.* I think Tommy was the bravest man I ever met.

When I knew him he was established in a flat on the Left Bank with Barbara, a charming gentle lady with whom he lived as man and wife until his death in 1964. It was a matter of astonishment to me that Tommy, who had done more for the Allied cause and for France than any other expatriate, was never invited to the Embassy on the Queen's birthday, simply because he and Barbara were not formally married. Could narrow official prejudice reach further?

At that time Tommy was the Paris representative of the CBI and I have no doubt British industry benefited hugely for he was held in universal respect and affection. Although a prey to frequent and painful headaches caused by his suffering at the hands of the Gestapo, mentally Tommy had completely overcome his experiences, of which he never spoke. Only once was I made conscious of the horrors inflicted on him and countless others. I had a friend and French colleague, André Feret-Patin also a prominent leader of the Resistance in West France, and as it happened, also an ex-inmate of Buchenwald. They did not know each other and I thought it might be interesting for them to meet. Finally I arranged this over a drink at the Crillon Bar.

They exchanged one question and one answer. It concerned the particular camp blocks they had inhabited. It established their credentials. Then they turned, smiling and in silence, to me; there was nothing more for them to say. I had conceived in my ignorance that their shared experience would develop into comradeship, that they would dive happily into reminiscence, but there was nothing whatever for them to say. In that instant I knew the

* First published in 1952 by Evans Bros.

depth of the terrible experience they shared. They were not as other men and I was far removed from them. Moreover, they were too kind to attempt to initiate me. I felt inexpressibly humbled, even ashamed. We talked of trivialities. I do not think they ever met again.

Tommy, needless to say, was deep in the confidence of the Paris Gaullistes, and gradually through him I met a number of his friends and contacts. It was a wide and curious conspiracy, or rather a number of uncoordinated yet often interlocking plots, generated and propelled by a wide range of personalities, some prominent in public life, some in the Army, some moved by a compulsive taste for rebellion. Their connection consisted in a mutual disgust with the impotence of the system and the conviction, shared by most, that only one man could resolve it. It was up to me to seek to follow their fortunes.

The extraordinary events which finally brought about de Gaulle's return were more reminiscent of the storming of the Bastille than of a colonial revolt, but to understand what happened one has to look at the course of the savage Algerian tragedy. This was not easy at the time. Apart from the gaulliste activists, Paris seemed mesmerized by the tergiversations at the Palais Bourbon and the Luxembourg. Even the brutal battle for Algiers, the FLN bombing and the equally merciless *"ratonnades"* against the Muslims and their property perpetrated by the Europeans failed to halt what de Gaulle once called "the absurd ballet" of the 4th Republic.

The Berber and Arab peoples of North Africa have a history of fierce independence. The revolt of Abd el Kadir which followed the French conquest in 1830 lasted 15 years, after which the 2nd Republic declared this vast territory a part of metropolitan France. The claim was never sustainable. Spaniards, Italians and Maltese as well as French, poured into Algeria where, known collectively as the *"Colons"* or *"Pieds Noirs"*, they maintained an obstinate and violent opposition to assimilation. Full French citizenship was never easily available to the Muslim population, and in spite of the advantages of French education and economic development, resentment grew. The defeat in '40 lowered respect for the *Presence Française*. Bad harvests in the war years while the Vichy Government purloined Algerian produce for German-occupied Europe stoked the fires of revolt. In 1945, at Setif, the boil burst. A hideous week of massacre, rape and looting of European property was followed by equally ruthless *"ratissages"* by the French Army which left several thousand Muslim dead. The FLN rebellion spread throughout the territory and into Algiers itself.

From the urban jungle of the Casbah an FLN terrorist leader, Saadi Jacef, built up an organization which was to launch a reign of reciprocal terror in the city. The bombs, placed initially by pretty Arab girls in European clothes, were first aimed at the known haunts of the *Pieds Noirs* but became increasingly indiscriminate. Women and children were mercilessly butchered. Reprisals by the *Pied Noir* mob against innocent Muslims and their property were equally horrifying.

In December, 1956, General Salan was appointed C in C. Justly or no his previous record in Indo China did not endear him to the *Pieds Noirs*. Soon after his arrival three incidents built up the crisis in Algiers.

General Jacques Faure, Chief of Staff of the Algiers division, a brave and popular officer but an extraordinarily inept conspirator, disclosed to the Secretary General of the Prefecture, Paul Teitgen, the existence of a plot to seize Lacoste, the Governor General, and impel Salan to establish a military government. After which, claimed the General, his political contacts in Paris, in particular the Senator Michel Debré, would lead a *coup d'état* and place the army at the disposal of de Gaulle.

This was immediately reported to Lacoste. General Faure was recalled and awarded 30 days *Arrêt de Forteresse*. Surprisingly, he was then appointed to a high command in Germany whence he later threatened to lead an armoured column into France in support of de Gaulle.

On 28 December, 1956, after the Faure plot came apart, Algiers was rocked by the murder by a Muslim assassin of Amédée Froger, a highly respected mayor. Scarcely was this outrage assimilated than Salan's *Chef du Cabinet*, a Commandant Rodier, was killed by a bazooka accurately fired at his office from across the street and certainly aimed at the absent Salan. This was a sophisticated remote-controlled device and, although the perpetrator was never certainly established, it was clearly the work of Colon extremists.

By January, 1957, the situation in the city was slipping out of control. Lacoste gave the Army full authority to restore order and Salan brought in the paratroops under their redoubtable commander, General Massu. The battle of Algiers began. By ruthless methods, including institutionalized torture, Massu's units, together with the security service, killed or captured the leaders of the FLN terrorist organization in the Casbah, including Jacef. The Army, rather than the civil power, was now clearly perceived to be in authority and the paratroops became the darlings of the *Pieds Noirs*.

Meanwhile, a strong political current was running for de Gaulle in Paris. Jacques Soustelle, a powerful politician, ex-Governor General of Algeria and champion of the movement for "*Algérie Française*", was working tirelessly and secretly for revolt in Algiers while at the same time using his considerable influence at the Palais Bourbon to demonstrate the impotence of the system and the need for change. A strong ally was Michel Debré, later to become de Gaulle's first Prime Minister; while the General's own small cabinet led by Olivier Guichard was also busy on his behalf, though without his knowledge.

Thus Paris as well as Algiers bubbled with plots. Tommy, and I with his help, stood on the edge of the pot, so to speak. Our Ambassador, Gladwyn Jebb, on the other hand appeared to accept the confident assurances of members of the Government that the situation was under control in Algiers and that a *coup de main* in Paris was out of the question. All turned as usual on the realignment of the parties and their respective leaders.

Referring to this period in his memoirs, Macmillan writes: "At the time I did not fully realize the true situation in France". Some of us at least were trying to enlighten him.

In fact morale in the capital was dissolving. The truth about the regular torture of FLN suspects by Massu's paras was at last emerging. Two highly respected senior officers resigned their posts. General Jacques de Bollardière, Grand Commander of the Legion of Honour and a Companion of the Resistance, surrendered his command at Blida in protest, returned to Paris and wrote publicly to Servan Schreiber, editor of *L'Express*. He got 60 days' fortress arrest for his pains. Meantime Paul Teitgen, who had protested consistently to Lacoste about police and army interrogation methods, finally resigned, claiming that over 3000 Algerians had "disappeared".

Early in February, 1958, a heavy reprisal raid by French B26 bombers flattened a Tunisian village called Sakiet near the Algerian frontier. The place had every appearance of a strong FLN base and two French reconnaissance planes had been shot down over it. The bombers destroyed the school which was full of children. Photographs of the pathetic casualties and damage appeared in the world's press. These reports and incidents, well articulated in the Paris press, had a profound and corrosive effect on French morale. In addition prices had risen alarmingly and in April, 1958, France was again shaken by massive strikes. The country, so it seemed to me, was rapidly becoming ungovernable.

Soustelle and his allies, who had succeeded in defeating the government of Bourgès-Maunory in September, 1957, subsequently overturned his successor Gaillard on 15 April the next year, just as the Algerian crisis was nearing flashpoint.

Throughout April and the beginning of May the situation had become increasingly confused. Various groups of "*activists*" were threatening to take control. The students of Algiers University were organized under Pierre Lagaillarde, a wild ex-paratrooper. A curious revolutionary theorist named Robert Martel had succeeded in setting up yet another secret army. Many of these "ultras" were far from being gaullistes, indeed they strongly suspected the General's intentions with regard to Algeria. Then there was the lawyer Biaggi, another revolutionary spark who had organized a tomato bombardment of the Governor General in February, 1956, an initiative which actually caused Guy Mollet, the Prime Minister of the day, to abandon his Algerian policy, thus indicating that real political clout henceforth rested with the tomato grenadiers.

On 5 May, 1958, President Coty, who had long favoured de Gaulle's return but whose main consideration as President of the Republic was to preserve legality, decided to sound the General out about the conditions he would require before accepting a summons to the Elysée. When these were explained, it became obvious there was no chance of arranging de Gaulle's investiture under the constitution. He would have no truck with the parties or their leaders and would only accept a written invitation from the President to form a Government. This seemed to close the door. Coty sent for Réné Pleven, ex-minister in de Gaulle's wartime government-in-exile and already twice premier of France for a combined total of two years.

Pleven made two unsuccessful attempts to assemble an administration on 5 and 8 May and it was in this vacuum, with departments still nominally controlled by Félix Gaillard's ministers, that the bomb finally burst in the Ville Blanche.

Two separate revolutions had for some time been in preparation in Algiers. On the one hand Léon Delbecque, Soustelle's unofficial representative, had formed a "committee of vigilance" which was to be transformed into a committee of public safety (*Comité de Salut Public*) to take power as soon as the *Gouvernement Général* had been taken over. It was hoped that Soustelle would then return to Algiers and take charge. Later the action would shift to Paris with the clear objective of bringing de Gaulle back to power.

At the same time the various groups of "Ultras", comprising secret armies, bands of students and groups of counter-terrorists, more or less under the control of Pierre Lagaillarde and his self-appointed committee of seven, were making their own preparations.

In the event the "Ultras" decided to forestall the Gaullistes. On the 13 May a mob rushed the *Gouvernement Général*, forced their way through all the entrances and took over the office of the Governor General, Lacoste, who had incidentally withdrawn secretly to Paris in despair. Chaos reigned. Lagaillarde demanded the establishment of his own *Comité de Salut Public*. General Salan, the Commander-in-Chief, arrived post haste, followed by General Massu commanding the paratroops. Meantime files and records were hurled from the windows.

The intention of Lagaillarde and his "Ultras" was to force Salan to join their Committee and thus wheel the army into line behind the coup. In the general confusion General Salan was pushed on to the balcony, only to be greeted with boos and insults from the crowd below.

After much heated discussion General Massu, regarded as a hero by the public, decided to take matters in hand, sat down at a table and asked Lagaillarde for the names of his Committee. These seemed to be mainly the people who had managed to push closest to the table. Massu then made his way on to the balcony to announce the formation of the *Comité de Salut Public* under his Presidency. Loud and prolonged cheers and the Marseillaise greeted this announcement.

Communications had not been severed and the officials of the *Gouvernement Général* had been in touch with Paris. Gaillard, still acting Prime Minister although he no longer commanded a majority in the Assembly, first delegated the civil power to General Salan, but, when told that Salan was not acceptable to the mob, transferred authority to Massu in a desperate attempt to preserve some semblance of legality. Massu appealed for calm, but Lagaillarde and his group insisted on exhorting their supporters to stay in the forum in order to keep up the pressure on the army.

Word reached the revolutionaries that they could expect the arrival of both Jacques Soustelle and Chaban Delmas. Léon Delbecque, whose Gaulliste initiative had been badly upstaged, then appeared and announced himself to the Committee as the representative of Jacques Soustelle. This quietened the Ultras and Delbecque succeeded in inscribing a number of his Gaulliste supporters and members of his *Comité de Vigilance* on to Lagaillarde's *Comité de Salut Public*. Delbecque's arrival was greeted by Lacoste's staff and also by General Salan with considerable hostility, but when he brandished a telegram from Army Headquarters in Paris to the effect that Soustelle was on his way calm was restored.

Darkness fell on the crowd milling in the forum. The street lamps had been destroyed in the initial assault and there was no means of lighting the balcony except from within. A series of orators had to announce their identity. Not even Massu was recognized. Around 10 o'clock Delbecque shouted to the crowd that Jacques Soustelle was expected at any minute, a palpable falsehood since his presence at the Palais Bourbon had just been announced over Paris radio. General Massu, warming to the task, ordered one of the Committee members to go with a detachment of his paratroops to take over Algiers radio. Meanwhile, crowds were still converging on the forum anxious not to miss the revolution as if it were a grand spectacle of *Son et Lumière* – "*plus de son que de lumière, d'ailleurs!*" wrote Serge Bromberger.

A telephone call from the airport disclosed that the long-awaited aircraft had landed. Soustelle was not aboard. Consternation greeted this revelation.

The same evening around 6 o'clock two of my Gaulliste friends, René Dumont and Geoffrey de la Tour du Pin, close associates of Jacques

Soustelle, were having a drink at my house in Rue Gambetta. They were questioning me about British reaction to the eventual return of de Gaulle to power while I was endeavouring to find out what was afoot.

Both were bubbling with suppressed excitement. The telephone rang. It was for Dumont. He listened for a minute, grunted, replaced the receiver and nodded purposefully to his companion. Both my guests rose, apologized, grinning all over their faces and left hurriedly without explanation.

At that moment no firm news of the coup had yet broken in Paris, but something was surely up and I reported as much. Chancery remained serenely sceptical. I learned subsequently that my friends had reached Algiers, joined Soustelle and both made it on to the notorious balcony.

Confusion reigned in the *Gouvernement Général*. Another Gaulliste officer, General Petit, who had arrived in the plane which was supposed to have brought Soustelle, joined General Salan and the rest to tell them Soustelle had refused to accompany him without the approval of de Gaulle. This had not been forthcoming and Soustelle had returned to the assembly. Morale amongst the Gaullistes slumped. General Petit sought to remedy the situation by drafting a telegram of appeal to de Gaulle which he offered to Salan. Salan read the text, changed a few words, crossed out de Gaulle and addressed the telegram to President Coty instead. He then left the room, telling Petit that he was taking a copy in order to prepare his defence before the High Court.

Total anarchy now threatened and there was a risk that the Ultras, supported by their paramilitary followers, and quite possibly also by the paratroops encamped about the forum, would swamp the Gaulliste faction.

Massu decided to take the initiative; he grabbed Petit's telegram, read dressed it to de Gaulle and despatched it. In fact it never reached Colombey until a fortnight later, which was perhaps just as well. Nevertheless Massu read it to the crowd, to wild applause. The revolution seemed to have been successfully hijacked for Gaullism.

Meantime Gaillard, as a last gesture and with the agreement of his eventual successor, the Alsatian Pflimlin, decided to cut all communication with Algiers by air and sea. This not unnaturally infuriated Salan and Massu who were still trying to preserve a tenuous connection with legality. Pflimlin was duly endorsed and immediately made matters worse by referring in the Assembly to the "treasonous" generals in Algiers.

Plans for the invasion of metropolitan France now began to take serious shape.

In Paris street demonstrations against the régime were becoming increasingly menacing and strongly supported by the *Anciens Combattants* (ex servicemen's organizations). Clandestine groups were reported by the police to be taking up arms. The threat seemed to centre on yet another more than usually insecure "secret" organization called *"Le Grand O"* which had been raised in Paris with the express purpose of overthrowing the Government in favour of de Gaulle. Tommy was well aware of its existence; so was I. The inspiration here had come from two more generals: Cherrières, lately retired from active service and president of an ex-servicemen's organization for Muslims in Algiers, and General Chassin, serving with the Air Force and known for his outspoken anti-communist views.

Both these plotters had narrowly escaped arrest when the police descended on the Chassin flat minutes after the General's departure. The *"flics"* were busy setting up a listening device when the bell rang. Who should step into the arms of the law but one Major Puga of the General HQ staff in Paris, clearly a suspect member of *'Le Grand O"*.

"I've come to see my mistress," stammered the unfortunate Major. Now this would normally be an entirely acceptable explanation in France but the only candidate available seemed to be Madame Chassin and she poor lady was in hospital.

"Madame Chassin?" asked the policeman.

"I'm on the wrong floor," said Major Puga desperately. He was promptly marched off to Fresnes prison and incarcerated for a fortnight.

As a result of various raids that evening some fifty members of the *Anciens d'Indochine* were arrested and an operation order discovered which provided for the capture of the Elysée and various ministries.

At this grave moment, with the Arc de Triomphe and the Champs Elysées bursting with *Anciens Combattants*, *Anciens d'Indochine* and their supporters, with the CRS anti-riot police drawn up in strength in the Concorde and with Algiers effectively in the hands of the revolutionaries, supported by the Army, the Assembly in Paris was still locked in debates on procedure and other banalities. Pflimlin, the new PM, had sought to make a statement to the Chamber about the dramatic events in Algiers but the President de L'Assemblée (speaker), Le Troquer, a socialist and fervently anti-Gaulliste, refused to allow it. In the course of a furious altercation Le Troquer asserted that he could not allow debate to be interrupted by the antics of a few treasonous generals.

But of course the news had leaked, even to the Chamber. Where was Chaban? Where was Soustelle? No sign of either.

Chaban Delmas in due course turned up to claim disingenuously that he had never instructed Delbecque to launch his coup in Algiers.

The new Minister of the Interior, Maurice Faure, had meanwhile placed Soustelle under strict surveillance. Eventually he managed to escape and, accompanied by several friends, crossed into Switzerland where they chartered a private plane and made for Algiers posing as journalists. He arrived on the 17th to a mixed reception from the Generals. A furious argument broke out at the airport as to the role he should play. Salan at first refused to entertain him, but, when the extent of his popularity became clear, offered him office. Soustelle refused, claiming he had simply come to try to reunite the people of Algiers. Nevertheless, his presence, which was immediately known in Paris, served to confirm the rift between the Government and Algiers, and thus to open the road for de Gaulle.

Meanwhile, two events combined to deepen the crisis. Salan, who until now had never uttered a seditious word and had tried consistently to cling to an equivocal appearance of legality, was finally driven by Pflimlin's bungling blockade, by the subsequent indecision in Paris and by the irresistible pressure from the *Comité de Salut Public* to declare publicly at 12.30pm on the 15th from the famous balcony – *"Vive de Gaulle!"*

This announcement at last broke the brooding silence of the Presence at Colombey. De Gaulle had repeatedly insisted that he would never respond to any initiative but a legal summons to power from the President. Now, here was the Commander-in-Chief, in whom civil as well as military power had been vested in Algiers, invoking his cause. The moment had come to speak. Since Salan's announcement the media were besieging the General's office in Rue de Solferino. At 5 o'clock on the same afternoon de Gaulle's pronunciamento was released.

"The disintegration of the State is leading inexorably to the alienation of her people; to trouble in the Army; to national dislocation and to the loss of independence. Faced for twelve years with problems too demanding for the political parties to resolve, France is embarked on a course to destruction. Lately, the country, from the depths of its being, has placed its confidence in me to lead the way to safety. Today, faced with fresh and mounting perils, I wish her to know that I am ready to assume the powers of the Republic."

This Olympian statement caused public euphoria and consternation in the Government. The powers of the Republic! What did he mean? Did he want to be both Prime Minister and President? The National Assembly was recalled to a special session. The Communists went wild. Dictatorship was at the gates. Pflimlin redoubled his efforts to maintain his majority and at the same time to make his peace with Salan. But any hope of arresting the course of events was effectively destroyed by the arrogant and aggressive attitude of the new Minister of Defence, de Chevigny.

De Chevigny had already discounted warnings of widespread disaffection in the Army. For him this was nothing but an insignificant group of treasonous plotters. He would deal with them. He would arrest ten Generals if need be. The Command as a whole was too intelligent to engage in such an adventure. Relying principally on the reports of his personally appointed Cabinet – a fearful weakness of the French system of Government – he failed on his appointment even to consult General Ely, Chief of Defence. On the 18th, at the height of the crisis, Ely resigned.

Towards evening on the 14th de Chevigny telephoned Maurice Faure to say he had the names of the two Generals who were leading the revolt. They were respecitvely Challe and Martin. Now General Challe, whose influence had been so decisive during the Suez operation, was the right hand of Ely and a formidable figure. Martin was his adjoint.

Faure, horrified at this report, sent his representative, Abel Thomas, round to Defence Headquarters at the Invalides where he demanded to see General Challe.

Challe, with General Ely's agreement, had called only a few hours before on Guy Mollet, head of the Socialist Party, to warn him of the deep concern at General Headquarters about the Government's handling of the crisis and to assure him of the Army's solidarity with the "treasonous" generals in Algiers. "Not a man in metropolitan France would march against his comrades in Algiers", Mollet was told.

Abel Thomas sought to warn Challe of the terrible risks involved in a military coup. It would mean the Popular Front. It would lead to civil war. The General agreed. There was, he said, no Army plot but the young officers were becoming increasingly impatient with the high command. They would not tolerate negotiations with the FLN, and they were behind the Army in Algiers. Moreover, the Government's decision to cut off supplies to Algiers had spelt disaster. Algiers could not last more than two weeks, and this would force the Army to act.

"How long would it take to launch a landing at Paris?" asked Abel Thomas.

"48 hours," replied Challe. "Two regiments of paras could be deployed by the weekend if Pflimlin was still in power."

"And if a Government of Public Salvation is formed?"

"You'd better act quickly; within the next 48 hours," Challe said.

"Why haven't you informed the Minister?"

"We have been trying to see him for two days but he chooses to believe other sources," replied the General.

Now it happened that General Challe had already ordered the transfer of 24 Nord 2501 Transport Aircraft, equipped to deliver paratroops, to Algiers on the 11 May. On the 14th, the day after the invasion of the *Gouvernement Génééral*, 24 more aircraft were sent. General Challe claimed the planes were needed because of the current threat to isolate French garrisons in Tunisia and Algeria, but the fact remained that they were there.

Abel Thomas returned to the Ministry of Interior, Place Beauvau, at 8 o'clock to report his conversation.

Support for de Gaulle was growing by the hour. His phrase *"Prêt à assumer les pouvoirs de la République"* had shaken the crumbling edifice of the Fourth Republic to its foundations. Panic was spreading among the political parties.

The only hope now, said Bourgès-Maunory to Guy Mollet, the socialist leader, was to form a Government of National Salvation and only he, Mollet, could do it.

Arriving at a Counsel of Ministers during the night of the 16th, Pflimlin announced that Mollet had agreed to join the government as Vice-President of the Council. During the days to follow Mollet was to play a critical role in opening the way for de Gaulle.

Various wild suggestions were made at this meeting. The Chamber should be asked the next day to vote a state of National Emergency which would carry powers of censorship, arrest, detention without charge, and so forth.

"The drama is," said Mollet, "that the Republic no longer has any Army at its disposal."

At this de Chevigny exploded again. The Army was entirely dependable. He had conducted his own enquiries. They could count on military force to resist any attempt from Algiers.

"Its distresses me to disagree," replied Mollet. "General Challe says the precise opposite."

After this meeting de Chevigny called Challe, abused him over the telephone and despatched a car to remove him to Brest, where he was to be placed in *"Résidence Obligatoire"* under the authority of the Admiral commanding there. The Admiral refused to respect this instruction and Challe stayed peacefully in the local hotel for the next two weeks.

Finally de Chevigny heard from the police that Challe was plotting to leave for Algiers. He ordered an officer from the General's own Cabinet to go to Orly Airport and set a trap for him. The officer refused point blank.

The debate in the Assembly continued unabated. Emergency powers of the most draconian nature were eventually voted. De Chevigny, not content with the departure of General Challe, proceeded to banish his adjoint, General Martin, to Metz.

"Why Metz?" asked the astonished Martin.

"Because it is at the opposite point of the compass to Brest," the Minister replied.

But voices of sanity were beginning, nevertheless, to be heard. Mollet sought clarification of de Gaulle's statement from Chaban-Delmas. Chaban implored the General by telephone to see him. De Gaulle refused. He would have no truck with any political leader. Nevertheless, and not for the first time, he changed his mind, took the suggestion seriously and in due course agreed to see Mollet.

Preparations for the occupation of Paris advanced rapidly on every hand. General Massu, who was now, to all intents and purposes, in command of the action in Algiers, while Salan still sought to preserve his tightrope act between legality and insurrection, despatched two paratroop officers, Major Vitasse and Captain Lamouliatte, by air to Pau where they were to land by parachute, liaise with General Miquel, commanding the paratroop base, and thence co-ordinate the action in Paris. Miquel's adherence was well established. The dropping zone at Pau was in constant use by paratroops in training, and it was thought the arrival of these two would attract no particular attention. By bad planning or forgetfulness, they chose Sunday the 17th. The plane was challenged. The two officers jumped anyway and managed to evade the police. In due course Lamouliatte made his way to Paris where he contacted Foccard, of de Gaulle's small staff in the Rue Solferino. The General's attitude, he was told, had in no way changed. He would not contemplate a return to office through illegal action by the Army. Nevertheless, preparations for the imminent arrival of the paras at Paris continued.

Meanwhile, in the Provinces General Chassin's frenetic efforts to raise the Resistance were beginning to pay off. The ex-Maquisards in their thousands uncovered wartime caches of weapons and explosives and posed in fearsome groups to be photographed by the foreign press. The Swiss became extremely nervous. The *Daily Mirror* announced that panic-stricken Parisians were fleeing the capital. They were. It was the weekend.

In true clandestine style, Chassin, chief of "*Le Grand O*", never slept twice in the same house. A courier from Paris sought him daily to keep him in touch with events in the capital. One night in a small village in mid-France the General was staying with the local Doctor.

In the middle of the night this courier in a 2CV Renault arrived and by mistake woke up the local vet who happened to live opposite the doctor and who came to the door in a state of considerable disarray.

"I am a friend of the Pope," said the courier.

'*Vous êtes fou?*" suggested the astonished vet.

"A friend of the Pope's I tell you."

"The Pope is over here," shouted a voice from the other side of the street. It was the Doctor.

"*Tous mabouls*! They must be bonkers," exclaimed the poor vet rubbing his eyes.

The Senior Command, both at Paris and in Algiers, were still deeply apprehensive of the consequences of what was afoot. The horrors of the Spanish Civil War were very real to Frenchmen, but the running was increasingly being made by hotheads and comparatively junior officers, Massu apparently at their head.

The need to panic the Government into expecting the paras was seen as an essential tactic.

Roger Frey, Secretary General of the *Républicains Sociaux* and the intellectual voice of Gaullism, had made his way to Algiers from Palma on the 16th in a launch belonging to a British cannabis smuggler. He arrived dishevelled and unshaven at the *Gouvernement Général* and immediately set about devising a deception campaign.

That weekend, on the Saturday I think, I dined late with Tommy Yeo-Thomas at his flat. I knew he was deep in the Gaulliste game; indeed he made no secret of it. After supper we sat with a bottle of whisky between us. Tommy produced a list of messages and telephone numbers. They read like a schedule on the BBC wartime programme for the Resistance – "*Voici quelques messages personnels*" – which presaged parachute drops, the arrival of agents and other secret operations. He had to pass them on, he said.

Nothing happened. We talked long and late. I was trying my best to find out what the messages might mean, but if the Gestapo torturers failed to extract any information from Tommy it was not surprising that I had no success either.

The whisky descended. Tommy, loaded I suspect with pain killers, went to sleep. What to do? Ring the Embassy? Tear up the messages and go home? The telephone rang. I decided, since I was a Gaulliste at heart, that I might just as well be an "*activiste*" too. Anyway I couldn't let Tommy down. I reached for the receiver.

After much crackling on a long distance line a voice said, "*Merde!*"

I took this to allude to the bad connection rather than the revolution.

"*Les carottes sont cuites – deux fois – tu m'entends?*"

"*J'ai compris,*" I said.

The line went dead. I looked down my list. Sure as fate, the "cooked carrots" had a telephone number, in the Midi it seemed. I dialled. A woman's voice on the other end this time. "*Les carottes sont cuites,*" I said hopefully. "*Deux fois. Tu comprends?*" She did.

I had another glass of whisky and passed two more messages. By this time dawn was breaking. Tommy had gone to bed. I felt I had done my duty and left, wondering dimly whether I had sent for the paras and what the Embassy would say if they found out.

Much later I discovered these messages were all part of Roger Frey's deception plan. They meant nothing at all but did serve to increase the general excitement in Paris and to persuade the Government that the paras were on their way.

By this time the situation in Corsica was also simmering merrily. Henri Maillot, a cousin of de Gaulle with a distinguished Resistance record in the island, had been busy fomenting support for the revolt. This was not difficult. There was a Corsican population of over 100,000 in Algeria and the island was in any case strongly Gaulliste.

The confused debate continued at the Palais Bourbon. Pflimlin, anxious to preserve an illusion of authority, agreed to a Socialist motion designed to bind the Army and its commanders to legality by sending a message of homage and gratitude to all ranks in the name of the Republic. The Communists, wishing to stiffen the Government's resistance, voted for it.

The motion, passed by a majority of over 500, alarmed those leading the revolt. Activists and young officers began to suspect collusion between Salan and Paris. There was a risk the whole enterprise might fizzle out through some devious compromise between the Government and the High Command. Moreover, the Army was deeply suspicious of this unsolicited expression of gratitude from the Communists.

Soustelle, Delbecque and Massu decided that a dramatic move must be made in order finally to break the dialogue with Paris and destroy Salan's ambiguous legality. There was still doubt in the minds of senior officials about the wisdom of the attempt on the metropolis. A rising in Corsica might do the trick.

At dawn on the 24th a plane took off from Algiers. The party included Pascal Arrighi, Deputy for Corsica and a convinced Gaullist, escorted by several officials, Colonel Thomazo, a leading activist who had joined the party at the last moment as an adventure, and a Captain Bauer who had until recently commanded the parachute battalion stationed in Corsica. They touched down at Calvi to be met by Bauer's successor Captain Mantei. One of the party contacted Maillot in Ajaccio to be told that his revolutionaries were already assembled in the bars and cafés waiting for the word to move. The successful coup which followed was aided not a little by the neutrality of the CRS company despatched from Nice by the government specifically to resist it.

Ajaccio fell without difficulty. Bastia proved more resistant, mainly because of the determined and irascible deputy mayor, Sebastian de Casalta. The mayor happened to be away and Casalta, supported by three Communist councillors encamped in the mayor's office, decided to defy the revolution. Their vigil lasted longer than anticipated. It was Sunday: *déjeuners de famille* and the call of the seaside dispersed the crowds. Also there was a bicycle race in the afternoon. The revolution was postponed till Monday.

Early in the morning a delegation from Algiers led by Léon Delbecque arrived at the mayor's office to be greeted by loud accusations of treachery. Now Casalta had a good resistance record and was well respected. Delbecque pleaded with him to leave. "No," he protested, "not unless you place a hand on my shoulder as a symbol of force. Then I shall descend the stairs and you will all follow me singing the Marseillaise."

After a long negotiation Casalta was persuaded to modify his conditions. He embraced his three supporters, draped himself in the mayor's official tricolor flag and descended in dignified state to the crowd below. His dramatic exit was well received, Corsicans being always ready, in Arrighi's words, "*pour se faire honneur*".

Next day the journalists pestered Pascal Arrighi for news. "Were many killed?" they asked.

"Eh non," said the Deputy. "This was a revolution, not the elections."

Meanwhile Colonel Thomazo, present purely by chance, found himself appointed Governor of Corsica.

The effect of the coup was just what the rebel leaders had hoped. The Coriscan revolt had been largely spontaneous, but at the Palais Bourbon it was hailed as the work of the treasonous generals. The breach between Algiers and Paris was now irreparable. Thus the defection of the Emperor's island and the imminent arrival of the paras in Paris combined to ensure the collapse of the Fourth Republic and the return of de Gaulle, but all was by no means over.

The operation against Paris was to be led by General Miquel, commanding the Paras base at Toulouse. Reinforcements would travel by road. The armoured formation stationed near Rambouillet would move in support and General Faure was reported ready to lead an armoured column from Germany. In Paris itself, the clandestine organizations, manned chiefly by the *Anciens Combattants* and the *Anciens d'Indochine*, had completed their preparations to attack the Palais Bourbon and the government offices.

All had been set to go on the 24th, but because of uncertainty over de Gaulle's intentions the operation was postponed to 30 May. The risk of chaos, even civil war, was real. No one could predict the outcome. The population of Paris was in no sense as well informed or prepared as many of the plotters believed. Strict and effective censorship of the media had been imposed. Indeed there was more news of what was happening in the foreign papers than in Paris itself.

Le Troquer, Speaker of the Assembly, was still implacably opposed to de Gaulle, as were Mendès France and Mitterand.

Pflimlin, on the other hand, was at last convinced that the only possible course was to resign in favour of de Gaulle. Through the good offices of President Coty a secret meeting was arranged between the two in Paris. Pflimlin's conditions proved unacceptable and, after long and fruitless negotiations, the pair parted at loggerheads. Later, however, de Gaulle agreed to see Guy Mollet. The meeting at Colombey went extremely well and from that moment Mollet dedicated his every effort to persuading the Socialist Party.

Early in the morning of the 29th President Coty called his advisors and showed them the draft of a statement he intended to send to the Assembly before the debate opened at 3 o'clock in the afternoon. In simple and dignified terms he informed them that their behaviour was leading France to disaster, that he intended forthwith to invite de Gaulle to form a government and to reform the constitution. If his proposal proved unacceptable to Parliament then he would resign that day. Indeed he had already given orders for his bags to be packed. He then telephoned Colombey.

France stood on the extreme edge of the abyss. No President had threatened to resign since 1875. Should Coty depart, Le Troquer, as President of the Assembly, would, under the Constitution, inherit the Presidency for a period of ten days. It was virtually certain that he would immediately seek to form a Popular Front Government to include the Communist Party and this in the teeth of the Army descending on Paris to prevent just such a contingency. Moreover, in such circumstances, de Gaulle had made it plain he would never agree to serve.

By this brave and dramatic gesture, the elderly President had provided a chance for France to escape from, at best, a south American-style military junta, at worst, civil war.

The statement was delivered to Le Troquer seconds before he was due to mount the rostrum at 3 o'clock in the afternoon. He read it to the Assembly at breakneck speed. Consternation on the Left. Triumph on the Right. Cries of betrayal! Blackmail! Dictatorship! Both camps in competition broke into the Marseillaise as though they were fighting for its possession.

The Government engaged in a further frenzied and futile discussion about counter-measures. They would remove themselves to the north of France. The legal Government should take to the Maquis. All in vain. They had been deserted by the Army, by the police and even the CRS. No means of authority remained to them.

At this juncture a crowd of some 500 students broke into the Cour of the Palais Bourbon. Dominique Padot, in her book *Le Treize Mai*, describes how two deputies approached a policeman on duty:

"Can't you clear the Cour?" they demanded indignantly.

"*Circulez!*" replied the Agent de Police with frigid authority.

"*Nous sommes Parlementaires!*" protested the deputies.

"*Eh bien alors, circulez plus vite que ça. On vous a assez vu!*"

By this time between four and five thousand activists had collected around the Place Vendôme ready to launch a demonstration which would lead to the takeover of Paris.

News of the President's initiative had already reached Algiers and at 11 o'clock that morning the order was passed to General Miquel to postpone Opeation "Résurrection" scheduled for that night. General de Gaulle arrived at the Elysée at 9 o'clock the same evening to be welcomed on the steps of the palace by President Coty with tears in his eyes. The relief in the streets was palpable. The Champs Elysées was blocked with cars, hooting their horns in triumph. I have to confess I contributed my own hoot. The CRS on duty in front of lines of their black transports, raised their arms in a "V" for Victory. France seemed to be delivered.

But not yet. There remained the crucial stumbling block of de Gaulle's appearance at the Palais Bourbon, and his Investiture. Coty and the General now withdrew to plan the next vital tactical moves. De Gaulle then received the old Socialist ex-President Vincent Auriol, whose patronage was evidently of importance to his Party, also, and, together, Guy Mollet and his chief doubter among the Socialists, Dixoneux. All were won over and left astonished at de Gaulle's liberalism, particularly with regard to the overseas territories. Mollet accepted the Vice-Presidency which indeed he deserved.

On 1 June the General appeared before the Assembly, mounted the rostrum and read his brief policy statement, after which he folded his notes, glanced haughtily round and departed. In an atmosphere of doom, gloom and surly uncertainty the Assembly proceeded to vote for the Investiture, 329 to 224.

The debate dragged on next day, interminably, over the precise powers which the new Prime Minister demanded. As the day wore on opposition mounted. Then in the evening in one of his not infrequent and surprising volte-faces, de Gaulle decided to return to the Assembly, this time to use his formidable powers to charm and disarm. He talked informally among the deputies and spoke again from the Government Bench. Panic and uncertainty subsided. He was accepted.

How close France was to an explosion of appalling proportions few at that moment probably knew. General Miquel, to whom had been delegated command of Operation "Résurrection", had indeed received the order to postpone the action. But the impetus which events had steadily built up since the initial revolt in Algiers and which by then had committed much of the

Army and many outside it was no longer susceptible to simple military orders. Passionate emotions were engaged. Miquel was subjected to the most intense and ceaseless pressure from all sides during that day to stick to the plan. To abandon now would be to betray everything. Those who had looked forward for so long to the day of reckoning with the Fourth Republic, to an end of weakness, double dealing and cowardice were not easily put off. It is immensely to his credit that General Miquel remained resolute. The Army stayed in its ranks and the activists poised round the Place de la Concorde, ready to do what they longed to do, what they had plotted and waited for so long to do, learned almost by chance that the assault on the Assembly for the night of the 30th had been cancelled. They retreated from the brink, too disheartened even to join the celebrations. It had been a close call.

De Gaulle was welcomed not as a politician but as a king. For France, his return spelt deliverance from perpetual friction and eventually, in spite of a further attempted coup in 1961, from the Algerian morass. For Anglo-French relations, and for Europe, the dividend was less certain. Guy Mollet, the Socialist Leader, was probably the most powerful and effective politician to survive the Fourth Republic. His influence for De Gaulle was decisive. He was also a strong European and a sincere friend to Britain. Had he and those who shared his view led France during the formative years of the EEC the Community would in all probability have been solidly based on a Franco-British understanding. For de Gaulle this could never be. Europe, whether it was to stretch east to the Urals or not, was to turn henceforth upon a Franco-German axis.

His motive for this shift in the course of European destiny may well have been mixed. Publicly he proclaimed the British were "not ready" for Europe. If by this he meant Federal Europe he was certainly right. But since he was an archetypal nationalist who surely saw Europe in terms of a union of nation states, this is uncertain reasoning. Probably he felt powerful enough to believe he could manage Germany better without us. Possibly his long and humiliating experience in the war years as a client and supplicant, in particular his morose relationship with Churchill, coloured the judgement of this immensely proud man. However that may be, he would surely have rejected much of the unnatural bureaucratic fantasy later peddled by Brussels in the name of Europe.

Yet it cannot be doubted that the federalist course upon which his compatriot Delors seeks to set the Community and the grave dangers which this historical aberration is likely to bring could never have happened had we and France seen fit to steer the European ship. It was not to be. De Gaulle saw to that. It is a sad irony.

*

40. My first wife, Sally, in Finland, 1951.

41. "In due course Neil arrived, then Carola" (p.144). My son and daughter, by then aged 8 and 6.

42. Lapps. "I journeyed to Lapland in both summer and winter" (p.151).

43. "In summer, I camped at night in the forests" (p.152)

44. "The Tenoyoki, a great river which flows from the Arctic Sea and marks the march with Norway" (p.153). My Lapp ghillie by the river.

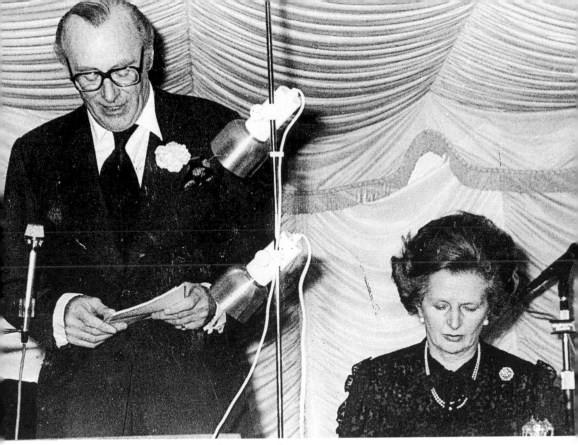

45. With Mrs Thatcher. Speaking at the rally during the Falklands War (see p.237).

46. With Lizzie Anne and Constituency Chairman Sir John Howard at my last General Election count.

47. With Lizzie Anne, Meribel, 1986.

Days after his accession De Gaulle attended a ceremony in honour of those killed in the Résistance or murdered by the Gestapo. It took place at Mont Valérien, near the wall against which so many were shot. The towering figure of the General led the way through a press of ex-Résistants and his most loyal supporters. He was followed by Pflimlin and a shambling file of shame-faced ministers. His speech was short and moving. The sense of comradeship and relief was unforgettable. Thanks to Tommy, I was allowed to be there. It was like liberation all over again.

Now there is a moral to this story. Increasingly we hear and read the case advanced for constitutional reform and in particular for Proportional Representation in Britain. The Liberal Democrats would make it a condition of their co-operation with any government. Clearly they see such a system as the best, if not the only, hope of office. But there are groups in both the Socialist and Conservative parties which lend the idea currency as well. PR is held to be "fairer" than the long-established system of first past the post. It is argued that PR would lead to more "open" government. The impression is sedulously created that the hour of this eminently sensible and logical notion has come, or if it hasn't it is only round the corner. Pure intellect demands it. We are out of date with our crude confrontational posture in the House of Commons – and why, anyway, should government reside premanently in the hands of two major parties?

When the war ended a constituent assembly was set up in France with a clean sheet to consider a constitution. They deliberated between 1944 and 1945. They had three aims:-

First to promote the development of a few large, stable, well-disciplined and responsible parties to replace the shifting groups of the Third Republic.

Second, to establish a new chamber to reflect accurately the opinions of the country so that whatever constitution was devised would enjoy the confidence of the people.

Third, to ensure that no single party would come to dominate the Republic.

It is against this background that the provisions of the electoral ordinance of August, 1945, must be seen. There were to be 586 deputies. Candidates had to stand as members of lists. Every list had to have as many names as the constituencey had seats. No candidate could stand in more than one department, nor on more than one list in that department. Electors could not vote for individual candidates but only for one list as a single entity. Thus all lists were rigid and blocked. After the count seats were distributed in two stages: by quotient found by dividing the total number of valid votes cast in each constituency by the number of seats in it. The second stage constituted distribution by the highest average of votes per list. You follow me?

This system, no doubt by the law of unintended effects, provided such bizarre results that it was modified by the new Electoral Law of May, 1951. This had the following consequences: in metropolitan France the constituency and distribution of seats was unchanged (except for one, divided into two).

But a new electoral system was introduced in Paris, where eight constituencies of the Seine and Seine et Oise were henceforth to use the PR system of the Largest Remainder, chosen because it tended to favour the smaller parties. It was held that under the 1945 system these had been under represented among the 75 deputies concerned; a provision which seems to run clean counter to the first guiding principle of the original Constituent Assembly.

These contrivances, based on the most laudable of objectives, led not to open government, but to a morass of intrigue and impotence; through death and defeat abroad to the very brink of civil war, averted only because the French nation, or most of it, turned in despair to a saviour, to one man, happily for them a remarkable man, of high principle and courage, but a man as fallible as any other.

Of course it will be argued that this exercise in French logic was flawed; that there are better, fairer, simpler systems of PR. Don't be fooled, citizen. Reject the constitution mongers in whatever forms they appear. Contemplate the blessings of relative stability gradually gained down the centuries while power devolved from autocratic Kings to the Lords and thence the Commons. Respect the precious balance which has evolved, and which effectively restrains the power of man over man; which permits the transfer of power without violence, and yet fosters strong government.

And if you don't easily accept that, take a long look at the Fourth French Republic.

———————|———————

12

CYPRUS

In 1958 I was posted to Cyprus. The island was locked in the bitter and, in the end, disastrous struggle with EOKA.

Enosis, or Union with Greece, was the spur to rebellion; independence from British rule the result; a further brutal partition of the island between Greek and Turk the consequence.

Grivas, the Greek guerrilla leader, was still at large. Makarios, that most devious of prelates, dominated the political scene. Field Marshal Sir John Harding had recently retired as Governor in favour of Hugh Foot.* There was a smell of compromise in the air.

Our security forces had learned much during the years of EOKA terrorism. We were probably within weeks if not days of capturing Grivas and if we had the subsequent negotiations for the island's future would have been a deal easier. Hugh Foot's cast of mind was vastly different to that of his predecessor. In fact as a colonial governor he seemed to me miscast. Certainly he enjoyed the occasional pomp and plumed presence in full dress. His speeches were sonorous and delivered with dignity. The act was excellent. But his true reactions seemed to me conditioned more by the radical left-wing thinking of his family than ever they were by a dispassionate assessment of his country's interests. To rise effectively to the top in what was the colonial service one surely had to believe, at least to some extent, in the mission which gave rise to it, not simply in the need to dismantle it.

Weeks after my arrival a shaky truce broke out. I watched Grivas, a jaunty little figure, preening himself in triumph, escorted to an RAF transport to be flown to Athens. The interminable negotiations for the island's future began in an atmosphere of smouldering mistrust. The Governor's talent as a conciliator was certainly valuable at this juncture, but it was only with the arrival of Julian Amery that the business of the island's disposal began to reflect the British interest.

* Later Lord Caradon

I was responsible for foreign intelligence. Cyprus was a handy offshore centre for all manner of Middle Eastern and Levantine plots and rumours, quite apart from the cauldron in the island itself. EOKA still simmered audibly, the long habit of murder and violence bubbling just below the surface while the ancient antipathy between Greek and Turk had increased to the point of combustion.

With the end of the emergency the need was to devise an acceptable future for the island's disparate peoples and to safeguard our defence interests.

Now that he had dispensed with Grivas, Archbishop Makarios' position was paramount in the Greek community. We were closely informed. It was our business to be. We knew practically everything he said to his aides and advisors, yet never throughout the interminable negotiation for the sovereign bases did we learn with any certainty what Makarios' next move would be.

True to Byzantine tradition he was ruthless, trusted no one, not even his closest collaborators and manipulated his opponents with a beatific charm. Women are said to have found him irresistible. One man alone took his measure. Julian Amery, then Under Secretary at the Foreign & Commonwealth Office, had been charged with the negotiations.

The idea of a sovereign base was originally one of several possible solutions advanced in London. Julian had to balance this requirement against a transfer of the rest of the island's sovereignty under the terms of a constitution acceptable to all three parties, Greek, Turkish and British. The Turkish card assumed critical importance.

The talks began in February and they were not concluded until the end of June. In the course of his protracted stay Julian frequently visited us at Kyrenia. Despite their tortuous nature the negotiations were courteously conducted. Only once, fairly early in the proceedings, did Makarios threaten mayhem. After an inconclusive morning meeting he came to Julian's room at Government House and told him that unless his conditions were met he would denounce British policy in his sermon the next Sunday.

"Was he going to call for violence?" Julian asked.

"Of course not," he said, "but violence will certainly follow".

Staking his political future, Julian then told the Archbishop that if he carried out his threat all British troops would be immediately confined to barracks. Turkish reaction would be swift. The current proposal was for a ratio of 70 Greeks seats to 30 Turkish in the Cypriot Assembly. But in Amery's view the Turks would cut Greek throats in inverse proportion. Makarios withdrew. There was no sermon.

In the spring Makarios tried another gambit. He broke off the talks altogether, gambling on the British losing patience. He nearly won. The pause lasted no less than 40 days. The British officials became increasingly restive. Telegrams flew back and forth. Julian explored the island, and together we organized suitable diversions to pass the time. The Governor inclined steadily towards surrender. Finally his nerve broke. There was a lunch party at Government House. Julian argued with him till two o'clock while the guests waited. Foot wanted to send a telegram to Macleod, Secretary of State for the Colonies, making his view clear that Julian should give in and grant Makarios' current conditions.

Macleod's past record as a rapid dispenser of independence boded ill for Julian's resistance but he succeeded in persuading the Governor to wait until the following Wednesday. Early on Wednesday Foot left for Larnaca to referee a polo match. No telegram had yet been sent. Later in the morning Julian was contacted by Glafkos Clerides, ex-RAF squadron leader, a member of Makarios' ruling committee and Julian's unofficial link. The Archbishop wished to reopen the discussions. Julian sent a despatch rider post haste to Larnaca. The talks began again next day. It had been a close-run thing.

The principle of the sovereign base was now accepted and agreement turned on its extent. Gradually the Archbishop ceded territory until, with the assent of the defence chiefs and by cleverly discounting an inland lake, a formula was set at 99 square miles, a delicate concession to archiepiscopal face.

In 1974, after the anti-Makarios coup which brought about the Turkish invasion, the Archbishop narrowly escaped with his life by helicopter – into the Sovereign Base Area at Episkopi! Julian met him on his arrival in London to be assured that on reflection the Archbishop now appreciated the merit of the sovereign base.

Julian Amery met him once more after he was restored to power. It happened that his visit to the island took place shortly after the conclusion of yet another attempted anti-Makarios coup, this time masterminded by one of the Archbishop's former and closest collaborators, Polycarpos Jiorkadjis, who had finished up drilled full of holes in a back street of Nicosia.

Before his interview Julian naturally asked the High Commissioner whether there was anything he should know with regard to the Archbishop. Well, said the High Commissioner, it would be tactless to mention the demise of Polycarpos.

Makarios greeted his old antagonist warmly and to Julian's astonishment opened the conversation with a question. "I suppose you want to know what happened to Jiorkadjis?" he said smiling. "Well, it was him or me!"

The Archbishop died of a heart attack, still in office, in 1977. Banished to the Seychelles by the British for subversion and subsequently restored to his see, a dominant figure behind EOKA throughout the emergency and a formidable opponent during the negotiations for independence; chased for his life into the British base by the Greek Junta in 1974 and again restored to power after the Turkish invasion in the same year, Makarios was surely among the most durable of our colonial opponents and subsequent Commenwealth Heads of State. His instinct for survival was unerring. His political skill surely rivalled that of any Emperor of the East. He served his people well, after his fashion.

The sovereign base at Episkopi has played a vitally important part not only in the defence of the British interest but also that of the West ever since. Julian Amery has never got the credit he deserved for this important triumph, and it is a poor reflection on the Convervative leadership that after the 1974 election he was left to languish on the back benches until made a life peer in 1992. His knowledge of foreign affairs, his intimate contacts with those who count in the world, particularly in the Middle East, his unerring and instinctive judgement and power of analysis of men and events should have long ago qualified him for the highest office in the field of foreign affairs or defence, well ahead of some of the mediocrities I have watched effortlessly hoisted up the ladder. Not for nothing has he been referred to in the serious press as "the best foreign secretary we never had".

Apart from my interesting and often intricate duties, the next eighteen months provided an idyllic opportunity to soak up something of Cyprus' kaleidoscopic history, appreciate its incomparable beauty and, in short, to fall in love with the island.

I do not know what ancient and powerful God must have taken offence but unquestionably a long-standing curse was laid upon Cyprus. The tides of every conquering host, of every civilized nation and religion in Europe and Asia, have swept over her and their remains still stand in awesome and ruinous splendour round her shores and upon her peaks. The island is basically Greek in the sense that the original inhabitants spoke a form of the language. Their ways are Greek, although many would detect a stark contrast between their Hellenism and that of metropolitan Greece. No great thalassocracy distinguished their bronze age as it did in Minoan Crete. Trade between the Mycaenean settlements flourished and the classic ruins of Salamis stand as a splendid reminder of Cyprus' onetime importance as a maritime market. Zeno, the first Stoic, developed a philosophy here which bore uncanny resemblance to the later teachings of Christ. St Paul, a Cypriot Jew, and his companion Barnabas began their mission in the island.

After the schism Cyprus fell naturally under the loose control of Byzantium and was ruled toward the end of the 12th century by a scoundrel called Isaac Comnenos, self-styled Holy Emperor.

Meanwhile things were going badly for the Franks. In 1187 the crusader army was decisively defeated at the Horns of Hattin by Saladin the Kurd. Guy de Lusignan, King of Jerusalem, was captured but subsequently released in exchange for the town of Ascalon and a promise (soon broken) never again to bear arms against Islam.

Only the coastal towns of Tyre, Tripoli and Antioch remained in Christian hands, plus a few strongholds like the Krak des Chevaliers.

These disasters inspired the Third Crusade led by Philippe Augustus of France and Richard I, Lionheart, of England. Bad weather delayed Richard's fleet and he spent the winter of 1190/91 at Messina. His mother, Eleanor of Aquitaine, profiting from this misfortune, hurried to Sicily with Berengaria, daughter of the King of Navarre, destined to be his bride.

On 10 April, 1191, Richard's fleet put to sea. Whether or not things went wrong between the betrothed, Richard decreed that Berengaria and his sister Joanna should sail in a different ship. They were caught in a storm and sought shelter at Lemesos on the Cypriot coast.

The villain Comnenos, by this time in league with Saladin, closed in, denied supplies to the royal ladies, robbed the wrecked crews and demanded that the women should land. Two gallant crusaders, Roger de Harcourt and William du Bois, escaped from their own wreck nearby and together with their men cut through Comnenos' lines to Berengaria's ship. Comnenos fortified the beach and put to sea in pursuit. But now, with a fine sense of timing, Richard arrived from the Gulf of Antalya and landed, horses and all. Isaac fled. The Latin merchants and native Cypriots, fed up with Comnenos, welcomed the Crusaders. Richard captured Isaac's camp, together with much booty.

On 12 May, 1191, in the fortress chapel of Lemnos, Berengaria married Richard and was crowned Queen of England.

Who should then turn up from Syria but Guy de Lusignan, still claiming to be King of Jerusalem. Urgent messages began to arrive from Philippe Augustus urging Richard to stop messing about in Cyprus and make his way to Acre to join the crusade. They seem to have had no immediate effect. Richard and Guy de Lusignan took Nicosia and drove Comnenos into his last refuge in Buffavento Castle where he eventually surrendered.

Thus the first British occupation of the island began. It lasted just two years, after which Richard, short of money to pay the troops, sold it to Guy de Lusignan. For the next three centuries the Lusignan dynasty ruled the island unchallenged. What a romantic and mysterious realm it must have been. One can imagine the austere regime of these Frankish warrior knights slowly seduced over the centuries by contact and marriage with the women of an older, more devious and lascivious Levantine world, until no strength remained to resist the pressures of the Italian maritime city states.

The Byzantine and Frankish occupations have left some of the most breathtaking examples of the medieval stronghold, rivalling all but the Krak des Chevaliers, and even that great fortress cannot compare for beauty with the Abbey of Bellapaix whence the soldier monks looked across the straits to the Anatolian shore, or Hilarion, whose baileys, curtain walls and towers seem to grow from the rock itself as if thrown up in the original upheaval which formed the two peaks upon which it was built. Didymus, the twins, was their name in Greek, misconstrued by the Crusaders, who called the great castle le Chateau de Dieu d'Amour. Our Richard the First captured it. One wonders how. The falcons wheel and cry about its broken turrets, swooping in and out of what were once the royal apartments whence there is a vertiginous glimpse of the sea a thousand feet below down a jagged and vertical rampart of rock. Who can guess what unfortunates may have been flung headlong from the eyrie after some misdemeanour at this Lusignan court.

East beyond Bellapaix in the Kyrenia range of mountains there rises the Pentadactylon, the five fingers, and next to their jagged peaks high above the pine forests clings another grim fortress; the last resort of Comnenos. Buffavento the Venetians called it; Bouffe le Vent was the Crusader's name; Wuthering Heights would have suited it well, glowering down its precipitous sides at Syria beyond the sea. To the east again stand the walls of Kantara. They built and defended stoutly, these long-vanished religious adventurers, and they held for over three centuries until the sad abdication of Catherine Cornaro and the coming of the lion of St Mark.

Venetian rule lasted for nearly a century until their defeat after a bloody fight with the Ottomans at Famagusta. The ruins of the city have never been repaired. The Turkish invaders simply squatted and built their houses among the old walls. They still stood when I was in Cyprus.

Turkish rule in turn lasted three hundred years. The Ottoman administration was tolerant, even lackadaisical, provided there was no undue provocation. If there was the reaction was apt to be definitive. The last time the contemporary equivalent of EOKA caused an unacceptable disturbance, the Turks took the reigning Archbishop, the Makarios of the day, and flayed him alive in the main square of Famagusta. There was no further trouble during the occupation.

I once witnessed a military display by the Turkish Army in the dry moat round Nicosia. In traditional uniforms and armed with pikes, the Janissaries marched past us to martial music. Every tenth step or so, upon a ferocious drumbeat, their ranks halted and turned outwards, pikes thrust before them, eyes fixed in silence on the bystanders. This display was employed throughout the Empire as an occasional reminder that, for all their lazy tolerance, disloyalty to the Sublime Porte could bring serious consequences. One still got the message and I quaked like the rest of the spectators as the Janissaries passed.

The second British occupation dates from 1878. Disraeli was convinced that in Cyprus lay the key to Western Asia and the passage to India. With the Russians at the Gates of Constantinople, the Turks were in no position to argue and, in return for a somewhat nebulous guarantee of help the Sultan of Turkey, agreed to recognize the de facto control of the island by Britain. Formal annexation had to wait until 1914 when Turkey joined the Central Powers.

British rule brought many practical benefits and some devoted Governors, in particular Sir Harry Luke and Sir Ronald Storrs, both historians. And if we were sometimes guilty of insensitivity to Greek aspirations, the island was in many ways a happier place than it is in the aftermath of the second Turkish invasion in 1974. For as I write, Cyprus is still brutally divided by a quarrel whose cloudy origins lie deep in history with the coming of the Saracen, the fall of Constantinople and most recently with EOKA and their demand for Enosis. Deserted Turkish villages fall into forlorn decay in the Greek south of the island while all trace of Greek habitation has been erased in the north. Between the two a fiercely policed curtain has fallen.

The two sectors say much about the respective characters of Cypriot Greek and Turk. In Greek Cyprus, and particularly along the coast, there is a continuous belt of garish and vulgar touristical prosperity. On the Turkish side, up the steep hill from Kyrenia, there winds and wallows a half-finished and unnecessary motorway, leading nowhere in particular. It stops abruptly near the top of the pass where once I listened to the little skops owls' sad and evocative hooting at night. Around Kyrenia hideous high-rise blocks, at various stages of completion, look as though not only their builders but they themselves have lost their concrete hearts; everywhere an air of amiable tasteless muddle. Yet, mercifully, Kyrenia's charming Venetian harbour has been jealously preserved.

There is warm welcome and friendship on either side of this sad frontier for the returning Briton, but otherwise little sign of reconciliation.

Thus the curse still lies upon the beautiful copper island and with it the uncertainty as to who truly has title.

We lived in a most attractive Turkish house near Kyrenia called Tat-li-su, meaning "sweet water". It belonged and still does to my friend Ali Dana, a distinguished Turkish lawyer. My wife Sally had arrived soon after the truce and this was one of the happiest times we had together. I remember vividly her beauty and radiance as she stepped from the aeroplane. Around Tat-li-su there ran an arched verandah shaded by a vast carob tree. This carob tree was inhabited by a colony of cicadas whose chirruping filled the evenings. I thought it a cheerful sound but it used to irritate our friend Geoffrey McDermott, the Foreign Office representative at Episkopi, who frequently stayed with us. Geoffrey was an authoritative and entirely untypical Foreign Office official. When he could stand the cicadas no longer he would stride to the carob tree and shout at the top of his voice "Shut Up!" Instantly they did. Sadly Geoffrey later left the office after some disagreement in Berlin. I have often reflected since that the Foreign Office could have done with his kind of authority.

My life in Cyprus brought some frustration, caused in particular by the childish rivalry between our various security services, (the disease is probably endemic) but also much pleasure and absorbing interest. Among my friends was Penelope Tremayne, heroine of the Samaria Gorge. She was then working as *Observer* correspondent and was living alone in Lawrence Durrell's house in Bellapaix, a notoriously pro-EOKA village, during the trouble.

When she returned from her office in Nicosia as like as not she would find daubed on the walls opposite the great "tree of idleness" made famous in Durrell's *Bitter Lemons* anti-British insults of a particularly unpleasant character.

One such occasion was shortly after the cowardly murder by EOKA of Mrs Cutlisse, the wife of a British sergeant. The event had caused widespread revulsion and, in order to distract attention from it, EOKA launched an entirely fictitious propaganda campaign alleging British atrocities in Famagusta. The graffito alluded to this and ended "Shame on the British". Under the eyes of those responsible who sat drinking in the taverna, Penelope climbed on top of her Landrover, crossed out "British" and chalked up "Shame on the Cypriots who murder women", glared at the watchers opposite and drove on up the hill to her house.

Her defiance constituted a most dangerous provocation as she was soon to have confirmed. She had a friend, one Collis, guardian of the ruined abbey, who, in spite of his affability and in typical Cypriot fashion, was also hand in glove with the local EOKA cell. Collis told her some days later that they had argued all night about whether, how and by whom she should be murdered, but came to no conclusion. "They are like a lot of women and I told them they should dress like women", he added cheerfully.

But the danger was real. One evening a week or so later Penelope was working late by the light of an oil lamp. There was no electricity. Durrell's house was built into the side of the hill so that she could see the bottom half of any figure outside the window behind the lamp. Suddenly she was aware of several shadows moving hesitantly about in the darkness. There are two versions about what happened next. Professor Yannis Cleanthou, a distinguished Greek Cypriot archaeologist whom I met on holiday in 1985 long after the emergency, knew of the incident. A charming and informative companion, Professor Cleanthou had formerly been an EOKA sympathizer. He told me that Penelope was certainly on Grivas' hit list. Indeed he had given orders that she was to be beaten up – "not killed", the Professor added carefully. Several young EOKA activists were despatched to carry out this attack on a defenceless woman. They arrived at Durrell's house and forced the door. Penelope, according to Professor Cleanthou, had just finished her bath and faced them clad only in her dressing gown. Their purpose was plain. Penelope was a beautiful woman. Without a word she let her wrap fall and stood before them in all her naked glory.

This exercise in heroic sexual psychology proved a complete success. The youths, overcome with embarrassment and modesty, are said to have fled.

Sadly Penelope's own version is less dramatic. Between the lamp by which she was working and the window through which she saw the moving shadows, there stood on a table the plaster reproduction of a figure from the Nicosia museum belonging to Durrell, head and shoulders, half life-size. Penelope waited, unarmed, expecting the worst. No attack came and the menacing shadows disappeared.

Collis, as obligingly informative as ever, subsequently told her that several youths had been despatched by EOKA to kill her but had soon come running back down the hill in a panic to explain they could not do the deed because there was a soldier on guard looking out of the window at them. Penelope had never admired the plaster cast which she said must have been a Byzantine civil servant. Whether or no, he stood her in good stead that night. She was never molested again.

On another occasion she certainly saved the lives of two British soldiers. She was sitting in a taverna in a remote village in the Troodos mountains arguing in Greek with the usual group of idlers, several of whom were armed. The matter under discussion was whether Cypriot people could be accepted as friendly and hospitable in spite of the emergency. An army jeep pulled up and two soldiers of the patrol, sub-machine guns at the ready, approached the taverna. Their purpose was unclear. That they were in instant danger of being murdered was not. There was a heavy silence. Penelope saw hands steal towards hidden weapons.

"Put down your guns," she said to the soldiers with quiet and deadly emphasis, "and sit down at that table." Surprised by the English voice and sensing danger, the two men responded. "Now," she said to the Cypriots, "you claim to be hospitable people. Here are two strangers. Who is going to prove it? Who will welcome them?" Grudgingly some of the Cypriots murmured a greeting and offered coffee. The tension eased. Death had again passed close.

By the spring of 1960 the situation in the island had eased. I planned a short week's holiday with six friends. We hired a stout seagoing boat and crew in Kyrenia harbour with the object of sailing to the Anatolian coast in search of classical remains and also in my case to skin dive for fish. As we were embarking a corporal on my staff came running with a telegram. It read, "Regret you are not required in South Harrow". I was mystified. I had no wish to be required in South Harrow. I felt much happier where I was. It was seconds before I connected this unsolicited dismissal with the Conservative Party. Some by-elections were pending and somehow my name must at last have come out at the top of a list. I put South Harrow behind me and away we sailed, as it happened to a minor adventure.

We cleared the ship at a small Turkish port and set out west along the coast where we visited the grim and evocative Saracen castle of Anamur standing with its back to the waves and its wide gates facing the valley and the land approaches. This was surely a cavalry fortress. The men slept above the stables and at the alarm four horsemen abreast could gallop out through the gates.

One evening Ivor Porter, a friend in the Foreign Office, and I had gone for a walk along the remains of what was surely a Roman road. As we wandered back in the setting sun midst the scent of rosemary and thyme we became briefly separated. Suddenly over the hill before me appeared four men. We had been warned by our Greek skipper that the natives were by no means always friendly but I thought it best to offer a hand. They grabbed both my arms and held on. Two of my assailants were fairly elderly, wizened and small, the other two young, gormless looking and fairly large.

"'Spion, 'Spion," shouted the oldest and most villainous looking. It seemed unlikely the Turkish Intelligence Service had animated this attack, nor was I in the hands of the police. The warnings of Andreas, the skipper, seemed all too well founded.

"Non 'spion," I said smiling hopefully. "NATO, NATO." NATO's southern flank remained unmoved.

"Passaporti," they shouted.

"In the ship," I said, making to move them towards the little bay below us where she lay.

"'Spion, 'Spion"!

Then the wizened one made a bad decision. He issued some gabbled instructions to the two youths, who turned back over the hill. Most Turkish

194

peasants in these parts seemed to carry an old gun of some kind. We had seen them. It was ten to one they were off to get one. After which I would have been marched fifteen miles or so to the nearest town and shoved in the local bug-ridden lock-up. Altercations with the Mayor would have followed, appeals to the Embassy, final release and retribution, but much unpleasantness and the end of the holiday. It was now or never. As soon as the two youths had disappeared I wrenched my arms free and banged the two heads together as hard as I could. One fell over, the other looked distinctly disorientated. I ran for the ship, followed in due course by a hail of rocks. Half-way back I saw a figure coming up the steep slope to look for me. It was Andreas, not, be it noted, any of my fellow English holidaymakers. I was full of gratitude. Andreas exuded hatred and mistrust of Turks. We pulled up the hook and sailed away before these hospitable people had time to return with their bundouk and shoot at us.

Years later when I returned to Anamur on a yachting holiday with Julian and Billy McLean, Billy pulled my leg mercilessly about this incident, in which I suspect he only half believed.

"Do you think it's safe for us here, Steve? They never forget anything. They may still have headaches."

We returned to Kyrenia at the end of our week to find another communication waiting for me. Would I present myself before the selection committee of the Conservative Association in Ampthill, Bedfordshire, the following Thursday. This seemed more promising. I booked a seat on a plane and went.

———|———

13

THE DISORDERLY ADMINISTRATION
OF DECLINE

During his tenure as head of the Civil Service Sir William Armstrong is supposed to have described his task as "the orderly administration of decline". Whether he was referring to the devaluation of the currency or to the dismantling of Empire I do not know, but the description certainly could not have been applied to our record in Central Africa.

Arrived from Cyprus I telephoned my boss at the Foreign Office, John Bruce Lockhart. "Good," said John, "I didn't know you were back. Meet me in the Ritz Bar at 12.30." I was there. He ordered two large martinis and launched into an unstoppable monologue. I was to be offered a splendid job in Africa. We were going to tour the southern half of the continent together and lay a lot of plans. It was only when he reached for his martini that I was able to tell him about my invitation to Mid-Bedfordshire. "You bloody fool!" he said. Perhaps he was right. John is still, I am happy to say, a close friend and far too kind a man to press his point. Anyway it was then or never.

The Selection Committee met in Ampthill. I knew nothing of Bedfordshire. Catherine of Aragon, the best-looking, probably the nicest and most intelligent of Henry VIII's wives, had beeen driven to live there, and at best escaped the axe. John Bunyan had wandered about there, and indeed is alleged to have based his imagery on the Bedfordshire countryside. If so he was easily pleased, for it is not the most scenic slice of England. Two vast sheds near Cardington, outside Bedford, had housed the ill-fated R101. The place still maintained a vestigial connection with ballooning. Indeed I had once made an ascent from there myself. The current theory in the service was that we could float secret agents over the Iron Curtain in this way and thus defeat the radar. Some of us were moved to experiment. It had been quite an experience. We had threatened to get entangled in some power lines and explode. There was a need to empty sand bags as rapidly as possible out of the fragile basket in which my instructor and I were swinging about. We lurched over a farmyard, terrified some pigs and showered their proprietor with sand before landing with a fearful thump in what was to become my constituency. Cardington was fixed indelibly in my memory. Nothing of great note that I knew of had otherwise happened in Bedfordshire.

I sat facing a semi-circle of twenty or so young to middle-aged people. Stick a pin into the map of England and mid-Bedfordshire is only a fraction east of centre. These folk in character and outlook, I came to recognize, were of the heart of England. Among them in due course I found some of the truest friends a man could hope for. But I was under penetrating, shrewd though kindly inspection. What did I think about this, or that or the other aspect of contemporary domestic Conservative Party policy? Nothing much, I was bound to admit. I had no benefit of Central Office brief. I had lived for most of a decade abroad. "Well can you tell us about that?" somebody asked rather desperately. I could – and did. It was quite a good story. "Tell me what your rank is?" asked a friendly looking Brigadier. "About like a Brigadier, Brigadier," I ventured. It was no better than a venture but it made everyone laugh. "What are your views on field sports, and particularly fox hunting?" asked a sharp-looking person in a tweed jacket. I scored ten for that.

There were more meetings, an address to a larger gathering and I was a selected candidate.

The retiring member, Alan Lennox-Boyd, a charismatic figure if ever there was one, helped me and my wife in every possible way, even to the loan of a house in the constituency. My resignation from the Foreign Office was formalized in an interview with a sour administrative person who clearly took pleasure in assuring me I should get neither pension nor gratuity for my twelve years' work, since, as he explained, I had not been requested or expected to leave.

On 16 November, 1960, there was a package of by-elections of which Mid-Bedfordshire was one. They went well for Macmillan's government. In Mid-Bedfordshire we even increased our majority. To Westminster I went, up the steps of St Stephen's entrance into a strange world, rather like one's first day at school; and this goes especially for one's first contacts with the Whips' Office. But my Conservative colleagues were unfailingly helpful and welcoming. Even opponents are kind to beginners. It is a honeymoon which lasts so long as one's particular adherence and idiosyncrasies are still a matter for speculation, but it is warm and genuine nevertheless.

The Palace of Westminster is a complicated place. I had been there only a week or two when a very senior member next to whom I was sitting in the smoking room leant across: "You're new aren't you?" I could scarcely deny it. "Very glad to meet you. How many lavatories have you discovered?" I was speechless. Was this some elaborate test? The Whips had said nothing about lavatories. I thought two, perhaps three. "That's it," said the sage. "I've been here over twenty years and I've got to thirty-eight. It's a question of urological drive and geographical experience. Of course if you count the House of Lords I'd be well up on that."

After my twenty-three years I believe I was still nowhere near his figure. Maybe this is a mark of failure.

Anyway things went with a swing to begin with. After a very short space I was elected Vice-Chairman of the Conservative Foreign Affairs Committee and invited to join various allegedly influential private groups. My maiden speech, not unnaturally in a defence debate, seemed to go well. All was set fair. Then came Rhodesia.

It was inevitable I should take an interest in Central Africa. Much of my parents' life was spent there, I had been brought to Rhodesia as a small child; my sister was born there. I had grown up with tales of the veld and the farm. The fate of the Central African Federation was already the cause of deep concern and controversy in the Tory Party.

In 1961 I accepted an invitation from the British South Africa Company to join a group of Conservative Members of Parliament due to visit Rhodesia. The three weeks' tour was efficiently arranged. We met everyone who seemed to matter, white and black. We were free to see what and whom we liked.

For the next fifteen years I returned frequently and travelled as widely as I could. I was captivated by the country, particularly the Zambezi and its tributaries. Whenever I could I set off into the veld, sometimes with my rifle, sometimes not. Of good companions none is more memorable than Romani, a Rhodesian "messenger" or sergeant of police, assigned to accompany me, and a great tracker. Six foot three inches erect he could move noiselessly through the tall grass, sometimes leaping to spy the game as his Zulu ancestors did when they closed on their human prey. We spoke little of each others' tongues but we forged an instinctive trust which belied the need for language. It is the harmony of the hunter. By day and, on one stimulating occasion, by night, we travelled the bush together. Best of all was the dawn. Whatever blights fate may have decreed for this tragic continent she has granted the African dawn. From the first cool whispering suspicion of light, to the time of creeping shadows, of stealth and movement, to the sudden presence of beauty poised among the dark Mopani trees, or tensed for flight at the water's edge, the wonder and excitement persist. All the veld is alive with fleeting mystery, until driven slowly into somnolence by the swelling orchestra of the day and the beating heat.

The 'Swana people have a saying for this magic overture to the African dawn – "*Ma kuku ana katsa kawnu*" – the time when a man first sees the horns of his cattle.

But if I was to come to any useful conclusions about British responsibilities there it seemed essential to learn something about the indigenous Africans. How otherwise was one to legislate for their future?

I was introduced to Doctor Mike Gelfand. Mike was a teaching surgeon at the multi-racial university in what was then Salisbury. A South African by birth, he had emigrated north because of antipathy to apartheid. An intelligent man and a gentle soul, his interest in and sympathy for the native African had led him to a profound study of their customs and traditions. Such was their trust in him that he was welcome at their most intimate ceremonies. He spoke fluent Sishona and N'Debele, the two languages of Rhodesia.

Hour after hour and more than once I sat on the stoep at June Hill, the British South Africa Company guesthouse outside Salisbury, listening to Mike while the sun – and the sundowners – descended. I read his books. He led me to others whose knowledge and interest in the people of Central and Southern Africa he regarded as serious. I travelled not only in Rhodesia but in Natal and the Transkei for the same purpose. These experiences led me first to a profound respect for the ways of the African, second to a recognition of the deep divide which separates us Europeans from him, and thence eventually to contempt for so much of the progressive doctrine peddled at the time in London.

Nobody familiar with Central Africa would then have denied that the African people needed help and that in different ways their lives and opportunities could and should be enhanced. But to be effective this help had to rest, not on the proposition that European ideas must be adopted, but rather that to achieve anything useful it was necessary for the European to understand the disturbing impact of these ideas on the African personality. Then and only then was it legitimate to decide how to help.

The Mashona and the Matabele are very different peoples. The first comprise a wide group of sub-tribes, the second are in fact the descendants of two Zulu impis or regiments which settled in Rhodesia in the 19th century. The entity of the chief is paramount to both. He embodies the spirit of the tribe. The Zulus select their chief by the simple method of primogeniture just as we do. The Mashona employ a much more complicated collateral system by which there are a number of related candidates for the succession. But the basic beliefs and instinctive knowledge of both peoples, indeed of all the Bantu peoples, do not differ so much. Once chosen, the chief expresses the will of the people. If his authority is weakened or usurped the cohesion of the tribe is threatened.

The mystical importance of the Chief had long ago burnt into my memory through a macabre story of my father's. History in Africa descends by word of mouth. When I was an infant at Marangoe, Lewis had a Zulu cook, a splendid old man called Hendrik. Sometimes after the weekly beer drink on Saturday evening he would make his way unsteadily up to the stoep, where my father sat with his sundowner. In his youth Hendrik had followed Frederick Selous, the great hunter and explorer whose pioneering first opened the road for the European into what is now Zimbabwe.

"Va is Selous?" he would bellow.

"Hendrik, Selous is dead."

"No, no, no, va is Selous?" the old man would cry repeatedly before wandering away fuddled and evidently grief-stricken.

But Hendrik's preoccupation with the past went further back than his devotion to Selous. In his more sober moments he told my father a story of the Zulu War, a story, the outcome of which sent reverberations through the chancelleries of Europe, caused intense embarrassment to the British Government and brought grief to Queen Victoria, a story the full, primitive horror of which was surely concealed at the time.

In January, 1879, in response to pressure from Afrikaaner settlers suffering from raids along the borders of Natal, a British force under Lord Chelmsford marched into Zululand. It was to be a short campaign against native warriors unfamiliar with modern firearms. The time had come to teach the Zulu a lesson. No forward scouts or formal reconnaissance seemed necessary. But the grass is high at that time of year and the Zulu, who had mobilized between forty and sixty thousand men, proved hard to locate among the broken kopjes and dongas of Natal. There followed the great Zulu victory and capture of the British base at Isandhlawana and the heroic defence of Rorke's Drift by the 24th of Foot. Reinforcements were hastily despatched and the Zulus thenceforth treated with respect.

In early April, against Disraeli's wishes and to the embarrassment of the War Office, there arrived at Durban none other than the Prince Imperial of France, aged twenty-two, son of Napoleon III. After the Emperor's death France had lurched back into republicanism and the Empress Eugenie, with her son, were living at Chislehurst under the protection of Queen Victoria, who had taken them to her heart. It was she who had insisted that the Prince, who had completed his course at Woolwich with distinction, should be granted his wish to see active service.

Lord Chelmsford eventually despatched him under the care and command of Colonel Harrison, the Quartermaster General, who had established a headquarters at Itelezi. He gave strict instructions that the Prince was to be closely escorted if he left the camp.

On 1st June Harrison sent him on patrol with a Lieutenant Carey and six troopers. Lord Chelmsford was not informed and it was not made clear who was in command, Carey or the Prince. In the heat of midday the Prince suggested they unsaddle and picket the horses by a river. Carey didn't like the place. The long grass was too near, but the Prince insisted. No lookout was posted. They rested there until well into the afternoon. About three o'clock Carey tried to insist they leave but the Prince said they should wait a few minutes more. Those were fatal minutes.

A Zulu impi of about fifty men was creeping towards them. Every so often a warrior leapt unseen above the grass to spy. The Prince and his party had saddled up and were about to mount when the Zulus swept into the open, assegais glinting in the sun, mouthing their terrifying ululation.

"Ride for it" was the only possible reaction.

Several of the Zulus had captured rifles and they opened a murderous fire. Two troopers were killed on the spot. The Prince, who was a fine rider, laid hold of a stirrup leather or strap on his accoutrements and was about to vault into the saddle when the strap broke. His plunging horse knocked him down and galloped away.

Accounts differ as to what happened next. According to Trooper Le Tocq who had pulled up his horse at the edge of a donga nearby and was the only eye witness, the Prince ran some distance, realized there was no escape and turned bravely to face his assailants. He was swiftly overwhelmed and died under repeated assegai thrusts.

The body was recovered next day and eventually delivered to Chislehurst. The Prince had been so badly mutilated that the family doctor, Dr Evans, could only identify him by a gold filling in a tooth. The Empress was not allowed to see her son but was assured that he had died bravely, bearing all his wounds in front.

Hendrik's great-grandfather was with that impi and the tale did not have far to travel down the generations.

"They killed a great chief, N'kosi."

"How did they know he was a chief?" my father would ask.

"It was his clothes, his uniform, they knew who he was," said Hendrik.

"What did they do then, Hendrik?"

"What they always did if they killed a great chief. They cut out his heart and ate it between them so that some of his strength should pass in."

★

The religion of the Bantu people is called Animism. The word commonly carries an implication of the primitive. I see nothing primitive in Animism. At least African belief demonstrates a consciousness of a metaphysical world which we have long lost. It is different, that is all.

Mike Gelfand understood: take our concept of the individual, his purpose in life, his ambition, even his immortal soul, that is for those who still believe in such a phenomenon. We can only conceive of any of these things in terms of a single entity. This is me, no one else. I represent a distinct and unique personality. To the African, such a concept is not just alien, it is frightening. Comfort can only lie in belonging to a communal personality, to the family, together with their ancestors, to the group, to the tribe. To be cast from this belonging is to suffer an unbearable defenceless loneliness, a state apt for death.

Because of our self-awareness, we gear all our activities, in no matter what sphere of life, to individual effort. We educate, exhort, reward or punish each other as individuals. The successful stand out, admired or envied as the case may be. No one is discountenanced at being considered an individual.

For the tribal African the reverse is the case. Any quality or achievement or possession which marks a man as unusual, as one who stands out from the crowd, is to be shunned, even considered uncanny. Extraordinary material possessions or success is thus dangerous. If disaster should strike – a drought, the death of the cattle – the cause must be identified and the elements or the ancestors placated by its removal. It is for the witch doctor to discover the source of the misfortune and he will look first for whoever is unusual. In days before the European administration the cause of the trouble could expect short shrift, just because he or she as an individual was deemed to have harmed the communal spirit. The conflict here is obvious. Full of good intent, the European administrator strives to persuade the African people to imitate and thus to gain, to be successful. If they fail they are regarded as stupid or lazy. The real reason may be confusion of mind. I visited a kraal once in the Transkei with a dedicated South African agricultural officer. His job was to help the people improve their crops, use fertilizer, modern soil preparation and harvesting techniques. There was a fairly general reluctance to conform, but one African farmer became an apt pupil. Indeed he was very soon a comparatively rich man as a result. The South African returned next season to find his friend sitting idle outside his house. He had planted absolutely nothing. "Why not?" "Well," he said, "after what you told me I made enough for three years, there is no need." Laziness? A guilty conscience? My guide had no idea, but at least it showed a charmingly modest assessment of need, somewhat alien to the European work ethic.

I talked long with Mike about concepts of good and evil. In modern times those who profess adherence to Christian belief have a clear idea of what they mean by good, a less precise grasp of evil. In the middle ages perhaps this still existed, but now "the Devil and all his works" is no more than a half-serious figure of speech. For African people the opposite is true; good and evil exist, of course, in equal balance, but whereas the principle of good is a cloudy one, evil is precise, close, always about us, in the veld, on the wind; it is abroad by night. Certainly those who are already dead can dispense it. It is an ever present force, able without physical presence to extract life itself.

And who are we to deny such powers? We have only to read our newspapers or watch television for one single day to wonder. Our church, engrossed in welfare politics, is no longer the bastion it was against "the Devil and all his works". We may hold African instinctive belief to be primitive, but if we can not recognize the force of evil in spite of its manifest presence among us who are we to judge?

In Central Africa strange powers exist. My father spent some time, hunting I think, in the territory of a somewhat isolated tribe living along the banks of the Zambezi. He got on well with their Chief. They had a God called Wachimomba. He lived in a small wattle house in discreet seclusion. He was very holy. One day, as a great favour, my father was permitted a glimpse of the deity. It was hard to tell in the semi-dark what shape he was but my father thought he might well have been the figurehead of a long-perished Portuguese ship. At any rate the reason for this reverence was clearly explained. Long ago, perhaps in the days of the great-great grandfathers, a dreaded Zulu impi had come marauding into their territory in search of the usual booty, cattle and women. Unable to resist, the people had fled into the bush leaving Wachimomba behind. The Zulus, contemptuous of local belief, threw him into the Zambezi and went on their predatory way. As the days passed one by one the warriors fell mortally sick. They died, inexplicably, where they lay; not one returned. Presently the people crept back to their kraals. After the rains the great river subsided. There was Wachimomba sitting on a sandbank. No wonder he was worshipped. I would not wish to be disrespectful to Wachimomba.

Missionaries have much to answer for. Heroic many missions may have been in early days and doubtless mission stations have often relieved physical suffering and furthered general education, but the state of defenceless grace attainable by true African converts to Christianity, deeply appealing though it can be, hardly equips them to stand the pressures of modern western life which crowd upon them, and it is no wonder that Africa abounds with strange half-invented versions of the Christian faith mixed with the old religions. Moreover, latterly too many missions openly and irresponsibly favoured African Nationalist extremism.

Obsessed with our long-evolved methods of government, we overlook the shattering effect all this has had on the African mind. We wrenched away his checks and balances, replaced them with the symbols and trappings of an alien and complex system of government, then simply walked away. We now behold the result. There is no need to emphasize the unhappy state of so much of post-colonial Africa.

In 1962 Iain Macleod, then Colonial Secretary, was in Salisbury at the same time I was. In the course of one my talks with Mike Gelfand I suggested he should meet Iain. Indeed it seemed to me essential.

"Oh, but I have met him," said Mike. There was a silence.

"Well?" I asked.

"'E went to sleep, man" said Mike in his lisping South African voice.

Now Secretaries of State are entitled to be overtired but I could not understand how anyone genuinely concerned about British policy in Central Africa should have failed to appreciate the importance of what Mike Gelfand had to tell. The next week Iain Macleod was widely reported cooking scrambled eggs for breakfast with Kenneth Kaunda, great friends and equals together on the march to liberal democracy. But, scrambled eggs apart, they were not equal; they were very different. I do not know whether Macleod's policies at the Colonial Office were motivated principally by his conviction that we should abscond from our responsibilities in Africa as soon as possible or whether he thought he could turn the African territories into something like the Home Counties by imposing our institutions upon them. In any case the result was the same. In his book Roy Welensky described Macleod as "a mixture of cold calculation, sudden gushes of emotion and ignorance of Africa". The last qualification was certainly true.

As I write, Kaunda's wretched regime has finally collapsed, leaving Zambia in ruins and its future bleak. Are we to congratulate ourselves?

In the context of British politics in the 1960s the white Rhodesians were naive. Their loyalty to the Crown and to the British Government had been unquestioning. Before all the Dominions and Colonies, Rhodesia declared war on Nazi Germany the day after Britain. Their contribution had been out of all proportion to their numbers. Thousands of RAF pilots trained there, including many Rhodesians, among them Ian Smith. Every man that could be spared went north to the African campaign and the outstanding exploits of the Rhodesian patrol of the LRDG have been well chronicled. All this was the natural reaction of a fiercely loyal and patriotic people. The attitude still lingered in 1960 although to me it already seemed sadly and nostalgically dated.

"Play up and play the game."

"My country right or wrong."
These nostrums, still familiar if already fading in my own boyhood, pervaded the mood and thinking in the Salisbury Club, among gatherings of Rhodesian farmers, on the rugby field or the cricket pitch. Greetings were open-hearted, handshakes were firm and uninhibited. In Rhodesia one was not just poured a whisky, one was handed a glass and the bottle (the stuff is like gold in Zimbabwe now). The ethic of Rhodesia was still Kiplingesque. I was minded the other day of how deep we have buried these attitudes. It was at the funeral of a farmer friend whose family I knew well, decent, well-to-do country folk leading entirely useful lives. During the service one of his sons read Kipling's "If", a well-merited tribute to his father's character. As an aspiration for manhood I know of no better advice in or out of scripture and said so afterwards to my friend's son. What struck me was his reaction and that of his contemporaries. It was as though they had discovered a long-buried treasure. Kipling's words and the attitude to life which they conveyed seemed to conjure a vision which they found entirely apt and attractive but had never heard expressed. They would have been happy in Rhodesia.

These travels in Central Africa led me to various conclusions. The tilt towards independence was already irreversible. In any case the impact of European ideas and administration had ruptured traditional African society to an extent that it had to be replaced by something else. The transition was likely to be long and painful.

The white Rhodesians had to be respected, not just because of their proven loyalty to the Crown and to Britain, nor simply because of their long record of successful self-government, but above all because they had accepted Duncan Sandys' 1961 Constitution which committed them to the advancement and encouragement of the African people. The process of African participation in business and government within the framework of the Federation had already begun. It seemed to me Rhodesia could serve as an example not only to apartheid South Africa but also to the British Protectorates to the north, where, despite increasing deference to African nationalism and much pious talk, considerably less had actually been done by the Colonial Office to advance African education or preparation for partnership in government.

But the one certain formula for disaster would be to introduce immediate majority rule as an alternative to a developing partnership. If we did this it would be to expose the great mass of tribal Africans to uncertainty and suffering. Their traditional and instinctive means of communion would be taken from them. The cohesion of their society and the root of their beliefs would be fatally shaken; and, worst of all, the place of the chief, mystical embodiment of the spirit of the people, would be usurped by some African nationalist man of power, divested of his native morality, yet immune to the constraints of European democratic government. Fear would rule, first by intimidation and then under tyranny – and that is precisely what happened.

The Central African Federation, so full of initial promise, based upon the principle of partnership, brought into being by a British Conservative government, was systematically betrayed by its successors, both Conservative and Labour, through a combination of weakness, ignorance and deceit, in the name of majority rule.

These were the ideas and events which impelled me into opposition to the Central African policy of successive British governments under Macmillan, Home, Wilson and Heath. It proved a long exile.

From 1960 until the final Lancashire House conference in 1979 my friends and I in Parliament did our best to support the Federation and subsequently Rhodesia and to introduce some balance into the increasingly rancid and emotional debate at home. Julian Amery, Pat Wall, Ronald Bell, I and other sympathizers were in constant touch with the Federal Rhodesian leaders. We were treated with raucous hostility by the Socialists, with polite disapproval by the Conservative management and by many of our colleagues. We were accused of right-wing extremism and blind support for what was disdainfully referred to as the Rhodesian "kith and kin". Personally I can see nothing disgraceful about support for one's kith and kin but the motive, so far as I was concerned, went wider and deeper than that.

The idea of some form of union or federation between Northern and Southern Rhodesia, based upon a gradually evolving partnership between the races, had originally been promoted by a number of far-sighted people, notably Roy Welensky, in the forties. The concept made both political and economic sense. Such a union could create a counterbalance of power to South Africa and a formidable base for the development of the whole of Central Africa.

In 1948 Dr D. F. Malan and his nationalist party came to power in Pretoria and the notorious apartheid legislation soon followed. It was fear that this policy would spread north which decided the British Government to overcome the qualms of the Colonial Office and to support Federation. Their condition was that Nyasaland (now Malawi) should be included.

The Central African Federation was enthusiastically promoted by Oliver Lyttelton and Lord Ismay at a series of meetings in London attended by Godfrey Huggins, Prime Minister of Rhodesia (subsequently Lord Malvern) and Edgar Whitehead in January and February of 1952. It was even made clear to Huggins that the British government would be prepared to override African opposition if necessary in the interests of all.

The federal constitution and the way forward were agreed at the first Lancaster House conference in April, 1952. The Rhodesian delegation included two African political leaders, Jasper Savanhu and Joshua N'komo. Savanhu made a profound impression and both agreed to the eventual proposal. In N'komo's closing speech he made clear that he regarded it as his duty to explain the advantages of the Federation to the Africans and this in spite of the considerable pressure being applied to him and Savanhu in London by the British left. N'komo may well have had cause in later years to regret his subsequent defection.

On his return, Godfrey Huggins made a ringing appeal for support in the Southern Rhodesian parliament. He prophesied a bleak future for Rhodesia if federation did not come about and if the European section of the population did not take steps to bring the African people into partnership. "We should have the courage of our conviction and attempt to set a pattern for Africa." Later in his speech he quoted Lord Bryce: "Do not give a people institutions for which it is unripe in the simple faith that the tool will give skill to the workman's hand. Respect facts. Man is, in each country, not what we may wish him to be but what nature and history have made him."

The aspiration was a noble one and Lord Bryce's qualification undeniably apposite. With the whole-hearted support of the British government all seemed set fair in spite of the genuine doubts among some influential Rhodesian politicians. Difficulties there would surely be, but no one then could have foreseen that the Macmillan government, "in a great betrayal," as the Federal Minister Julian Greenfield put it in his memoir*, "would go back on all the assurances and pledges which their predecessors had given to Southern Rhodesia when Federation was inaugurated."

At a second conference in London in 1953, firmly conducted by Lords Swinton and Salisbury, both of whom were strong supporters of federation, the dead hand of the Colonial Office and the Commonwealth Relations Office officials began to emerge. At their repeated insistence a fateful decision was taken to review the federal constitution in not less than seven and not more than nine years. This was to prove the kiss of death.

In a subsequent referendum in February, 1953, the Rhodesians voted for federation by a majority of 63%, supported in parliament incidentally by Ian Smith.

Lord Malvern became the first Prime Minister of the Federation, to be

* *Testimony of a Rhodesian Federal* by J. M. Greenfield, published by Books of Rhodesia, 1978.

succeeded in 1954 by Roy Welensky. Julian Greenfield, Federal Minister of Law, was given the heavy responsibility of drafting an electoral law applicable to the three disparate territories of Southern Rhodesia, Northern Rhodesia and Nyasaland. That he succeeded in the teeth of many difficulties put in his way by the Colonial Office officials in the protectorates was a tremendous achievement. At the first full Federal elections in 1958 the United Federal Party won a large majority overall, and there was even an African elected for the opposition Dominion Party. It had been an objective of the electoral law that cross-party allegiance should be non-racial. Welensky appointed two Africans as junior ministers. A beginning had been made and partnership was on course.

Next year, 1959, brought two ominous deelopments. My predecessor as member for Mid-Bedfordshire, Alan Lennox-Boyd, Secretary of State for Commonwealth Relations and a strong supporter of Federation, retired from parliament. Duncan Sandys replaced him at the CRO while Iain Macleod was appointed Colonial Secretary. By 1960 there were ugly signs of unrest, instigated initially by supporters of Dr Banda in Nyasaland and inexcusably condoned, if not tacitly encouraged, by the Church of Scotland missions, whose ministers preferred to court extreme African nationalism rather than risk losing ground to the Marxists. In spite of warnings from the Federal authorities the Governor and the Colonial Office allowed the situation to deteriorate. Eventually riots were put down with some loss of life. Both Banda and Kaunda were arrested. Furious protests ensued from the Labour Party and the Colonial Secretary felt obliged to set up an enquiry. Patrick Devlin, a judge of the High Court, was appointed and in due course produced one of the most ridiculously lop-sided reports of modern times. It was not accepted by the Conservative government but proved a gift to the opposition. The responsibility for the trouble lay plainly with the colonial administration, yet the Devlin Report effectively and unfairly shifted it on to the Federal government.

In September, 1960, soon after my election to Parliament, Macmillan and Home set up Lord Monckton's Commission to look into the affairs of the Federation. Apparently they felt that an independent enquiry might persuade the Labour Party and the African Nationalists to temper their opposition. An election was pending and Macmillan feared Labour might make an issue of Central Africa. He and Lord Home gave repeated assurances to Welensky that secession by any of the territories would be specifically excluded from the terms of reference. But later, under close questioning by Labour in the House of Commons, Macmillan implied the precise opposite. During the period the Monckton Commission was in Salisbury, Harold Macmillan travelled through Africa to the Cape where he chose to make his "wind of change" speech. However accurate his predictions might have been, this was an irresponsible pronouncement at the time, which could only give direct and immediate encouragement to every African Nationalist extremist.

In October the Monckton Report was published. Not only did it anticipate secession but recommended parity of black and white seats in the Federal assembly. All Julian Greenfield's painstaking negotiation was undone. The report was a disaster and it was rejected as such by Welensky. But the damage proved irreparable.

However the matter is presented in the various memoirs of those involved, it is abundantly clear that British ministers during this period decided to abandon the aim of partnership between the races and to substitute majority rule. They must have realized this would spell the inevitable end of the Federation, yet from 1961 to 1963 they continued to pay lip service to the federal idea and to assure federal ministers of their wish that it should succeed.

For part of this period the influence of Macleod was probably critical, although Sandys, Home, Maudling and eventually Butler all played their part. Lord Home certainly realized the dangers. In his memoir* he wrote, "It seems that we were almost crazily quixotic to persuade ourselves that such political refinements as tolerance of parliamentary opposition and restraint in the use of political power, which it had taken us six hundred years to design, could take root in one or two generations". Probably he gave way with reluctance but he was unable to check the course of events.

R. A. Butler was appointed by Macmillan as the undertaker. His attitude and true objectives were characteristically opaque. Welensky believed that had he been involved earlier he could have helped the situation. Sir Albert Robinson, Rhodesia's extremely capable High Commissioner in London, rejected him as devious and concerned simply to rid himself and his government of an intractable colonial problem.

But the overall responsibility for this betrayal rests squarely with Macmillan. He and his colleagues were simply overborne by African Nationalist extremism. They closed their eyes to the vicious intimidation which lay behind the demands of men like Kaunda and Banda, nor were they ever prepared to give credence or lend adequate support to the moderate Africans who were genuinely ready for partnership. They succumbed to the clamour of the Labour Party and the extreme British left. They lacked the courage to carry through what their predecessors had begun, nor could they bring themselves to admit to the Federal Government or the Rhodesians that they had in effect decided, in Greenfield's words, "to substitute black domination for partnership".

* The Way the Wind Blows, Bantam, 1976.

By their various accounts British ministers maintain in effect that they were faced with the inevitable. Of course the psychololgical pressures exercised by the African Nationalist leaders were considerable, but they were not irresistible had the British government been determined to stick to its guns. The true reason why the Federation was abandoned is not to be found in Macmillan's fine words about the British "duty to spread to other nations those advantages which through the long course of centuries they had won for themselves" but rather in Duncan Sandys' candid admission to Roy Welensky over lunch at Muzinda in 1961. Welensky had just given his opinion that with firmness it would not be difficult to keep Nyasaland in the Federation. "No, Roy," Sandys answered; "you see, we British have lost the will to govern."

Things reached a farcical limit of misjudgement in February, 1961, during the Northern Rhodesia constitutional conference in London.

Macleod was determined to grant a franchise which would ensure an immediate African majority in Northern Rhodesia. Meantime Duncan Sandys was making excellent progress in parallel constitutional talks with the Southern Rhodesian government in Salisbury. Indeed unanimity on his proposals, including the agreement of Joshua N'komo, seemed virtually certain.

Macleod's scheme, in Welensky's view, would have two effects: the breakdown of the Southern Rhodesian talks and the eventual destruction of the Federation. He and his ministers warned and protested vehemently. For a time it looked as though Macleod had been checked. Further negotiations with Sandys by telephone and telegram appeared to have averted a crisis. Meantime Macleod was subjected to a searching examination by a hostile backbench Commonwealth Committee. I remember it well. He seemed to take account of our misgivings and gave an assurance that his proposals would accord with the principals of Alan Lennox-Boyd's White Paper of 1958. Later Macleod angrily accused Julian Greenfield, the federal minister in London for the conference, of having promoted Tory backbench opposition. There had been no need; enough of us were already deeply suspicious of the Colonial Secretary's intentions and manoeuvring.

Talks between the federal ministers and Macleod became almost incoherent. Indeed Greenfield and Roberts, the other federal representative in London, reported to Salisbury that the Colonial Secretary was in such a state of nerves that at times he was almost unintelligible. To quote Welensky's book, "The climax came when the Colonial Secretary declared, 'I'm not going to be blackmailed by you or Welensky or anybody else. I'm going to make my decision on Tuesday and I'll lay it on the table that afternoon.'

Roberts stood up. 'If that's your decision, Secretary of State, our ways must part forthwith; goodbye,' and he turned to go. 'Come back,' shouted Macleod, 'come back!'" At the end of this embarrassing and futile interview Roberts was left with the feeling that the Colonial Secretary was in such a state that he might attempt to go ahead with his proposals athough there was still a chance the Cabinet would restrain him.

Meanwhile on 10 February Kaunda issued a press statement warning that unless he was granted an African majority forthwith there would be an uprising in Northern Rhodesia "which by contrast would make Mau Mau a child's picnic". Perhaps this lurid threat carried greater weight than the arguments of the Federal Ministers.

It was during these exchanges that Roy Welensky received a report that the RAF were concentrating troop-carrying aircraft, Comets and Britannias, on the airfield at Nairobi. A Rhodesian Air Force Canberra was sent up to investigate. It was clear from the embarrassed and evasive attitude of the British crews that something was afoot and it could surely only be the imposition of Macleod's proposals in Northern Rhodesia by force if necessary. On their way back the Rhodesians photographed the British planes on the airfield. Welensky took appropriate measures to deny the federal airfields to any such landing. When, later in March, Welensky dined alone with Macmillan at Admiralty House he raised the matter and, again to quote his book, "The tears rolled down Macmillan's cheeks. 'Roy, do you really believe that I, who have seen the horror of two world wars, would have tolerated a situation in which Britishers would have been shooting down Britishers, their brothers alongside whom they had fought on many a battlefield?'" Welensky then disclosed that he was in no doubt about the presence of the aircraft or of the purpose for which they were gathered there. Macmillan's answer: "But of course Roy we all make mistakes. Those aircraft and those troops weren't to be used against you. We were collecting them in case you needed help and we should have had them there ready for you." But help against what?

Welensky subsequently learned from two British Cabinet Ministers that indeed there had been a contingency plan but that when it reached the Cabinet wiser counsels had prevailed.

The truth of this murky affair is hard to determine. It is possible the RAF at Nairobi were given a warning order or at least had heard of this contingency. But no aircraft could have been moved to Kenya without the knowledge of the Secretary of State for Air, Julian Amery. It is a fact that the Chief of Air Staff, Air Chief Marshal Sir Thomas Pike, called on Amery as a matter of urgency to report that he had been requested by the Colonial Secretary to prepare contingency plans for intervention in Rhodesia. "But that's politically mad!" said Julian. "Well," replied Pike, "that's not my business, but they had better realize there are several Rhodesian officers on the planning staff, so there is not much chance Welensky won't hear about it. Perhaps you'd better stop it." Julian went straight to Harold Macmillan and Macleod's insane proposals were effectively scotched.

Once the Federation was dissolved and independence granted, the trappings of democracy disappeared predictably and virtually overnight in both Zambia and Malawi, while the Federal Party gave way to the Rhodesia Front in Salisbury. Even then Winston Field, the new Southern Rhodesia Prime Minister, declared his willingness to stand on the 1961 constitution agreed by his predecessor with Duncan Sandys. It was not enough. At the Falls Conference, called in June, 1963, to dispose the assets of the Federation, independence was granted to both the protectorates but denied to Southern Rhodesia.

Both Welensky, Greenfield and Sir Albert Robinson urged Winston Field not to attend the Conference unless he had an assurance in writing that Southern Rhodesia would also be granted independence. Even Macmillan, recording his diary notes of a cabinet meeting, wrote that the Rhodesian request was made "with a certain show of reason".* Field and his Cabinet gave way.

Jack Howman, Rhodesian Minister for Community Relations, in London to give a lecture, broke the news to the High Commissioner. It happened that Clifford Dupont, a member of the Rhodesian Cabinet, was also in London. Both were horrified. They telephoned Field, who was extremely short with Dupont, telling him to resign if he didn't like it. Robinson well understood Butler and the British ministers. He told the Rhodesian Prime Minister that the British Government was completely committed to granting both Kaunda and Banda their independence, and that, provided Field accepted certain minor constitutional changes, he could safely make independence a condition of attendance. Field finally agreed to review his decision.

With relief, Robinson sought a meeting with Butler the following Monday. R.A.B. was installed in the old India Office. The approach to his desk involved a walk of many yards. Butler waited in his chair. Finally arrived before him, Robinson announced that the Rhodesian Government was not prepared in the prevailing circumstances to attend the Falls Conference. Butler rose, grinning, scrabbled up a piece of paper in his arthritic, claw-like grip, advanced round the desk and did a sort of dance of triumph round the High Commissioner. "I've got it, I've got it," he chanted, "an hour ago from

* Robert Blake, *A History of Rhodesia*, 1977

our High Commissioner. They have agreed to attend!" Completely discountenanced, Robinson could only apologize for taking up time and withdrew.

Under pressure the Rhodesians had lost their nerve and with it their strongest card. The terms subsequently offered by Butler were no longer minor. They went far beyond the 1961 arrangements and all concerned knew they would prove unacceptable.

———————|———————

14

THE DISUNITED NATIONS

In the midst of this turmoil, with the existence of the Federation increasingly threatened, I decided to visit Portuguese East Africa or Mozambique and then Angola, to try to form some impression of Portuguese intentions and capacity to hold their African empire. A welcome was no problem. The Portuguese authorities were more than helpful. My father had told a story of his only encounter with them in Mozambique. He had been given permission to hunt across the Zambezi in Portuguese territory and thought it only courteous to call on the Portuguese governor at Beira to express his thanks. He was bidden to dinner. Communication was difficult since neither spoke a word of each other's language but the occasion was none the less impressive. The Governor appeared in full Admiral's uniform and bare feet. Much vinho verde was drunk and after dinner the Admiral's pet lion was led in on a chain by an enormous African to be fed the leftovers.

I could hardly hope for such a demonstration but found much to delight and interest me.

First stop was Quelimane, an attractive small station on the Indian Ocean. I was met by the local Portuguese governor who was kindness itself and spoke good English, even if he lacked an Admiral's uniform. The main industry was coconuts, grove upon grove of tall palms from which the nuts were gathered by small boys who shinned up the trunks like squirrels, each shod with serrated, scythe-like steel crampons with which they gripped the tree and literally leapt upward.

My host wished to introduce me to various local dignitaries. We began, evidently by careful design, with a gentleman who lived on the outskirts of the little town in a street which I was told belonged exclusively to him and his family. The street comprised about four houses either side. A good many children were running about. I was intrigued to notice they were of different colours from near white to very black.

We came to Senhor Karel Pott's house at the end of the street. He was

48. Charlie — Fitzwilliam Team Event, 1983 (see Ch. 17).

49. Charlie — Fitzwilliam Point to Point, 1984.

50. Charlie surveys the opposition.

51. Charlie — bronze by the author.

52. Milton (see Ch. 18).

53. The Thatchers at Milton, July, 1994. With the Bishop of Peterborough, Lord Renton, Lord and Lady Westbury, Lizzie Anne and the author.

sitting on the stoep and rose to greet us. He was large, black, of impressive mien and beaming his welcome. He addressed me in good French.

"How is Lord Exeter?" he said. I was stumped. I didn't know Lord Exeter. Later, as it happened, David Exeter became a good friend and neighbour in Cambridgeshire, but that was many years away.

So far as I knew his lordship was well, I thought. Was he a close friend?

"*Mais bien sur*," replied my host. "He won the Gold in the four hundred metres hurdles at the Amsterdam Olympics in '32. I got the Silver." He was full of good talk and I enjoyed my visit immensely. Later I was impressed to learn that not only did the houses in the little street belong to him but all the children as well. What a splendid stud of potential athletes the Portuguese had to call on in Quelimane.

I spent several days in Lourenço Marques (Maputo), a merry place then with little sign of disaffection or rebellion. This was soon to come.

Thence I journeyed up the coast as far as the Isla da Mozambique, a strip of Africa perhaps three miles long and no more than a few hundred yards broad at its widest point, lying a mile offshore and connected by a long bridge to the mainland.

In the southern tip and for a mile or so to the north lived the Makua people. Their narrow streets and wattle huts were dug down below sea level to shelter them from wind and weather. Shiny black with open friendly faces, the women swathed in bright cotton with coloured scarves about their heads swayed provocatively past. Everywhere there were smiles and the muffled beat of drums.

A mile to the north the Makua dwellings shaded off into the Arab quarter, pale faces from the Gulf, the men in galabiehs with their tarbush or cap wound about with a bandanna, their expressions grave and speculative.

When the Portuguese ships first put in to this natural harbour the island and hinterland lay under the sway of the Arab slaver Moussa ben Bekka, hence the name of the province. This was one of the busiest slaving ports and a string of forts connected it and other harbours to the mysterious city of Zimbabwe whose sinister ruinous walls surely bear witness to a terrible trade. Here on Moussa ben Bekka's island lived the descendants, one must suppose, of the traders and their victims. I felt happier among the Makua.

Further north appeared the houses of the Portuguese administrators and a charming small bungalow hotel where I stayed. One walked straight from the front door on to the beach. There were lobsters cooked on a charcoal fire with hot piri piri sauce, and all night long the breeze from the Indian Ocean whispered and sang in the tamarisk trees.

On the rock-strewn northern tip of the island stood a great fortress, its curtain walls some twenty-five feet high and five feet thick. At each embrasure stood an ancient cannon or culverin, the ball shot still stacked ready to hand. One entered below the teeth of a heavy portcullis and above the gate in tall engraved lettering was the legend "Vasco da Gama 1498".

This had been the great adventurer's last port of call before he set off across the Indian Ocean into the unknown. Here his carracks had anchored and victualled before making passage to and from Goa – and here a somewhat sleepy Portuguese garrison still lived.

Not for the first time I felt awe at the achievements of these wandering seafarers in their tiny ships, despatched by Henry, their strange navigator prince, from the rocky promontory at the foot of Europe, to brave the greatest oceans in the world and leave their mark at every distant landfall round the coasts of the African continent and from China to the Americas. It was a century or more before any other nation ventured after them.

But seamen they were, neither soldiers nor administrators, at least to judge from my short stay. I was allowed to visit their military base at Nampula and to accompany a patrol. The Frelimo communist guerrillas already infested the bush in Tete and Mozambique and there were reports of a Cuban presence. Portuguese army tactics, drill and general demeanour gave me little confidence, in spite of brave stories of their success against the terrorists. Nothing much had been done to improve communications, housing or schools during their centuries-long sojourn and it proved easy for the infiltrators to establish themselves among the tribes. Ken Flower describes an exchange between General Costa Gomes, the Portuguese Commander, and his ADC after Gomes had seen something of the Rhodesian Army in the Zambezi valley. "But do the Rhodesians really expect us to follow their example, living like animals in the African bush merely to confront guerrillas?" His ADC replied, "No, senhor, it is a quite magnificent example and it suits the Rhodesians who are Anglo-Saxons but they don't really expect that sort of behaviour from us Latins."

There was an air of detachment among the Portuguese. The pomp and circumstance of the Governor General's reception in Luanda, where next I called, seemed of another age. It was as though such rituals were by themselves enough to maintain the empire and to hold history at bay. Full of foreboding I left Angola via the enchanting Benguela Railway, another experience from the past.

Indeed it was not long before the Portuguese nerve broke. In April, 1974, their President, Caetano, was replaced as head of state in a coup by Generals Spinola, Costa Gomes and others. In fact Spinola was in the hands of a number of junior officers of the "*Movimento des Forcas Armadas*" who had had enough of the war in Africa and were ready for peace at almost any price. The Frelimo and Zanla guerrillas were steadily gaining ground and

Portuguese troops were withdrawn after the coup from the border areas. Negotiations with Frelimo were soon initiated in Lusaka. A final half-hearted conspiracy by certain Portuguese officers in Mozambique aimed at rejection of the Lusaka agreement and a more gradual approach to independence failed in 1974. By June, 1975, full independence followed and with it the steady infiltration of thousands of communist-trained guerrillas across the Zambezi, from their bases in Mozambique into Rhodesia.

But however mismanaged the Portuguese withdrawal from Africa may have been, it was surely a model operation compared to what had taken place in the Congo. Almost without warning at midnight on 30 June, 1960, this vast territory was declared an independent republic by the Belgian Government and all power handed to African Nationalist leaders of whom Kasavubu, Lumumba, Mobutu and Tshombe rapidly became household names. Within days the whole apparatus of government collapsed. The Force Publique mutinied, killed their white officers and embarked on an orgy of looting and rapine. The Europeans fled in their thousands either over the Congo River to Brazzaville or to the Federation. About six thousand were rescued by the Royal Rhodesian Air Force.

The Belgians flew in paratroops and a fearful row broke out at the United Nations. The only man to make any attempt to restore order was Moise Tshombe, president of the provisional government of Katanga province, bordering Northern Rhodesia. On 10 July he appealed to Britain and the Federation to send in troops to help him. On the next day he declared Katanga independent.

Meanwhile the Security Council had decided on massive intervention. The British Government, anxious as usual to placate the Afro-Asian block and to keep in step with the United States, declined to help Tshombe and asked Welensky's advice on recognition. Roy Welensky advanced convincing arguments in favour, based on his exact knowledge of what was happening in the Congo, of the threat of further instability and Communist penetration. The British Government temporized.

The UN presence grew rapidly and with it the appalling muddle it induced. Tshombe built up his own strength, worked hard to secure some sort of *modus vivendi* with Leopoldville and at least succeeded in maintaining law and order through 1960 and into 1961. He was no puppet and subsequent events proved beyond doubt that he had a loyal and powerful following in Katanga.

Born in 1919 of a wealthy family, Moise Tshombe had failed as a businessman. He turned to politics in 1950, eventually becoming president of the *Conféderation des Associations Tribales du Katanga*, an African political grouping.

At the conference so hastily convened in Brussels to discuss provisions for independence, he and others had argued for a loose confederation. Their proposals were rejected in favour of Patrice Lumumba's demand for a centralized state. It was a bad judgement and much evil flowed from it, including Tshombe's temporary detention and ill treatment in Leopoldville. Lumumba was a pathologically unstable character who never succeeded in establishing full authority even in Leopoldville. At the end of November President Kasavubu ordered Lumumba's arrest. He was brutally treated by his Congolese guards and transferred by air to Elisabethville on 17 January, 1961, accompanied by a Congolese National Army guard. Tshombe had no warning of this and had previously refused to have him in Katanga. On arrival he was hustled away by car to a house on the outskirts of Elisabethville with two of his companions. All three were murdered. Whether Tshombe knew what was afoot or not may never be known, but certainly the deed was carried out by what passed for the authorities in Leopoldville.

Outrage at the United Nations. The Security Council passed a resolution calling for the withdrawal from the Congo of all Belgian and other European military and political advisers and mercenary officers and a second authorizing an armed force to proceed to Katanga "in order to prevent civil war", of which contingency there was little serious risk.

Meantime the UN officials in Leopoldville stepped up the pressure on Tshombe to implement their resolution and demanded the expulsion of all his European advisers. On 29 May, 1961, Doctor Conor Cruise O'Brien arrived in Elisabethville as the UN representative in Katanga. The build up of UN forces in the province continued apace. By August there was an Irish and a Swedish battalion and at least a brigade of Indian troops supported by field guns and armour.

On 28 August the UN launched their first attack on the Katangese. The aim seemed to be the occupation of key points in the town and the arrest of all Europeans still serving Tshombe. The Katanga gendarmerie were instructed to surrender and all consulates to hand over any nationals who sought refuge with them. UN patrols appeared in the streets firing indiscriminately at Europeans or Katangese alike. The Katangese gendarmerie held firm and little was achieved by the UN.

A second attack was carried out on 13 September aimed at capturing key points and this time arresting members of the Katangan Government. O'Brien was quite certainly responsible, though whether the UN authorities in New York knew about it is uncertain. The United Nations troops behaved with inexcusable brutality. The gendarmerie resisted fiercely. For instance it took two companies about four hours to capture the post office which was manned by only forty Katangese without a single European officer among them. When they finally surrendered they were shot. A crowd had gathered in the street and they saw the last prisoner, a Katangese gendarme with his hands above his head, prodded at bayonet point until he fell from the roof to his death. Cries of "murderers" were followed by a volley from the UN Gurkhas on the roof. Several civilians were killed. This was only one of a number of carefully attested atrocities for which the United Nations were indisputably responsible.

An uncertain ceasefire was gradually established. It was after these first attacks and before the final UN onslaught that I arrived in Katanga.

Roy Welensky had arranged for me to be flown up to a landing strip in Northern Rhodesia just south of the border where I was to be met by a guide. My entry was, so to speak, informal, no passport necessary. We simply walked through the bush into the outskirts of Elisabethville and thence by a circuitous route to the British Consulate. My guide seemed wary of meeting anybody. The place was pretty deserted. Every now and then the silence was broken by distant rifle shots and once by the chatter of a light machine gun. The town, or what I saw of it in the European sector, comprised modern buildings and villas spread about like a garden city. Clearly it had been a prosperous place. The Consulate was a modest suburban house not far from the Belgian Governor's former residence, now occupied by Tshombe and his retinue. The Consul, Mr Dunnett, was kindness itself. He was well informed, in close touch with Tshombe and in receipt of what seemed to me ridiculously conflicting and unrealistic instructions from the Foreign Office. He clearly thought so too but was too loyal and discreet to complain about it. What he told me of the position in Elisabethville confirmed everything I had learned in Salisbury and worse.

There was no doubt the UN force was intent on destroying Tshombe. Dunnett testified to the solid support enjoyed by Tshombe and the bravery of the Katangese gendarmerie. The resistance they had put up against the UN could not possibly be explained by the presence of a few Belgian officers.

I asked whether I could get access to Tshombe. Certainly. The Consul knew how to get into the residence and would send a guide. But caution was advised. The UN patrols were apt to open fire on anyone without challenge. A number of totally harmless Belgians as well as Katangese had been mown down. We crept cautiously around several corners up to the imposing gate of the residence. My guide explained to a sentry who took me straight into the hall. Two or three Katangan soldiers looked morosely at me and I was ushered into a long and imposing drawing room at the far end of which sat half a dozen Africans. A tall figure detached itself and walked towards me. It was Tshombe.

He greeted me in impeccable French, introduced his Cabinet or Chiefs of

Staff, apologized for the lack of anything appropriate to offer me. The champagne, alas, was finished. Supplies were difficult "*à cause de cette guerre d'ONU*". He shrugged his shoulders and smiled. I asked him about the current state of affairs. He said he only wished he could enlighten me. He had been attacked without warning. Destruction in the town was serious. He had tried to negotiate with "Monsieur O'Brien" but his initiatives had either been rebuffed or ignored. His only wish was to establish acceptable conditions for the end of secession so that life could return to normal. But the UN authorities seemed determined to prevent him getting in touch with Kasavubu, the State President.

I was immensely impressed with Tshombe. Here was a man under appalling strain and personal threat. He had already been arrested once and held under cruel conditions for weeks in Leopoldville during which time an attempt had allegedly been made to poison him. Now in the middle of his own province, threatened with house arrest, his security forces under sporadic attack, he was unable to negotiate with the command of an international force manifestly out of proper control, and was prevented from any regular contact with his friends outside Katanga. So far as I could see he had no means of communication with the outside world except a tenuous link to the Federal Government and another to the British Consul. Yet his manners remained impeccable, his calmness, self-control and sense of humour unimpaired. He made an unforgettable figure. Months later I heard him address a packed committee room in the House of Lords. He spoke in faultless French and held his audience, comprising members of both houses, effortlessly, indeed dominantly.

I have no doubt Tshombe was as wily and perhaps as ruthless as some of his rivals in the Congo; indeed he would have needed to be to survive as long as he did. But here was a highly intelligent and civilized African leader, prepared to reason, able and willing to overcome all the prejudices of race on both sides of the colour barrier and anxious to collaborate with Europeans. He was, in short, exactly the sort of figure so desperately needed by this so-called world authority to help ease the fearful transition into which his country had been thrown. Instead they destroyed him.

After Tshombe I was determined to meet Dr Conor Cruise O'Brien. This proved more difficult to arrange. The UN headquarters staff proved both obtuse and evasive. Who was I? What did I want? What authority did I have? Dr O'Brien was very busy. Finally I got through to O'Brien's office and told his staff officer that unless I was granted an interview I would have to tell the House of Commons that, while I had been treated with the greatest courtesy by Tshombe, the reverse was true of the United Nations representative and that in my view his forces were out of control. A date was fixed for the next day.

While this negotiation was proceeding I decided to have a look at what was happening in and around Elisabethville. The Consul had a jeep and accompanied me. I had no idea just how accurate my assumption about the UN forces would prove to be.

We came on an Irish battalion more or less dug in among their vehicles in an open space in what seemed to be the suburbs. A mortar crew was sporadically shelling a row of houses about a quarter of a mile away. The fall of shot seemed haphazard. There was no movement I could see among the houses. We found an Irish major. I tried to explain who I was and asked if he could tell me what his unit was doing. He produced a map and showed me where he thought he was.

"We're guard'n this sector," he said, indicating the surrounding area. Bang! went the mortar some thirty yards from us.

"Who are you shooting at," I asked. There was a longish pause. The major gazed vaguely at the line of houses.

"Sure I don't know who they are but they've bin shoot'n at us." This seemed to sum up the tactical situation as far as he was concerned, nor was he anxious to pursue the matter further. We left him and moved on.

Near the middle of town was a large open space. It looked to be about a mile across. It was literally teeming with Africans. Makeshift tents and flimsy shelters abounded. Smoke from a number of small fires rose lazily into the heavy still air. It was very hot. The people seemed desperately poor. Most were dressed in rags. They eyed us with a mixture of fear and hatred.

"I don't think we should go any further," said Dunnett.

"Who are they?"

"These are the Baluba. They are tribal rivals of the Lunda, Tshombe's people. Somehow they got the idea they were going to be massacred. The UN told them to move in here where they would be under United Nations protection. They are near starving. Nobody has given them enough to eat and they are said to have turned cannibal."

"Were they going to be massacred?" I asked.

"I don't think so," said my friend. "It was probably a panic. Nobody knows what to do next here."

"What about the UN protection?"

"They are over there."

We were near what looked like a command post. It was manned by a Swedish detachment. Their battalion lay in a defensive position, well dug-in, with their machine guns pointing into the middle of this mass of resentful and suffering humanity. Their positions were manned day and night. So much for the protection of the UN. It seemed a toss up who would massacre the poor Baluba first.

Next day I finally got to the UN headquarters in the Avenue Fromont, a high-rise block near the city centre. It was heavily guarded. I was shown into an open plan office full of typists. Eventually Dr Conor Cruise O'Brien appeared.

Since meeting him I have admired much of what Dr O'Brien has written. His articles in *The Times* and elsewhere have repeatedly struck a note of perceptive realism on politics and foreign affairs and for that all sensible people should be grateful. Roy Welensky, who clearly found him difficult, believed he was motivated by hatred of the British Empire and of the Conservative Party. I am bound to say his writings scarcely bear this out. But equally I admit that my only meeting with him in Katanga was both short and, from my point of view, unsatisfactory.

A tall, pale, slim figure, he seemed resentful that he should have had to grant me an interview. In reply to my questions he had no acceptable explanation of the role of his UN force. He referred to Tshombe in pejorative terms. He claimed the Baluba had been saved by the UN and were now in good hands. The Irish battalion knew quite well what they were supposed to be doing. He looked at his watch.

I learned later that he was already contemplating the final assault on Tshombe's forces and a complete take-over of Katanga. This would undoubtedly have inhibited him from talking frankly. Nevertheless the impression I took away was of a man in a high state of nervous uncertainty struggling with a responsibility he was quite unfit to discharge. He was not a soldier; he was not an administrator; he was not a policeman; he had no direct political experience I knew of. He was simply a highly intelligent academic and, of course, a protégé of the Secretary General. Hammarskjöld had insisted on his appointment, and here he was dealing out death and destruction in the name of a world assembly which had been set up, so I believed, to preserve peace.

I flew out of Katanga full of apprehension. When I got home I did my best to explain about my experiences and conclusions to the Conservative Foreign Affairs Committee. I think it caused quite a stir. There was plenty of suspicion to build on. Shortly afterwards, Alec Home, then Foreign Secretary, accepted an invitation to meet the Committee. Our doubts about the conduct of the UN and the treatment of the federation were given a forceful airing.

Alec Home looked worried. Most of us will have thought he understood and indeed had much sympathy with our views, that he saw the danger ahead, but nothing changed. The Macmillan government clung to the American connection and apparently did not dare upset the Afro-Asian block. A few warnings were doubtless covertly conveyed. They had little if any effect.

Tshombe later came to London where he made what I have described as a lucid and effective appeal for help. The effect on his audience was considerable, the practical result negligible.

The situation dragged on until December. On the 5th a strong column of armoured cars and troop carriers left the UN headquarters and barracks to attack a Katanga-held road block. Fierce fighting ensued. The Katangese gendarmes launched a counter-attack on the UN headquarters. Swedish and Indian Canberras strafed the airfield at Kolwezi. This was outright war. Again it failed. Tshombe's government survived for a few more weeks, but on 28 December a final attack with massive force was launched. After two days organized resistance collapsed. Tshombe escaped to Northern Rhodesia and announced that Katanga would fight on. And indeed they did for several years from guerrilla bases in Angola.

Tshombe eventually escaped to Spain whence he was kidnapped in 1967 and brought to Algiers. Repeated attempts were made by Mobutu to have him extradited and tried in Leopoldville. He died in Algiers under house arrest; they said it was a heart attack.

Of all the traumatic and disgraceful episodes in the process of African independence, Katanga was surely among the worst. Tshombe's tragedy and the fate of the Central African Federation effectively closed the door on any attempt at genuine power-sharing and partnership between the races.

On my way home from the Congo I made two interesting stops, the first at Brazzaville, capital of the ex-French Congo named after the intrepid Italo-French explorer Pierre Brazza de Savorgnan, rival of both Stanley and King Leopold during the struggle for the Congo.

President of the Congo Brazzaville at the time was the Abbé Youlu. Our ambassador arranged a precise time for my interview with him. I think it was eleven o'clock. The waiting room or rather waiting space appeared to be a farmyard. We sat on a wooden bench. Chickens picked and clucked about, a goat came and inspected us, its yellow eyes full of mad suspicion. The ambassador kept looking at his watch and apologizing. Poor man, he was used to the European circuit where such delays virtually rated an international incident. I said I understood how it was in Africa. At a quarter to twelve a smiling official in an galabieh bowed and ushered us into what had been the French governor's office, where he left us, still smiling, without a word. Nothing continued to happen.

After another twenty minutes' clock-watching, a door burst open and the prelate appeared. His entry took one's breath away, not simply because of its dramatic suddenness but because of his equally dramatic appearance. The abbé was short and nearly spherical. His face shone like long-matured and varnished teak. He wore a little embroidered cap, but the full glory of his presence lay in his soutane. It was of shimmering brocade from neck to floor. We were introduced. He rustled behind his enormous desk and sat there silently smiling.

My attempts at a serious political discussion were not successful. His answers to my questions were elliptical. He never stopped smiling. It seemed all was well in the Congo Brazzaville. How could it be otherwise under the care of this saintly and effulgent personage?

Defeated, I thought I would try another tack. I told him how much I admired his soutane. The smile stretched even further. "*Cela vous plaît? Eh oui,*" he said glancing coyly down. "*C'est par Dior*".

This seemed to clinch good relations and we withdrew. The ambassador still looked deeply disapproving. I did not envy him his post.

Further on the flight home I spent two nights in Lagos where Anthony Head, then High Commissioner, kindly put me up. There was a grand dinner party attended by several Nigerians of importance. Talk was flowing freely when someone asked what countries I had visited. "Rhodesia," I said. A silence like the pall of doom fell upon the guests; knives and forks clattered reproachfully. Explanations seemed superfluous; the word itself was enough. I tried the Abbé Youlu; that didn't do me any good either.

Next evening I made excuses and went off into the town, still prosperous and humming with activity. I picked up with a party of young Nigerians in a bar. They exuded the sort of uninhibited friendliness that I think only black people are capable of. We spent one of the merriest nights I can remember together. It was a real wrench to say goodbye.

My only other memory was of the market: the streets and alleyways full of bustling women shoppers dressed in bright colours, baskets on their heads. When a woman carries a basket on her head she holds her body straight and proud above the waist; below everything else sways and undulates in compensation. The scene was one of bright, uninhibited, billowing sexuality enhanced by many smiling, challenging, unselfconscious glances. I would have liked to stay longer, even though I had visited Rhodesia.

———|———

15

U.D.I.

Of course it need never and should never have happened.

I called on Lord Malvern once in his office in Salisbury before the dissolution of the Federation. "The trouble is," he said, "these people [Whitehead, Welensky and the Federals] don't know how to deal with the British. You never want to waste time arguing with them. Whitehall does not understand this country, never did and never will. It is best to agree with them and then proceed to do what you think best." As a formula it had been well tested since 1923 but by now it was too late. For the new men ruling Rhodesia escape from the toils of Whitehall had become an obsession, independence an irresistible challenge.

The possibility was clearly in the minds of Macmillan and his cabinet at this juncture. By denying independence to the Rhodesians they took a calculated gamble and lost. Winston Field resigned in April, 1964, to be succeeded by Ian Smith. You can argue that Smith was mistaken, but the position of the moderate Rhodesian leaders had been destroyed. By their repeated retreats and deception the British Government had created a mood of desperation and total mistrust. U.D.I was the result and the hysterical accusations of disloyalty with which it was greeted by the Wilson Government, and indeed though in more moderate terms by the Conservative official opposition, seemed to me as hypocritical as they were unjust.

I listened to Ian Smith's broadcast declaration over the radio at the Salisburys' house in Swan Walk, surrounded by the Cecil family whose commitment and service to Rhodesia needs no emphasis. It was an unreal and emotional moment. How could matters have been brought to such a point? Conditioned as we all were by years of what we saw as a progressive deception of the Rhodesians, there was no question where loyalty and duty lay so far as we were concerned.

We may have felt some sense of foreboding but we could not foresee what bitter tragedy would strike the family in the cause of Rhodesia's defence.

Next day in the House of Commons Harold Wilson, the perpetual actor, making great show of loyalty to Queen and Commonwealth, produced his sanctions policy with a flourish of would-be Churchillian aggression. Gasps of liberal horror were followed by solemn statements at the dispatch box, and then, upstairs, by a subdued meeting of the 1922 Committee.

What Ian Smith had done was indisputably illegal. It was a repudiation of the authority of the Crown and this understandably worried the colleagues. Moreover, there was a somewhat awestruck reaction to the Wilson sanctions proposals. Was Rhodesia about to be destroyed? How was Smithy to be turned back?

It was at this point that several of us stepped out of line. A glance at the map of Africa should have been enough to convince anyone, even if he had never been there, that sanctions could not conceivably work. Rhodesia was surrounded by friendly European controlled territory. Ports, communications and supply routes were available to her as before; there was not the faintest chance of either South Africa or the Portuguese territories supporting sanctions. British imports would very soon be replaced either from South Africa, by smuggling, or from internal resources, and so of course it proved.

Some of us pointed this out as forcefully as we could both in committee and on the floor of the House. We were not popular. The Conservative opposition supported Wilson uneasily but nevertheless officially. Meanwhile the activities of what became known as the Rhodesia Lobby grew apace: meetings all over the country, car stickers, a sustained and furious debate in the press, much turmoil in the Conservative ranks. Great rallies were held in London, one at Central Hall, Westminster, another at the Albert Hall. I was asked to make the closing speech at both. Emotions were in overdrive and I must admit the meetings were a stimulating experience.

At Central Hall a large mob from the CND did their best to wreck the proceedings. We saw them off. They trooped out stamping and shouting but nevertheless eliminated. No formal check was made but I guess we had over three thousand in the Albert Hall. There were too many speeches and I was getting increasingly apprehensive about my own chances as they droned on. Inexplicable disagreements began to break out between different factions in the body of the hall. What they were about I never learnt, but at one stage they produced one of the most cowardly and astonishing physical assaults I have ever witnessed. There was an interval between speeches. A man with a fanatical expression advanced on the platform. Whether he intended to speak, to congratulate us or to attack us I shall never know, but when he was no more than ten paces away a rival of some kind felled him from behind with a mighty right to the back of his head. His assailant then shot off down one of the subterranean gangways and disappeared. The victim presently staggered to his feet, looked about him in utter bewilderment, gave us all a sheepish grin and withdrew unsteadily whence he came.

At last it was my turn. I did manage to keep them quiet and got a standing ovation for it. Things calmed down and I received a charming letter afterwards from Dick Coleraine who had been in a box at the back with Lord Salisbury. It concluded, "Heath will never lead the Tory party; you could". Coming from a Conservative elder statesman and the son of a Conservative prime minister it was a note to treasure. But I must admit we were all a bit over the top that night.

One of our closest and most loyal allies during the Rhodesia debates was Reggie Paget (later Lord Paget), the Labour Member for Northampton. He knew Rhodesia well and made one of the more effective speeches at the Albert Hall. Later Reggie asked if I would address his constituents on the subject. I agreed. There can I suppose be few precedents. I arrived at the appointed hour to find the assembly room of a large school packed to bursting with Reggie's admirers and Labour supporters. I told them in truth that I was delighted to be able to take his place (he had some other engagement) and I do not think he would have disagreed with a word I said on his behalf. At least the reception I got was warm proof that support for Rhodesia was not confined to the Conservative ranks. The event even made the Peterborough column in the *Telegraph*. They said it did credit to both of us.

There followed the first Conservative conference after U.D.I. in 1964. The Tory management was understandably apprehensive. A number of us who opposed sanctions were called – Patrick Wall, Ronald Bell and others. My turn came. Feelings were running high. The time allotted was extremely short – five minutes or so. I had the unusual experience of orchestrating the applause. Cheering broke out at every pause. All realized that time was of the essence, so each time the cheering started I put up a hand. It stopped. I got through to a tumultuous reception and I felt at least that I had articulated the true feeling in the hall. The climate behind my back was glacial.

The managers of the Tory conference are skilled producers. I was never called to speak on Rhodesia again.

The sanctions policy proceeded to fail as predicted.

The Rhodesians proved themselves more than a match for world authority or, in plainer terms, for the CRO and the Foreign Office whose denizens pursued their futile campaign with a bitter zeal which went much further than the dutiful detachment for which senior foreign office officials are normally and respectfully known. I found this astonishing. It was impossible to talk rationally with them. Their hatred and resentment of the Rhodesians and their friends was palpable. And all this unnatural and unattractive emotion stemmed, one must suppose, from a determination to bolster their delusions about the Commonwealth.

South Africa had no option but to permit widespread sanctions-busting. The Portuguese, as Ken Flower, head of Rhodesian Intelligence, put it in his excellent book*, had both an ideological and a commercial interest in flouting sanctions, and Zambia, like it or not, had to do the same or perish. At the height of sanctions goods trains continued to roll past the frontier at Victoria carrying copper from Zambia and Zaire and returning with food, coke and explosives vital for their mining operations, while the Zambian economy would have collapsed without Kariba power.

No better example of the futility of international sanctions could be presented than that of the two existing superpowers. An intense competition arose between the United States and Russia to procure Rhodesian chromite. Both had of course signed the sanctions resolutions. The United States subsequently amended their Strategic Minerals Acts in January, 1972, to legalize the purchase of chromite from Rhodesia rather than have to buy it at a higher price from the Russians or accept an inferior Russian product. "And," wrote Ken Flower, "when the Mozambiquan border closure in 1976 finally stopped the export of chromite through Lourenço Marques a considerable stockpile was promptly paid for by Russian agents and clandestinely removed in Russian bottoms."

When ministers and those in a position to influence them lose their sense of the anatomy of power they threaten disaster. Those senior officials who must have advised Harold Wilson that he could safely tell the House of Commons that sanctions would bring Rhodesia to her knees "in weeks rather than months" were in precisely that category.

There followed a series of tragic missed opportunities on both sides.

I believe Harold Wilson genuinely did his best to reach a solution. The negotiation on *Tiger* initially succeeded, and only collapsed when both principals had to confront their colleagues. Ian Smith made no serious attempt to carry his cabinet. The majority was probably in favour of acceptance, but the vote was swayed, principally by Clifford Dupont, an intelligent though bitter little English lawyer and a latter-day settler, whose influence over the course of events was, I suspect, generally unhelpful. Wilson, on his side, was probably overborne by the ideologues in his Cabinet.

By this time it must be said the Rhodesians probably believed their successful defeat of sanctions precluded any need to compromise further. Moreover the operations of the small Rhodesian security forces were completely and impressively successful demonstrating how right Roy Welen-

* *Serving Secretly.*

sky had been when he advised Sandys that "with firmness" the Federation could have been held together.

Two years after the meeting on HMS *Tiger* Harold Wilson, like others in trouble both before and after him, sought the help of Arnold Goodman. Would he go to Rhodesia and see Ian Smith secretly to discover whether there was any basis for renewing negotiations?

In his fascinating memoirs Lord Goodman sets out the tragic story of what could have been achieved and yet failed, due to the bigoted opposition of the British left, of the Labour leadership and to the inexcusable incompetence of the Foreign and Commonwealth Relations Office.

Between 1968 and 1971 Arnold Goodman visited Rhodesia repeatedly at the behest first of Wilson and then of Ted Heath.

He got on well with Ian Smith whom he plainly regards as a man of integrity, even if he could not accept Smith's antipathy towards black rule. (Smith, incidentally, stated publicly that Arnold Goodman was the only person involved on the British side throughout the negotiations whom he could trust.)

The package originally brought back by Goodman together with Max Aitken, who accompanied him because he had been a friend of Ian's in the RAF, led to the talks aboard HMS *Fearless*. They broke down almost certainly because of the refusal of the Labour cabinet to allow Goodman, of whom they were jealous and mistrustful, to accompany the team.

In 1970 Rhodesia was declared a Republic with the incongruous Dupont appointed titular head as "Officer administering the Government".

After the Conservatives came to power, Arnold Goodman again agreed to seek a solution. He paid four visits to Rhodesia in 1971 accompanied on the last occasion by Alec Douglas-Home, then Foreign Secretary. They produced what should have been a final breakthrough.

The agreement was based on five principles of which the most important was unimpeded progress towards majority rule. The proposed constitution was inevitably complicated, but in Lord Goodman's view, which I certainly share, it would probably have led in time to a division of the European electorate, to an alliance of some kind between white and black electors and thus to shared power. Now the tribal African may not understand the subtle and to him incomprehensible intricacies of British democracy but he does understand power.

The last principle set out that the British government would need to be satisfied that the proposal for Independence was acceptable to the people of Rhodesia as a whole – and this opened the gates to all those on the British left who were determined to destroy the agreement.

If British ministers, once satisfied as they should have been, had possessed the determination to outface the opposition, if their Foreign Office advisers had made the slightest attempt to understand Africa and the Africans, then genuine partnership between the races might have flourished in Rhodesia and perhaps much further afield.

It was not to be. The government appointed the Pearce Commission to "test opinion". They returned convinced the Africans did not want the deal. No one had attempted to explain its advantages to them while the African extremists had certainly been busy. Lord Goodman was specifically forbidden by the Foreign Office to talk to the Africans and during the final phase of the negotiations they attached to him as an "expert" an official who had never even been to Rhodesia.

Lord Goodman sums up his view of the Foreign Office thus: "It would be unfair to say that I have formed a low view of the Foreign Office; rather I have formed the view that Foreign Office acticities have in some way become totally disconnected from the human race."

With the advent of the Callaghan Government Dr David Owen entered the scene. Together with some of my friends, I had one meeting with him at the Foreign Office. I had just returned from Rhodesia. However impressive Owen's subsequent political evolution, the combination of arrogance and ignorance with which he confronted the Rhodesian problem carried little hope of success. He eventually produced a ridiculous proposal for the transfer of power to Field Marshal Lord Carver, who was to be resident commissioner, while Smith was to relinquish power and preparations were to be made for a one man vote election. The proposition stood no chance and was not greatly helped by Carver's overbearing attitude in Salisbury.

By this time, after the Portuguese and Belgian collapse in Central Africa, and in default of any sign of deterrence from Britain or the Western Allies, the infiltration of Communist-trained African guerrillas had amounted to a flood. The nature of the veld and Rhodesia's vast frontiers made control impossible. The achievements of the Rhodesian Army were remarkable. Anti-terrorist operations were repeatedly successful against massive odds, but with every able-bodied man who could be spared, and many women, engaged in defence the strain on the Rhodesian economy was mounting.

Life on the farms I visited in the threatened districts became increasingly difficult. Each was in fact an armed fortress behind barbed wire and floodlights. No one ventured far after sunset. Once, on a coffee plantation in the Vumba hills belonging to my friend Mike Kealy, he, Richard Cecil and I were sitting over our drinks looking across a deep valley towards the Mozambique frontier when heavy firing broke out below us. Richard grabbed his Israeli sub-machine gun, clearly hoping for some action.

"Do put that thing away," said Mike who had commanded a battalion of the Devons. "It makes me nervous. It's only the farmers down there shooting at each other. They get like that whenever they've had their sundowners and hear noises in the night." Nevertheless one of the main infiltration routes from Portuguese territory passed close to Mike's farm and it was a miracle he was never molested.

It was soon after this that Richard went into action with a Rhodesian counter-terrorist unit and was killed, bright star in a dim firmament, snuffed out in a hail of Russian bullets. Mourned today as when he fell, full of romance, bravery and laughter, Richard's death seemed at the time to have a symbolic quality amid the sordid manoeuvring over Rhodesia's fate.

In September, 1976, Kissinger came and went. His apparent conversion of Ian Smith probably owed more to arm-twisting by Vorster, the South African Prime Minister, than to his own powers of diplomacy. Nevertheless, they did succeed in shifting the log jam. Smith announced his agreement to African majority rule after a two-year interim, a far less advantageous deal than he could have had earlier from Alec Home.

There followed the abortive Geneva Conference.

From 1973 to 1976 Smith conducted veiled and intermittent negotiations with some of the African leaders, particularly Sithole, N'Komo and Bishop Abel Musarewa, head of the African National Congress. Musarewa was once described by his ex-colleague Zvobgo who had defected to the Communists, in these terms: "I believe the Bishop is a man of courage and sincerity but remember he is not being schooled in the crucible of real nationalist politics. He is not able to speak with more than one voice. He is sincere in what he says." Zvobgo added, "The whites must be led down the garden path to the place of slaughter. Morality doesn't come into it." The first description certainly fitted my own impression of the Bishop; the second says a great deal about the nature of the insurgent movements.

Early in 1978 an internal agreement was finally reached and the brave little Bishop became the first black Prime Minister of Zimbabwe-Rhodesia. International reactions varied. American policy in Africa at this time was, to say the least, opaque. Owen and the Labour leadership refused to encourage the Musarewa government. The situation may not have been ideal, the risks still very great, but at the subsequent election Musarewa was supported by a sixty percent majority. The agreement represented an unprecedented advance and was welcomed by both Sir Alec Home and Lord Carrington in Parliament.

In view of what subsequently happened it is perhaps worth quoting what they said. Lord Carrington: "It must be said that there has been inadequate recognition of the remarkable achievement of the internal settlement and too much support for its opponents. If in the end the Patriotic Front (Mugabe and N'Komo) refuses to be associated with a settlement which is in accordance with the conditions laid down by both Conservative and Labour governments, if these two leaders insist upon force as the only means of settling the issue there is only one honourable course for the British Government to take and that is to support the internal settlement, however difficult that might be."

Sir Alec in the Commons: "In Rhodesia they are faced with a new prospect by Mr Smith's action which has dramatically reversed previous attitudes to African majority rule. Why are there hesitations and doubts? Dr Owen and Mr Young want to bring Mr N'komo into the settlement because that is the way most likely to end the war. In their view Salisbury should make the concessions to Mr N'komo and his army, and concessions to force and communism. The United Nations put the responsibility for the future of Rhodesia on the British Parliament. It is therefore Parliament's responsibility and no one else's and Russia should be told plainly that Britain will not tolerate intervention in a country for whose future the responsibility lies with her."

Both statements seemed entirely justified.

In May, 1979, the Callaghan Government fell and Mrs Thatcher appointed Lord Carrington to seek a final settlement. The Lancaster House Conference which followed was a triangular affair. In the centre sat the British, on the right Bishop Musarewa's Government, on the left the Patriotic Front led by Mugabe and N'komo. The result was a sad and complete reversal of the Conservative party policy as stated in opposition. Musarewa was abandoned. Christopher Soames was sent to Salisbury with the difficult task of overseeing a general election. When this took place, and in spite of assurances to the contrary and an attempt at supervision by British police and troops, the process degenerated into a competition in brutal intimidation. As N'komo said at the time, "A gun is worth any number of votes."

My friends and I did our best in London to advocate patience and support for the Bishop, to no avail. At one juncture Peter Carrington told Ken Flower, "I hope you're not being misled by those right wingers, Julian Amery, Steve Hastings and Co." Ken replied, "Not at all, they're only trying to be helpful, which is what I thought the Conservatives were meant to be over Rhodesia, and they've never failed to speak well of you – or of Mrs Thatcher – so there's nothing wrong with their loyalty and I'm astounded you should query their actions."

I do not blame Peter for his question. He was faced with an appalling problem and ours is an old friendship which can certainly withstand an occasional disagreement. But I was grateful to Ken Flower for his reply.

So the brave little Bishop resigned and Zimbabwe/Rhodesia was no more.

Of course the Rhodesia Front leaders were guilty of serious errors of judgement. But my conviction remains as strong today as it was then. It was the vacillation, indecision and unnecessary deference to the delusion of Commonwealth, to the Afro-Asian lobby and to the Americans, by a series of British governments from the inception of Federation to the Falls Conference which sowed the seed of the U.D.I. Rhodesia reaped the consequences, and much of the moral indignation to which we were treated in the House of Commons and by the Left in general over those years had for me a contemptibly hollow ring.

The fate of the Federation and ultimately of Rhodesia stemmed in large part from the muddled motives of the departments involved. The Colonial Office was generally devoted to the welfare of its dependant peoples and to the administration of justice. The achievements of its often isolated District Commissioners in Africa were beyond praise. They understood the African people, ruled with justice and firmness and remained true to their Imperial duty. The old Diplomatic Service, subsequently the Foreign Office, traditionally and consistently pursued what they saw as their country's interests. All this changed with the creation of the Commonwealth Relations Office, staffed by a random selection of officials, many of whom had neither the traditions nor the experience of either the Colonial or the Foreign Office. The subsequent amalgamation of the Foreign and Commonwealth Offices caused mounting confusion and finally blunted the whole thrust of our foreign policy.

Whatever the objectives of the Commonwealth may have been, and there is room for a good deal of guesswork, it is certain they did not necessarily or even generally coincide with the British interest. Had the British Government shown any consistent sign of knowing what it was up to with the Commonwealth a great deal of trouble might have been avoided. If they had decided to sink the national interest into some great and convincing supra-national entity based on the old Empire the intention at least would have been clear. But the Commonwealth related to no such thing. It had no common institutions other than the Commonwealth Office if you could so describe it, no constitution, no accepted system or standard of liberty and the law, no authority whatever except a nebulous acceptance of the Queen as "Head of the Commonwealth", whatever that might mean. In spite of the Queen's evident popularity and success as a social symbol, the Commonwealth possessed no common loyalty to anything or indeed anybody.

Rub out the sentiment which initially marked the striking of the Union Jack and the hoisting of some new multi-coloured flag of independence and the only explanation for this political aberration was the need to cover ourselves with some half-respectable blanket beneath which we could divest ourselves of our colonial responsibilities as soon as possible. But for the inhabitants of these colonies, particularly in Central Africa, there was much pain to come.

At the N'daba the people arrive at a communal decision. They approach it crab-wise, they inch towards it. The elders and the wise men have their say. Finally, as he must, the chief will express the view of all, but the decision once taken, to oppose is not only wrong it is dangerously immoral. So where is the place for Her Majesty's loyal opposition? No wonder the nationalist leaders to whom we ceded powers had little difficulty in establishing the one-party state.

If my analysis of African belief and tradition is anywhere near accurate it will be realized that what we regard as the foundations of liberty are in more than one respect not only alien but regarded as positively dangerous by the tribal African, the concept of property and the formal acceptance of opposition for instance.

The idea of a qualified democracy resting on the maintenance of liberty under the law might have worked, given the will to sustain it. The one certain way to invite chaos and suffering was to cede total democracy, one man one vote, before the conditions for its survival had been established.

I do not regret the stand my friends and I took over the years and I shall always wonder what might have been if the path of partnership so bravely undertaken had been allowed to evolve. Alas, such a course demanded more vision, courage and understanding than the successive British Ministers responsible were ever able to command.

———————|———————

16

PARLIAMENT

My political life started during a period of compulsive national retreat, presided over by clever and able men of good faith and intent, but, so far as I could see, little confidence in the future. It was a time of weariness, well expressed in the titles of the memoirs of two of the principal actors, R. A. Butler and Sir Alec Douglas-Home. Their respective books were called *The Art of the Possible* and *The Way the Wind Blows*. For me that sums it up.

I felt myself out of sympathy with this mood and I suppose my efforts on behalf of Rhodesia were in part born of reaction to it. Politics are often a matter of fashion and perhaps my views did not always accord with the trend, or at least with its interpretation, in the Whips' Office. But, for the fact that I never had the chance to achieve high office I really have no one to blame but myself. I was twice invited to become a Parliamentary Private Secretary and once to join Heath's Government. I refused on each occasion for what at the time seemed good reason, but what in retrospect I recognize as foolishness. The Rhodesian saga probably did not help, but politics is a lottery. Members of Parliament are there to stand by their judgement and it will be a sorry day for the system should they ever lose the habit.

I found the experience stimulating, often exciting, sometimes like everyone else frustrating. Towards the end of my twenty-three years' stint I confess I found the reflex routines of Parliamentary duty increasingly tedious, other interests beckoning. I happen to be scribbling this high up in the Andalusian hills. Behind me rise the bleached spines of the Sierra de Libar. History has swept back and forth across them since before the Roman legions. They carry the secrets of empires long gone, of the passage of armies and of battles whose din and trumpets echo no more. Time weeps here in Spain. The hopes, frustrations and occasional small triumphs of my momentary brush with history on the hoof seem insignificant to say the least. And I have no intention of trudging back through Hansard to prove any points now.

Public men are supposed to yearn for a lasting impression on the chronicle of their time. Perhaps my yearn was not strong enough. In any case few achieve it. I met only two who certainly will.

The first was Winston Churchill. One day as a new and relatively young Member I was deputed to escort him into and out of the chamber. His infirmity was advanced and this provision was essential. I had to walk across the bar by his side as far as his place on the front bench below the gangway, hand him his order paper and sit behind him. I think he was quite unclear about the business but gazed frequently round the chamber and mumbled occasionally to his neighbour. He did not stay long. He seemed unsteady as he rose to leave. I tried gently to take his arm, but was peremptorily shaken off. What touched me most as we regained the bar was the solicitude of the Labour Members on the Opposition bench. "He turns now; he wants to turn," they whispered to me, anxious lest I should frustrate his known routine.

Slowly he faced the table, the mace and the Speaker. He did not exactly bow as is the custom. His bent shoulders straightened a little and his old rheumy eyes fixed not on the Speaker but on the Chamber as a whole, as if he knew it might be the last time. Soon after that day, it was.

The second is Margaret Thatcher. History will certainly judge her to be great. They may argue that her achievement was some kind of aberration, a blip so to speak during a long period of national decline, a last flourish of the trumpet, or that it was the beginning of a return to the native courage and vigour, which down the centuries have so often astonished the world. It is too early to judge. We may have to plumb the depths again before we appreciate what she gave us. But that the spirit of a once great people stirred under her leadership, there is no doubt. The sight of her slight figure at the Despatch Box always smart, impeccable, enduringly female and attractive, facing this massive assembly of male ambition, often unruly and aggressive, is unforgettable, that she came to dominate it a matter for wonder. Who that heard or watched it can ever forget that last speech as Prime Minister?

My first serious business contact with her happened soon after she was elected leader. I had written something, or spoken in the House, not for the first time, about the subversive menace to this country presented by the Soviet Union and the Communist Party. The efforts of the KGB and its satellite services to manipulate the British left wing establishment and to use the Communist Party with its various front organizations to undermine the stability of the state, was at that time both penetrating and effective. A new threat – "the agent of influence" – was increasingly in evidence in the media and in broadly left wing circles.

Margaret asked me to prepare a report on security. I was given a small subvention from Central Office funds to cover incidental expenses. I collected a team comprising Nicholas Elliott, a retired senior officer and ex-colleague from the Secret Intelligence Service*, Harry Sporborg of Hambros, one of the principal architects and directors of the wartime Special Operations Executive (SOE), and Brian Crozier, an acknowledged authority on extreme left wing groups and personalities. We also had the invaluable help of Charles Elwell, an ex-member of the board of MI5 and a strong and constructive critic.

Crozier has since written a highly coloured and somewhat tendentious account of this initiative in a book about his achievements. But it was a serious exercise. The work took nearly a year. I began with a guide to historical materialism and an attempt to define how the Communist mind worked, for it is impossible to appreciate the diabolical nature of the Soviet Communist conspiracy without some idea of the twisted philosophy from which it was devised and practised.

My report sought to describe the enemy's resources and methods, followed by a review of our own security services, their strengths and weaknesses as we had known them. I handed it to Margaret's private secretary, Caroline Stephens, in December, 1978.† A week later Lizzie Anne and I were invited to one of the traditional Christmas parties given by the leader for Conservative Members and their wives. Margaret made her way through the throng.

"Stephen," she said, "I've read every word and I'm shattered. What should we do?"

Well, I had been asked to report, not to propose. "Perhaps you should appoint a committee," I said.

So a committee there was, comprising Willie Whitelaw, Peter Carrington, Keith Joseph, myself and, on occasion, my small team. After discussion of the paper, I was asked to suggest counter-measures. With some misgiving, because I was fairly sure that proposals of any kind from outsiders on this subject would be unwelcome in Whitehall, we did so.

With Harry's clear head to guide us, we produced an outline scheme for the formation of what could have been described as a Cold War equivalent of the SOE. We called it the Counter Subversion Executive (CSE). Further papers followed.

Peter was, I think, inclined to discount the extent of the threat, and probably saw our proposals as a potential challenge to the omnipotence of the Foreign Office. In the latter case he may well have been right.

What Willie thought I could not guess for he never said. Keith was

* Nicholas's book *With My Little Eye* contains several fascinating accounts of his work in SIS.
† Now Mrs Richard Ryder.

237

deeply interested and I know that Margaret herself took the matter very seriously.

But before we got much further Callaghan's Government fell in March, 1979, and this effectively put paid to the exercise. Most of our ideas were lost in the fever of electioneering and subsequently the impact of power. But I do believe the work served its purpose. Margaret had been fully alerted and now had a basis upon which to build her long campaign against Soviet and Communist subversion. I sometimes wonder whether our effectiveness against international terrorism and the IRA might not have benefited from something like the CSE.

The greatest challenge of Margaret's years in office was surely the Falklands War. She refers in her book to Enoch Powell's demanding assertion in the House at the outset of the campaign. He was referring to her "Iron Lady" label. "In the next week or two this House, the nation, and the Right Honourable Lady herself will learn of what metal she is made."

In the evening of 23 April we held a large rally at Shuttleworth Agricultural College in my constituency. Some five hundred people were seated at dinner in order to celebrate the fact that the seat had been held for fifty years by the Conservatives, during which long time there had been only two Members of Parliament, Alan Lennox-Boyd and myself, with over twenty years each. Margaret had agreed to speak. I was prepared for a message that, with the task force at sea, she would have to cut the date. To her great credit and my relief, she and Denis came. I quote again from her book. "That evening I had to speak at a large rally in Stephen Hastings' constituency in Bedfordshire. Stephen and his predecessor Alan Lennox-Boyd spoke magnificently. I was given a wonderful reception. No one present had any doubt of the justice of our cause nor that we would eventually win through. I felt proud and exhilarated, but I felt too an almost crushing burden of responsibility. I knew that the task force would enter the waters around the Falkland Islands the following day."

She and Denis stayed the night with us at Milton and a message arrived from Downing Street at breakfast next morning to announce the first successful attack on the airfield at Port Stanley.

In my speech I had slightly altered a passage on England by the American poet and staunch anglophile R. W. Emerson – "She sees a little better on a cloudy day, and, in storm, battle and calamity, she has a secret vigour and a pulse like a cannon".

The words seemed apt enough with this courageous and outwardly serene woman sitting beside me, upon whose slight shoulders rested at that moment the destiny of our ships and the lives of so many men. Her presence among us that evening was the act of a great captain, yet she found time to spend several minutes talking to the catering staff and to those who had waited upon us.

We knew then of what metal she was made.

There was a surge of support for Margaret during the campaign, although this was not always reflected in the media. One happening still lives with me. The disgraceful neutrality of the BBC had irritated many of us. Their commentators seemed to have set themselves up as international arbiters rather than supporters of their country. Finally George Howard, the Chairman, was invited to attend the Conservative Foreign Affairs and Defence Committee. He did so, together with several of his top people. I have never witnessed at any Commons committee such a roasting as they got from the Conservative Members present. I had my chance. Their attitude at the outset was one of truculent arrogance, but by the end they were, I think, deflated.

After the campaign was over the BBC commissioned Ian Curteis, a renowned scriptwriter, to undertake a drama for television based on the Falklands War. His achievement, *The Falklands Play*, was the result of deep and fascinating research. It was initially welcomed with enthusiasm by the then Director General, Alistair Milne, but was subsequently replaced by a pacifist travesty called *Tumbledown*, the whining story of a misguided young officer, and incidentally an insult to my own former battalion the 2nd Scots Guards who had captured Tumbledown Hill in a brave assault suffering a number of casulties. In spite of appeals by many responsible people, the BBC has repeatedly declined to restore the balance and put on what would unquestionably constitute an absorbing historical serial. If this was its revenge it cannot be denied that it does those concerned little credit.

Of course Margaret Thatcher made mistakes, but in the end she will be remembered across the world because, by her vision and courage, she broke through the suffocating bonds of a moribund yet almost universal social doctrine and rekindled the practice of liberty. Her name and her policies are invoked wherever men seek to reduce the state and restore the individual and so it will continue to be.

The picture, undoubtedly true, of Margaret sitting at her desk in Downing Street in tears, writing letters of condolence in her own hand to the families and wives of those who had been killed in the Falklands provides a true insight into her character. Iron Lady she may have seemed to her adversaries, but beneath the armour there is a warmth and sympathy for ordinary people which her superficial public image has effectively and unfairly concealed.

Historical figures apart, the outstanding parliamentarians were those who could fill the Chamber whenever they rose on the back benches. It is relatively easy from the Despatch Box. There were not many.

Enoch Powell of course, with his massive castles of logic steadily constructed rampart upon unassailable rampart, yet sometimes founded on some simple, instinctive, romantic conviction. Indeed it is this quality as much as his faultless oratory which endears and distinguishes Enoch.

"Hinch" (Lord Hinchingbrooke) sometime Member for Dorset South, was perhaps the last to speak with the style and resonance of the nineteenth century parliamentarian. I see him declaiming from his great height and measured stance before the front bench below the gangway, inclining with open disdain towards the hunched backs of Macmillan's ministers beside him. Referring repeatedly in terms of patrician contempt to "this *liberal* Conservative government", "Hinch" used dismissive sarcasm, without ever losing wit or dignity. The benches filled rapidly on either side when he was called.

Nigel Birch was another. (Member for West Flint, Nigel resigned as a treasury minister from the Macmillan Government together with Enoch Powell on a matter of principle in 1958.) Near blind towards the end, he would soon abandon his myopic attempt to follow his notes, and in low conversational tones, which nevertheless carried to every corner of the Chamber, he would present his argument as an act of clinical dissection. His was a truly mordant wit. I do not believe Macmillan ever recovered from Nigel's devastating attack delivered to a hushed house after the Prime Minister's attempt to salvage his waning authority by sacking half his cabinet – "We can not just have business as usual. I feel the time will come very soon when my Right Hon. friend ought to make way for a much younger colleague. I feel that ought to happen. I certainly will not quote at him the savage words of Cromwell, but perhaps some of Browning's words in his poem *The Lost Leader* might be appropriate:

> "Let him never come back to us!
> There would be doubt, hesitation and pain
> Forced praise on our part – the glimmer of twilight,
> Never glad confident morning again."

Never glad confident morning again!

Michael Foot, the involuntary radical, hopeless in authority, as loose a poltical thinker as he is ostentatiously untidy in appearance, nevertheless held the house. His spontaneous torrents of emotion could be hilariously funny, effectively wounding yet often generous as well.

And it is surely this quality above all which marks the true parliamentarian. For through it he expresses the underlying spirit of the House of Commons. For all the cut and thrust, the boorishness, the heaving and overacting, this is a very human place. The House responds to humility, is quick to accept genuine apology, ready to forgive. Despite its size, it is an intimate place, and this reflects its shape, for try as many do, it is less easy to get away with humbug when you must face your opponents across the floor rather than mounted on a podium before some great impersonal semi-circular audience.

Apart from the Rhodesian saga my career on the back benches had its moments.

In 1969 came the drama of the third London airport. The civil servants had decided that Heathrow was bursting at the seams. Something had to be done. Their choice fell first on Stanstead, but, after a formidable resistance, the people of Essex saw them off. They returned to the attack, this time with four alternatives. They included Stanstead yet again, a site north of Bedford, the Vale of Aylesbury and the offshore site on the Maplin Sands at Foulness. All three inland sites bordered my constituency. I decided to oppose them.

The Labour Government set up a commission under Mr Justice Roskill to recommend a solution. He and his advisors deliberated long and deep, for two years in fact, during which they invented a tortuous system of calculation called a "methodology". That was menacing enough. Their methodology dealt in "benefits" and "dis-benefits". That was worse. Everything had a price, except the disappearance of 20 thousand acres of the countryside. Early in the Roskill deliberations there was a strong suspicion that the "benefits" of submerging the Vale of Aylesbury beneath the concrete would outweigh the dis-benefits, unless Foulness were chosen.

We formed a resistance movement. It had two separate arms. In Parliament I set up a committee of those members whose constituencies were threatened, mostly, though not all, Tories. Numbers swelled as we went along and we managed to rake in some early environmentalists. Desmond Fennell QC, then a busy barrister of the Inner Temple, who lived in the charming Buckinghamshire village of Winslow, scheduled to become a "dis-benefit", became Chairman of the Wing Airport Resistance Association (WARA) and handled the action in the field, so to speak, with immense skill and persistence. He and his associates constituted a formidable body. We worked closely together.

Our objective was in no sense negative. We did not dispute the need for this airport, though in retrospect perhaps we should have done. We held simply that this is a crowded island, the countryside under mounting pressure, particularly in the south-east. It was only sensible to put the dreaded thing off shore if this were practicable, and clearly it was. At Foulness only the whitefront geese seemed likely to suffer a "dis-benefit", and even they were more than likely to find suitable grazing elsewhere.

The officials in Whitehall still favoured Stanstead, but it seemed odds against Roskill returning to the same charge, methodology or no. The site north of Bedford was always an outsider. As the months went by and as rumour increasingly pointed to the Vale of Aylesbury, so the resistance flourished.

At the rough end was an admirable guerrilla force comprising local farmers and other militant rustics who would turn out at a hint on the telephone, armed with pitchforks and other suitable weapons to confront the media, swearing to die on the bulldozers, and take a civil servant with them. The media would report these dire threats to Desmond and me for comment. Of course – tut tut – this was none of our doing, but it did express the depth of local feeling, did it not?

At the height of the campaign Desmond received a telephone call from none other than Captain R. Maxwell, then Labour Member for Buckingham. He wished a meeting to discuss the campaign. Knowing the Captain's reputation, Desmond wisely took a high-powered delegation from the top echelon of the resistance movement with him.

They repaired as instructed to the headquarters of Pergamon Press in Fitzroy Place at the appointed hour. Maxwell was late. Beautiful secretaries brought tea and serial apologies. At length the great man appeared, announced that he had only fifteen minutes to spare before leaving for the airport, and then delivered what could only be described as an ultimatum. He was dissatisfied with the conduct of the campaign. None of "his people" was involved. Who was the President? Desmond told him this was David Robarts, Chairman of the National Westminster Bank, which, incidentally, was financing Maxwell's current attempt to buy the *News of the World*. Maxwell was unimpressed. The President, he said, should be someone with national prestige, "and I," he added with emphasis, "have enough prestige to sink a battleship".

Desmond and his colleagues were told to think this over, and that he had arranged for his political agent to pass on their answer. If they did not accept his proposition, he would proceed to take over their campaign and replace them. He then left in a flurry for Tokyo.

Desmond had never been spoken to in such fashion before. He rang me up. He claims that I remonstrated with him because his call came in the middle of the Cup Final. I must have overcome this lamentable lapse because I told him that if Maxwell were to be taken on board, every single Conservative member of my committee would resign. That seemed to clinch it.

Desmond then rang the Labour agent and announced himself, expecting a ready ear and a difficult time of it. "Who are you?" asked the agent. Desmond did his best to explain. "We support the airport," said the agent bluntly. "I think there must be some mistake," protested Desmond. "You'd better telephone Captain Maxwell in Japan". "I'm not going to telephone anybody for you," said the agent.

That ended the matter. Nothing more was ever heard from Maxwell.

There followed many rallies supported among other celebrities by Cleo Laine who sang songs of defiance with her husband Johnny Dankworth. We repeatedly demanded a debate in Parliament. The Labour Government refused.

Eventually the great Roskill report appeared at a cost of well over two million pounds to the taxpayer. It ran to inordinate length and duly recommended Wing near Aylesbury. Within an hour of publication we had a motion down on the order paper of the House of Commons, signed by nearly two hundred MPs refusing to accept Roskill and insisting on Foulness. The 1970 election intervened. The Tories were back. Apart from the merits of the case, the new government was not going to open its account against that sort of opposition. Foulness had it and the methodology was rolled up for ever.

The resistance movement had triumphed and a great celebration was held in Buckinghamshire. Bonfires were lit. Sir Colin Buchanan, a member of the Commission, who alone had written a dissenting report, turned up and was feted as a hero. Much good ale disappeared and Cleo Laine sang more songs.

The fact that Foulness was never constructed is another story. The civil servants quietly and surreptitiously extended Stanstead, which is what they had always intended to do.

To be a good constituency Member should be the pious ambition of every MP provided it doesn't interfere with independent judgement. It was not ever thus. In 1714 a group of Mr Anthony Henry's constituents wrote asking him to vote against the budget. He replied as follows:-

"I have received your letter about the excise and I am surprised at your insolence in writing to me at all. You know and I know that I bought this constituency. You know and I know that I am now determined to sell it, and you know what you think I don't know that you are looking for another buyer. I know what you certainly don't know that I have found another constituency to buy.

"About what you said about the excise may God's curse light on you all and may it make your homes as open and as free to the excise officers as your wives and daughters have always been to me while I have represented your rascally constituency."

Well, well! We are all geared to the market these days, so perhaps the Speaker's Conference should have another look at the system and privatize the franchise so to speak. The Treasury would be delighted and it might help to solve the de-selection problem.

My friends in the constituency stood by me through the long Rhodesian saga; they saw me through a sad divorce. For a long time my only home was at Southill Park near Biggleswade with Jane and Sam Whitbread, my Chairman for 8 years. As time went by the pressure of the election campaigns was eased by a feeling of belonging. However the argument and the dreaded polls developed, there was always a tour of old friends one saw all too seldom and visits to pubs where one was instantly welcome. Whatever the demands on time and patience, the surfeit of wine and cheese, the personal tragedies, the impotence I sometimes felt, there were nevertheless occasions when in small ways one could help.

But I would never have achieved much without the help of Pamela Fleming, my private secretary and minder for eighteen years. Together we faced countless "surgeries". It is an unattractive description. I tried to introduce the term "interviews" but it would not stick.

Grievances of every imaginable kind were deployed before us together with much good advice. If I got too entangled Pam had a genius for wrapping up the interview firmly with some authoritative assertion like "The last one of these we referred to the Minister for Sport". The supplicant soon got the message that he or she was no longer unique.

Pam kept close contact with Government departments. We had trouble over a factory outside Sandy which made glue from what was delicately called animal waste products. Doubtless the glue was useful but the smell was overpowering. When the wind was in the west half the town needed gas masks. We had to know the Department's policy. The Minister responsible at the DOE, David Howell, had just been appointed. Pam rang the private office to ask what he thought. "The Minister is new," came the reply. "We haven't yet told him what he thinks".

Some of our visitors were regulars. Whenever we held our sessions, never mind the time, they were there. Let us call him Mr Chesterton. Mr Chesterton had one overriding pleasure in life: to ride his motorbike through the countryside: "Not fast you understand, I have never been a danger to the public". But in order to get the full benefit from his excursions it was essential for him to wear a cloth cap. It was the natural headgear. It enabled the wind to play about his head. It made him feel free. Now, horror of horrors, the nanny state was going to introduce compulsory crash helmets. What was I going to do about it?

I wrote the Minister of Transport without much hope. Why should there be a compulsory rule? Why should not Mr Chesterton fall off and crack his skull if he was inclined to? I received solemn statistical replies. There seemed no escape for Mr Chesterton. I discovered that the Sikhs also objected strongly, but this was for religious reasons. The crash helmet would not fit over their turbans, or their hair, or it was impracticable to wrap a turban round a crash helmet. I suggested Mr Chesterton get in touch with them. I even hinted he might become one. But no, this would not accord with his principles. His case was different. Ministerial authority remained stonily adamant. In the end I had to tell him firmly that there was nothing to be done. But this in no way deterred Mr Chesterton. Back he came, in sorrow rather than in anger. He was always the soul of politeness. Finally he confessed to me that his conviction or obsession, however you chose to look at it, had become too much for his family; his wife and children had left him in exasperation or despair. Yet even this didn't stop him. He continued occasionally to recur, not, I think, because he harboured any hope, but because he felt we were vicarious fellow sufferers. If we had had a motorbike we would have felt the same as he.

In my last Parliament I used to bring Kenny, my labrador, with me. However indignant any visitor might be, Kenny was a match for him. He had a way of sidling up and sitting beside the visitor in the middle of the discussion, fixing him with his imploring brown eyes and then raising one foreleg in a sort of Hitler salute. I never saw this fail. He did it to me once at a large open air meeting at which I had to speak from a stage. I was making what I hoped was a serious speech when suddenly my audience dissolved into helpless giggles. So far as I knew I hadn't made a joke. I looked down. There was Kenny, who had somehow found his way onto the platform, paw in the air, apparently beseeching me to stop.

In my last years at Westminster much of the interest in parliamentary life evaporated. The catalyst was horses. I had long been a member of the Guards' Saddle Club and took to riding out from Knightsbridge Barracks in the morning and feeling much better as a result. The familiar smell of saddle soap, the creak of leather, the sound, feel and power of a horse beneath me did the trick. There is no antidote. What, I asked myself, had I been doing all those years?

Soon, thanks to the kindness of David and Caroline Keith, I was hunting regularly with the Quorn Hounds, returning tired out just in time to bathe and make the ten o'clock vote in the House of Commons.

One late evening after the debate I was sitting in Pratt's Club talking to Edward Boyle, one of the nicest men ever to hold high office.

"What are you up to, Steve?" he asked.

"I'm going back to foxhunting."

Surprisingly Edward didn't laugh. "You are not the first," he said.

"Probably more my scene now."

"I've always thought of you as an intellectual manqué," said Edward.

Perhaps he had a point. There can be no doubt about the "manqué". I thought back a little ruefully to my attempts at further education. But to what profit. Perhaps there is no irredeemable contradiction between intellect and horsemanship. What matters above all is to go on being interested.

"Have another drink," I said.

A friend in the Whips' Office told me one day that my name had cropped up at the regular Whips' meeting that morning. It was thought I might be useful for this or that forgotten purpose. Anyway where was Stephen Hastings? There was a pause. "Quorn Monday," said someone. There was general laughter. It was, I suppose, a sort of footnote to a political career of sorts. "But," said my friend, "it was not unkind laughter."

Anyone who has followed the Quorn from Parson's Thorns across the vale will understand my absence. Anyone who has spent as long as I did in the House of Commons would have been grateful for the kindness.

I left Parliament with a profound respect for the House of Commons. It is, for all its foibles and drawbacks, still the most civilized method yet devised for limiting the power of man over man.

Our curious constitution is a unique achievement and still the model for much that is good or at least full of hope in the world. But it is a brittle and sensitive construction, always endangered and in need of constant and watchful protection. It is threatened today and the threat is more subtle and menacing than most of us realize or are prepared to admit.

I was once asked to give a talk at Hatfield to the assembled Monday Club. This group came together as a spontaneous reaction to the Government's treatment of Rhodesia but grew rapidly into a medium for the expression of certain traditional strands of Conservative thought. At the time it was not without influence. I was trying to articulate a view of the proper use of power. What I said seems to me to have been borne out.

In this country – perhaps in the West as a whole – we have elevated "democracy" to the level of a religion. Nothing is supposed to work unless it is "democratically" organized. No authority is morally justifiable unless it is "democratic". We bow to this political icon without much thought, indeed we seek to encourage it, if not to impose it across the world: Hong Kong provides a questionable example.

During my time there has been a growing tendency to fabricate the appearance of majority opinion. Protest, the judicious use of opinion polls, media pressure of every kind, can and does represent itself as the expression of democracy at work. It is nothing of the kind. All too often it is no more than a promotion by some ill-informed, selfish and bullying minority.

The word from the Greek means "rule by the people" and the Athenian practice discounted a large helot population. Total democracy in my sense of the term is still a comparatively recent experiment (after all women only got the vote in 1928). It is not even a clear political objective. It is justifiable and respectable only if it is rooted in liberty, and liberty, to its maximum practicable extent, rests in turn upon two foundations: the concept of property and the rule of law. When these are in place the free flow of opinion and aspiration is safe. Should they give way before the pressure of greed, ignorance or ambition then liberty is borne away in the flood – and the collapse is all too often hailed in the name of democracy. Both these foundations, for instance, are under direct and violent threat in our own countryside today. The protection of the institutions which have hitherto defended us against this inundation should constitute the first charge of good government. Central to these institutions stands Parliament, but a Parliament today whose defences seem to shake under a remorseless stream of antagonistic criticism. A fundamental transfer of power is taking place from parliament into a confusing web of contradictory interests possessed of unprecedented powers of persuasion – the media.

Of course this vast industry includes many brave men and much honest endeavour, but the effect of its ubiquitous activities is often overbalanced towards the irresponsible, the malicious and sometimes the plain evil. We are subjected to daily assault both visual and in print by a hydra-headed monster whose only common purpose is to engage our attention and make us pay for it, whose ultimate masters are hard to identify and whose activities proceed without public sanction.

We live through a period in the world's history of absorbing interest, of great danger and of unprecedented challenge, yet our attention is everlastingly attracted to prurience. Even the quality newspapers, for whose resistance hitherto may God be praised, are impelled into shamefaced coverage on some inner page of the latest obscene manifestation of human nature gloatingly revealed by the tabloid press. Moreover, the presentation of fact seems to have given way to ceaseless introspective comment and criticism of our familiar institutions and beliefs. (On a recent visit abroad I got more hard news of what is happening in the world in a few minutes from the front pages of the *Oman Daily Observer* than can be extracted in half an hour from amongst all the voluminous expressions of opinion and half-informed analyses dished up for us daily and twice on Sundays at home.)

When sections of the media, motivated by heaven knows what obsession, can isolate and threaten the Crown itself, central focus of our constitution and nationhood, and do it apparently to greater effect than was ever achieved by the armed might of Nazi Germany, then something is seriously amiss.

Of course one reason for all this may be the impact of television. To read requires at least a minimum intellectual effort, to watch the television screen – none. Such is the miasma created by television that people now live their lives vicariously, no longer fully able to distinguish reality. The instant, colourful and inevitably superficial impact of what passes for news and current affairs programmes has driven the serious papers into competition by comment and the tabloids into their ceaseless presentation of scandal and sex.

You do not have to be a prude to deplore all this, you simply have to be sane. Yet we do tolerate it. I have yet to learn of an issue of the *"Daily Slime"* burned at the printer's gate. Complaints about TV bias, violence and obscene language are acknowledged, absorbed and ignored. The Governors of the BBC govern very little.

And where is this leading us? Ministers of the Crown fear to speak frankly even off the record or at private functions and as a result appear either indecisive, stupid or cowardly. Parliament is increasingly hypnotized, politicians of any stripe fawn before the arrogance and ill manners of their media inquisitors. Policy no longer reflects the real world but rather the supposed pressures of public opinion as asserted by those who seek to form it. So many people one talks to fear the media, but where is "the great silent majority" now? Very silent indeed.

Be careful, citizen. The hubbub may appear "democratic", but it is the bulwarks of our liberties and the anchors of our civilization which are giving way.

This is a retrospective comment. My time in public life has long receded. I miss the companionship of good friends in Parliament and indeed in my constituency certainly, but not the constraints of public life. In this I am lucky. There is life outside politics and to prove it I am going to tell you about Charlie.

———————|———————

17

CHARLIE

"Where in this wide world do you find
nobility without pride, friendship without envy,
or beauty without vanity?
Here where grace is laced with muscle
and strength by gentleness confined."

Ronald Duncan – "To the Horse"

So there is life after politics, and, in my case, unsurprisingly, this has quite a lot to do with horses. To my eye a mature and well conformed thoroughbred horse is the most beautiful creature on earth. To behold a stallion like Royal Academy for instance is to catch your breath. His presence provides an intellectual satisfaction, a feeling of exhilaration which lasts well after the horse has returned to his box. To watch them grow from foals to yearlings in our paddocks gives a pleasure which mercifully compensates for the all too possible disappointment and sense of loss when, sadly, they leave us for the sale ring.

Keats has it that beauty equals truth and vice versa, indeed he says that is all we need to know about life. It is an attractive idea but alas does not apply to horses, or the bookmakers would long ago have left the business. Yet just sometimes it holds good.

It was on a Friday in January, 1980, near Lowesby in Leicestershire that I first met Charlie. I was in urgent need of a good quality hunter and the need had been placed in the ever capable hands of my friend George Rich, a brilliant horseman and a dealer who had a genius for fitting horses to people. He was riding a tough looking chestnut with a lovely head.

"I think you'd better sit on this one" he said. I looked again. The horse seemed small for me and I said so. "I think he's got a bit of a motor," said George. "Hurry up, you can have 'im for twenty minutes, there's another after him." George generally said that. We swapped over. I found I had a minor earthquake beneath me.

"What's his name?" I asked.

"We call him Charlie."

With that I heard the horn, hounds were away and there was no more time to enquire into Charlie's antecedents. Indeed no time for anything except to try to steer him.

Lowesby is a lovely bit of rolling grass country scored with stout hedges and rails. We were heading for a stout hedge. Charlie had taken a decision about this without reference to me. We whizzed over it, shot past several surprised and hard-riding horsemen and found ourselves lined up for a fairly solid set of rails. My attempt to check Charlie was unavailing. I left him to it. He met the fence on the wrong stride and decided to ignore it, he simply galloped through it. Splintered pieces of rail shot into the air. I tensed for the inevitable somersault. Charlie barely checked his stride, on we went. At the end of twenty minutes I had lost George and nearly caused several accidents, not least to myself.

Somewhere near White's Barn there was a merciful check. Charlie, clearly irritated at this unnecessary interruption, turned round in circles, throwing up his handsome, intelligent head, ears pricked, lower lip trembling with perpetual excitement.

George appeared. "Do you want him?" he asked. I was in two very different minds. On the one hand here was a horse full of matchless courage and enthusiasm, on the other, I had only one neck.

"He doesn't know much," I said.

"He'll learn," said George. "He's got a motor."

It turned out Charlie was just five years old, had inevitably come over from Ireland, and then been sold, "to a man in the north who couldn't get on with him". I had some sympathy with the "man in the north". Charlie was by an Irish thoroughbred stallion called Prince Rhoy. No one knew who his mother was, or if they did they weren't telling. "He jumped that big drop fence superb," said George. I guessed that George had fitted him to me. Filled with many versions of reasonable doubt, I said, "O.K."

I was currently going through my phase as a geriatric jockey, trying to make up for a career as an amateur rider cut short by the war and sadly never resumed.

Six weeks later Charlie and I entered the Harborough cross country race, a form of the original point to point over four and a half miles of Leicestershire. This was the way of it:

Two horse boxes pulled into Tony Murray Smith's drive at Gumley that March morning – John Wood, the box driver, in good time with Michael, one of the lads from Milton, who "does" Charlie. In the other box was Joss Hanbury's mare over from Burley-on-the-Hill. Joss had finished third on her in the Melton ride the week before and I wondered how many fields ahead of me they would be. She was a wiry looking little brown thoroughbred, which had already made her mark in point to points as well – but this, after all, was a handicap.

Tony, hospitable as ever, asked us in for a drink; it did me no harm at all. There were some officials and friends over to watch the race and I tried to cover my nerves with the usual kind of mindless jokes.

The fact was I did not yet know Charlie's capacity. Good looks he certainly had; and he was strong, close coupled with a good nine inches of bone and lovely quality head and neck. I'd hunted him a few times by now. He could certainly gallop, but his jumping, though powerful, was chancy. We'd hit a few hard the last half day with the Quorn, a very good hunt in heavy going. The horse had been unnaturally run up afterwards and it took a fortnight at Milton to put the condition back on him. Nervous, he would begin to sweat when his mane was plaited-up before going out and now I looked apprehensively to see where he had broken out on the journey. John, our stud groom, assured me he had travelled fine and he looked calm enough. They were tacking him up. Time to put on my crash hat.

It was half a mile hack to the start. I rode down with Joss Hanbury. His long legs hung well below the girth on the little mare, but he's built like a bean pole and weighs nothing. Not for the first time I envied those with small bones. We turn down the lane and finally into a big grass field on the right where the start is to be. We are early. The rest of the large entry has assembled on the Saddington road and is being led down by a mounted steward. Plenty of time to contemplate those 25 fences spread over 4½ miles of the best of the Fernie grass, but passing over three formidable hills with steep gradients. Luckily a sharp north wind had dried out the land and except for a few places the going was good. I tried hard to memorise the line I had decided when we walked the course.

We check in at the Secretary's Land Rover to draw our number cloth. Each weight in the handicap wears a different coloured sash, white for heavyweight, yellow for middle and green for light. Charlie starts to play up when I try to put the cloth on. Someone kindly takes his head, but he breaks loose. Eventually I have to get off him. He is over excited as usual and has started to sweat. I take him down the field and give him a canter. The wind cuts through my jersey. Below Gumley Wood I see a great concourse of horsemen and colours bobbing down the road towards us. There are 65 starters. I try to walk Charlie about and calm him down. The tension mounts. Presently the others file through a gate towards us and mill about the Land

Rover to draw their numbers. Girths are tightened. Hunting friends greet one another. There are faces I never see except when we line up for this race. We grin at each other. The first fence, a solid enough hedge, stands out black below us.

At last the churning tossing crowd of horsemen is ready and Tony Murray Smith calls us through a gate and down to the start. "Get over there heavyweights. Make a big circle round me. Middle weights behind them. I shall call you up as soon as I let the heavyweights go. Are you ready now? Line up the heavyweights. Don't go till the flag drops. Come up now. GO!"

I squeeze Charlie's sides and drop my hands. He leaps sideways, gets the idea and surges forward. About eight of the twenty two heavyweights get away ahead of us, but we are no more than 3 or 4 lengths behind the leader at the first. My ears are full of the thrilling drum of hooves. As I feared Charlie is going too fast at it. No chance to measure it. We hurdle through it. The horse is tough and though he screws a bit he doesn't miss a stride, but it's not the best of omens. We swing left downhill over good level turf at steeplechase pace. I see Sam Vestey's red jersey ahead on the left. Peter Cairns is well up and Christopher Sporborg is cutting it out on his good horse, Tobermory, which led from start to finish last year. We meet the second just right and Charlie gives me a splendid leap. On downhill to the third, a good hedge with a ditch on the landing side. A big bay horse keeps crossing in front of me, his jockey either undecided or out of control. I have to pull right. Charlie surges at it and jumps me up level with the bay. We swing uphill right under Gumley Woods, towards the first "in and out" over the gated road.

Here three of them line up to follow the leader over a smallish timber gap in the hedge. But there is no way I can check Charlie. I had decided on a place near an oak tree where the fence was lower but fail to find it. We take it at its biggest and thickest with a wicked uphill take off. Charlie lands in the middle of the road and swerves. Thank God the jump out is only a sunken hedge and ditch. I manage to straighten him and we are over into the field. I have made a length or two.

Uphill now over ridge and furrow to the second, bigger double obstacle at the Kibworth road. I track Christopher who leads about 6 lengths. I see him jump the first then veer sharp right and jump at a worrying angle. Why? I land in the middle of the road again. Charlie ducks left and tries to gallop down it. I manage to turn him to face the ditch and hedge on the other side, but we have lost all momentum.

The hedge stands 4'6" against us with a ditch towards. All I can do is ask the horse to go. He gathers himself and to his eternal credit leaps it from a stand. I bless his agility and courage. It was a bad moment. I swing right now, up the first long hill over ridge and furrow again. I have lost some ground and am following Christopher and the big bay horse. I see others making to our left where the route is shorter, but the hill much steeper. I am sure they are wrong and the proof is soon there as we gallop through a gap in an old blackthorn hedgeline round the contour of the hill and steep down towards the deep dyke at the bottom. Only one of those who turned uphill is still with us. Charlie is pulling as we gallop down at the dyke. I drop my hands, hold my breath and leave it to him. We are well over and heading uphill again to a simple hedge with the hint of a gap. I follow three horses through it. There are others in the next field to our left.

The hill continues very steep. At the top is a massive hedge and timber fence which I fear more than any other in the race. I give Charlie a breather and for the first time he is temporarily off the bit. I feel it's safe to drop back a little. The others seem to me to be pushing too hard and there is still a hell of a long way to go. At the top I see the leaders gather themselves for what at the end of such a gradient must be a formidable fence. There is no give in it. I see one refuse and another somersault, hooves thrashing above the hedge. I line Charlie up at a place where the staring rails are covered by a thornbush. He stands back and dives at it – too far, I think for one awesome moment – but no, he judges the drop.

We swing sharp right over a low timber jump and then uphill. In front stretches a long ridge with Saddington village clear before us over the valley. About ten are still with the leading group. I am getting closer and Charlie is still pulling on. I see Christopher look back. Over the crest of the ridge we gallop together stride for stride. We are facing a line of three stout cut and laid fences, black against the sky. All will be jumped at speed and we have to be accurate. As we come into each the horse's stride lengthens. I sense that magic moment when you know he has it measured, feel the great gathering of strength beneath the saddle, the thrilling thrust into the air, the thrash of the thorn beneath us and the thunderous landing beyond. On we speed stirrup to stirrup, both horses in perfect competitive rhythm.

As we run downhill towards the canal I take a pull. This is a problem. Approached down an uneven slope there is a wide and straggling watercourse with a steep bank along the landing side. At an angle to the hill is a narrow hump backed bridge with a loose stony surface, beyond a water splash then up another bank to the lip of the "canal", a carrier some 4ft wide with a fast flowing stream and the ground rising on the landing side again. On my walk I had decided on the bridge since the bank of the first stream was either boggy or dangerously steep.

I see Christopher take the bridge, pebbles flying. He is followed by the bay and then by Charlie and me. I see someone in trouble at the water's edge. I kick up the bank to the canal nearly level with the bay and again thank God for my horse's athletic agility. We are well over, but I see another horse crumple to my left. We turn up a long grass incline where, for the first time, the going is really holding. I give Charlie his second breather. Over a hedge with a strong guard rail on the crest and down steeply again into a narrow trappy gap which conceals a second water carrier, not wide, but sudden with a bad take off. Charlie's impetus has carried us too close to the horse in front and we take it together girth to girth where no real room exists, but we survive. Ahead rises the last hill before the course drops to the long run in over five level fields. I take a strong pull to let the bay go on and to give Charlie his last long breather. We drop back. I see Christopher and Tobermory still holding his lead, the bay horse, being pressed a bit too hard maybe, and one other rider who has taken the direct route to our left.

It is a long pull. We reach the Saddington Road at the top and I line Charlie up at a simple post and rails. I seem to be closer to the bay than I had expected. Once over we round the shoulder up the hill and below stretches the glorious grass of the vale towards John Ball's covert and the finish. It is then I see the bay blow up. His stride slows and there is that heart-rending gargling gasp for oxygen as I gallop past him. Every moment I am expecting the middle and lightweights to sweep past me, but all I can see is Tobermory galloping easily down towards the stiff thorn hedge at the base of the final hill. He is perhaps 10 lengths ahead, takes it well and continues straight on. What's left of my rational memory shouts that we ought to tug sharp left after the fence. I do so and watch Christopher follow a wider arc to my right.

Now there is no more than half a mile to go and by the next I am four lengths behind him. We land in a patch of soggy ground, Christopher goes through it without trouble but by the next, a big "tiger trap", I am only two lengths adrift. Both of us land safely and for the first intoxicating moment I think we are going the stronger. I sit still, switch to the left to give the horse a clear run at the next. He jumps it perfectly and I am now a length and a half behind. The going is deep and I think I see Tobermory labour a bit. "Take him now", I say to myself and ask Charlie the question. His powerful stride stretches immediately and in seconds we are at Christopher's girth.

"How are you going? Better than me that's for sure!" he said as we pound past him. I am alone with two to go: a tiger trap and the last long sturdy hedge. I push him on with hands and heels and he feels amazingly strong. We meet the tiger trap wrong and he raps it hard. This gives Christopher hope behind me, but Charlie never misses a stride and we gallop on to the last. All my concentration centres on this solid black fence, straightforward, but so critical. I sit quite still and let him stride on naturally. To my joy he quickens well away and already I know he's timed it. We are over safely. How far off the flags of the finish look. Now for the first time I risk a look over both shoulders. Nothing there. We are going to win. I ride him out with hands and heels and not for a second does he falter after that gruelling 4½ miles. At last we are there and I can ease him.

There is no great crowd or shouting. Only jockeys' friends and a few enthusiastic supporters, all horsemen and horsepeople, but they will know better than most racecourse crowds what joy that moment brings. No Grand National winner ever took a more loving and admiring walloping than Charlie from his admirers; and there is Elizabeth Anne running down the hill towards us.

There are unlikely to be many more comparable joys for a jockey of 60 years!

George Rich is hanging about near the finishing post as, elated, I jump off Charlie, his sides heaving, head still high, lower lip going like a clapperboard.

"He's got a bit of a motor," said George.

Five times we started in the Harborough race, finishing second and third and winning three times. Now there is a cup for the winner, in Charlie's honour.

There were other triumphs, and could have been more but for pilot error. Charlie's only sin lay in his boundless courage. Just occasionally there was this tendency to ignore an obstacle if it seemed likely to prove inconvenient rather than break his stride. But mercifully, so far, we have always bounced together.

Of all the forms of competitive horsemanship in which I have been lucky enough to take part, nothing can compare with the cross-country races. The Melton and the Harborough rides are perhaps the best known but there are others. Long may they flourish, for they summon the pure spirit of sportsmanship. Most jockeys start without hope of victory or even a place. They ride for the thrill and the honour alone, to finish if possible, or at least get as far as they can. There are no prizes, except perhaps a bottle of champagne for the winners. No money involved, no crowd, no television, no press, no railed course, just a couple of coloured markers on trees perhaps and some reinforced hedges along the way. The route you take is mostly your own choice, and woe will certainly betide those who do not trouble to walk the long course, map in hand, before the day. Risks there are aplenty to horse and rider but among those who frequent or take part in these rides physical risk is part of the balance of life as it should be. Not for them the feather bedding which pervades so much of our existence. There are hospitals, so I am told, where those who hurt themselves in such events seem scarcely welcome, so incorrect is it held to be to risk life and limb without comprehensible reason. Of course if you smash yourself on the motorway that is entirely acceptable.

But such thoughts will never mar the spirit of those who gather round the trailer where drinks are dispensed to the survivors near the winning post, standing among their steaming horses after the Melton or the Harborough ride and for me they stand tall; above the gladiatorial self publicising triumphalism and commerce of what is termed sport in most other fields today.

Nobody needs to punch the air as they gallop down towards John Ball's covert or between the posts at Lowesby.

Charlie and I are still together, our joint ages not so far from the century. The years have inevitably blunted his jockey's ambitions; his seem unchanged.

When I stand with him in his box, his lovely neck arched, as he pokes in my pocket for apples, I know a pride and a companionship that no one else can share. His eye is as true as his heart and sometimes when I meet it I believe he understands.

———————|———————

MILTON

It is far now, in time and space, from the boom of Big Ben, the shrilling of the division bell, the ushers' stentorian summons to the lobbies. I wake to the mellow chime of a stable clock. It was started in 1690 and has to have a rest now and then. In my dwindling dream its note is redolent of a quieter time, of a different pace, of carriage wheels and hooves on the cobbled yard, of voices speaking a measured English, full of courtesy. I hear pigeon flapping noisily into action. Dogs bark. Not any dogs, our dogs. I am awake. One lands on my head, a wriggling furry lump distributing a damp and imperative greeting.

Our house belongs to three labradors. We stay there in happy accord provided we stick to the rules. If we don't, we are patiently and insistently smothered until we do. The rules involve punctilious observance of certain routines timed with an accuracy to match the stable clock – except when it stops.

They include: "It's time for a small walk." "It's time to welcome our friend Harold." (He's the house painter and enjoys a special status.) "It's time for small pieces of cheese after lunch." "It's time for a long walk." "It is certainly time for supper."

We abide by the rules and are rewarded with a bond and trust which is certainly super-human; and with a sensory understanding of our every mood and much of what we say. They collaborate in everything, invited or no. I do exercises in the morning lying on my back. One of them lies alongside and paddles with his legs in the air. Another one articulates. All dogs talk with movements of their ears and bodies; this one does it with noises as well. We could compile a dictionary.

"It's time to go to bed" is the last routine. This generally happens during the nine o'clock news. It is quite easy to sabotage the tele, if you climb onto the viewer's lap and persistently lick his face. No bad thing since attendance only spoils a much better version of events in the decent newspapers the next morning.

Two of our companions are first class retrievers. Their father could have been a champion until arthritis crippled his back and twisted his poor limbs. But it will never destroy his pride, his independent spirit or his dauntless courage, and he can peel tennis balls as if they were oranges.

Our labradors have peopled the district with their children and grandchildren.

The carriage wheels rumble only in my dreams but hooves still strike the cobbles in the yard and the early morning is sharpened by the clink of stable buckets, the blowing of equine noses and a blessed ammoniac smell. The stables live.

All this happens beside the great house with its three separate faces representing the changing fortunes of the family it has sheltered since the sixteenth century. Widespread and serene, its long Tudor front and the warm ochre of its Barnack stone facing blend with the park and the woods as if the whole edifice had risen from the earth with the great twisted oaks which surround it. They were standing when Wolsey's retinue camped among them while the Cardinal dispensed Maundy money to the folk who lived by the fens nearby.

They cast their shadow over Sir William Fitzwilliam, appointed gaoler to the unhappy Queen of Scots, as he rode back and forth to Fotheringhay nearby. At her tragic end she left him her seal and a portrait of her son. They are still here at Milton.

But there is more to the house than memories. This is the centre of a community stretching across the corners of three counties, a community which still lives by the rhythm of the seasons and the long ago traditions of the countryside. A wide variety of people draw a measure of fulfilment and happiness from their connection with Milton, so we trust.

Bus loads of small children from the city watch wide-eyed and breathless with wonder at lambing time, amongst the cattle, in the stables and the kennels. For to children, even to those who have never seen such things, and most have not, the ways with animals and the workings of nature are seen instinctively to be right.

The hounds live in the park and their passage in autumn and winter weaves much of the fabric of our community. I see them now at exercise emerging from the mist into a patch of tinted sunlight, sterns waving, a panoply of colour and movement flowing over the grass. They have been here four hundred years at least. Of course this is but an instant in the history of man and his hounds, but it impels me to tell a story of long ago, almost eight hundred thousand years to be modestly exact, when palaeolithic man was doing his best to survive. A poor thing, ugly, hairy and inept, armed only with a club, he and his friends scuttled after such small creatures as they could trap or catch for meat.

Hungry and envious, they watched the cleverest and boldest of the hunters – the dogs. Saw them select and separate their prey. Watched their matchless teamwork as first one then another led the pack in relentless pursuit, until their quarry, however formidable, was finally turned and brought down. And the men learned to run after the dogs, to surround their kill, drive them off with their clubs and drag the meat away to their fires.

Cheated and exhausted, the dogs followed the men to their caves where, skulking in the darkness on the edge of the firelight, they hoped for scraps from the kill. And the men threw bones to these hunters, upon whom increasingly they depended both to find and to run down the quarry they were unable to catch themselves. When they could they stole the puppies, and thus the first partnership between man and the animals began. In time there were always dogs about the camps and settlements so that hundreds of thousands of years later when man began to evolve what we call civilization the understanding and purpose shared between him and his hounds evolved with it. This was the beginning of the chase. At least that is what I think. It is only a best guess but I know of no other explanation.

At any rate the Pharaohs hunted and left vivid illustrations to prove it. Hunting was debated with approval and understanding by Plato and Socrates. The Consul Arrian, interpreter of the philosopher Epictetus and historian of Alexander, wrote a famous treatise on the care of hounds, in the second century AD.

Thus from ancient Egypt through the burgeoning of Greece and Rome, the Renaissance and the flowering of Europe, through the age of Shakespeare and throughout the bounds of Christendom man followed his hounds as part of the accepted rhythm of civilized existence.

Strange that it is only now, in late 20th century Britain where the inexorable advance of science and technology has devised new ways of living, closer to the ant heap than to traditional dwelling, and where man is condemned to lead his life ever further from nature, that hunting should arouse hysterical disapproval and suffer violent attack.

What has changed? Have we experienced a sudden moral revelation, some fresh and unsuspected insight into the laws of nature? If so I seem to have missed it and the media clearly indicate the opposite.

It is not the immemorial traditions of the chase nor the ways of the countryside which should give us cause for concern, but the warped attitudes induced in urban man. Worse still there are those in public life and in considerable authority who know this to be true but dare not say so lest they appear politically incorrect.

Of course there have been some earlier opponents of hunting, I must admit, but their eccentricities have not always done much for the cause. A famous 19th century antagonist was Jeremy Bentham, though I do not suppose many hunt saboteurs will have read him. First of the utilitarians, his doctrine is a justification for the suppression of minorities and a soulless alternative to religion. At his death his skin was stuffed, at his behest, and he sits in the entrance to University College, London, a warning to the credulous and a temptation surely for the next Guy Fawkes night.

Another strong supporter of the movement of course was that well known vegetarian and humanist Adolf Hitler.

Beyond the kennels lie the stud paddocks, shrine of hope. It is mid-June and for once, for this evening hour at least, it is an English June, serene, all green, from the dark hues of fir, oak and ash to shadowed viridian. There is a hum of insects. For once no lameness, no runny noses or staring coats to be seen. It is gate-leaning time.

The mares move, slowly grazing, long thoroughbred tails aswish, ears flicking, summer coats shining, chestnut and bay, portly brood mares now, the clamour of the trainer's yard and the racecourse long behind them. At peace, replete with motherhood.

Beneath them, about them, feed and scamper the foals. Small questing faces like fawns, they come to be petted, apt always for flight, ready with their heels, full of innocence and mischief like all baby things.

And as I watch them judgement turns slowly to dreams. I hear the drumming hooves and quick breath, see necks arched, eyes starting with delight at the speed bred in them as they strive up the level turf of Newmarket or the downland gallops of Lambourn. Little racehorses in the making.

I see distant shifting colours on the Rowley Mile, straining through my field glasses to find the one who started life here. I see the panoply of Ascot, horses in the paddock, lean and burnished, tuned to the moment, nervously waiting for their supreme trial. Could one of these little creatures be there one day?

I hear the roar as the field thunders down Tattenham Hill, past the crowded Downs at Epsom . . . That long elegant little bay colt . . . That lovely chestnut filly leading the dance . . . Could he or she be the one?

North of the house among the oaks, longhorn cattle move among the sheep. Great placid beasts, their herds fed England for centuries. Wherever there is still a drove road there they passed; maroon, roan and white they have not changed in form or colour since the seventeenth century and perhaps long before. They peopled the west when America was young.

Among them, brown and white, the Jacob's sheep watch, multi-horned, yellow-eyed, Pan-like. Nobody knows where they came from. My guess is Arcadia.

Beyond the lodge gate and down a lane which runs beside a brook, its rambling marked by stunted willows, there stands a small church in a field. The tower was built in Norman times, probably on the site of a Saxon chantry chapel. The nave dates from the 13th and Sir William Fitzwilliam added the chancel in the 16th century. The churchyard is sheltered by aged cedars and on the iron hand gate there is a notice "Please close both latches". This is because the cows can open one of them, then graze among the graves and eat the flowers planted there. They also eat radio aerials off the worshippers' cars parked among the cowpats. St Mary the Virgin is a rural church.

Within are many effigies. There is a somewhat dubious crusader with a broken sword in the side aisle, and in the chancel elaborate memorials to members of the presiding dynasty. They lend an air of quiet patronage and the flow of time. There is a feel of the year's rhythm and of the presence of generations of dutiful spirits, of quiet acceptance that all is in its place. Of course it is not; all that has changed. Our friends who come to church, people from the village and elsewhere, are properly rooted in the twentieth century. All kneel as equals now in life as well as the eyes of God, but the gentle aura of past centuries pervades our church and brings with it a precious peace and a whispered sense of simple, oft-repeated prayer. Here we are close to those who have passed before; indeed they kneel all about us, it seems to me.

Some years ago in the age of rampant socialism the local authority must have believed the family could not survive for they planned to turn Milton into municipal offices. In the war it housed the Jedburgh teams training to be dropped by parachute in occupied France. Last year the survivors held their reunion with us. That was Milton's war work, but it could not survive as a municipal office. Its soul would wither.

May the great house live on, warm, unhaunted, beautiful and welcoming, home to those who by right, and for a time, are lucky enough to be its custodians.

———|———

POSTSCRIPT

Leonardo said, "Experience has been the mistress of whoever has written well."

I have done my best. The difficulty is to decide what matters.

Few of us are lucky enough to be certain they understand the human condition. But if you've knocked around as long as I have you are bound to finish up with some opinions. If we were on the racecourse I would offer them as sound bets, but as we all know history and horses often beat the punter.

They relate in turn to the three parts of my life as a soldier, as an intelligence officer and as a Member of Parliament.

In this sad and unnecessary era of national doubt and self-criticism our armed forces constitute the one institution which has not only maintained but enhanced its standing among us. Their efficiency, bravery and adaptability are recognized across the world. Their importance lies not only in their professional capability but in the essential backing which they give to our diplomacy, and perhaps even more significantly because they present a shining advertisement for the rewards of discipline, a quality in short supply in our society.

Of all the political slogans I remember the "Peace Dividend" is probably the silliest. Of course the collapse of the Soviet Empire means a radical reassessment of the danger but that it should herald the onset of peace is manifestly ridiculous. The reverse is the case. The nuclear weapon has simply changed the rules.

The phase through which the world is passing fits all too neatly into Arnold Toynbee's massive analysis of the rise and fall of civilizations (broadly "empires" in our terms). The intervening period between collapse and re-emergence he describes as the "interregnum" during which we may expect the appearance of "ephemeral states". Few of them prove viable; conflict between them inevitable. Many disappear. At the same time there begins a

"*Volkerwanderung*", or wandering of peoples along and across the old frontiers. Further conflict results. This disturbed period always has and will continue to unfold until the pattern of the next dominion becomes clear.

This apocalyptic picture drew much subsequent criticism. He was accused of being short on facts and to have placed too much emphasis on spiritual motivation. The causal connection between historical events may be too capricious to sustain such a vast organic vision and Toynbee's recommendations for the survival of western civilization are certainly flawed. But equally, it is possible to draw the wrong conclusions from too close inspection of any period of history. Try sorting out the mixed motives in that kaleidoscopic holocaust, the Thirty Years War.

Toynbee's importance lies in the very breadth of his canvas. He makes us stand back and, if his interpretation of the human drama can be accepted, we get a chilling perception of the state of the world through which we are passing.

It is the dissolution not only of the Russian Empire but of the European empires post-war which has caused the present "interregnum" and the phenomena in Toynbee's analysis are all in plain evidence. What will constitute the next dominion? What indeed? It is folly in such circumstances to neglect, distort or reduce our Defence Forces and in particular the traditional regiments on which our strength, on land at least, has always finally depended. To do so in favour of our bloated system of welfare subsidies is to disregard reality.

My service with secret intelligence remains a closed book, not least because in my case the habit of secrecy leads swiftly to amnesia. I have little time for those who exploit their experiences in this complicated field, and even less for self appointed "intelligence experts", that is to say hangers-on with no professional experience who seek to make money out of reporting such gossip as they can pick up on the work of the security services with small risk of challenge or denial. For those who have truly served silence is not only golden but obligatory.

The occasional public appearance of failure attracts immediate adverse criticism in the media from people who in the nature of things can have no full knowledge of the facts. The remarkable successes achieved over the years against the German Abwehr, the mighty KGB, its satellite services and in other fields may never be known. No credit accrues to those responsible, all of whom are required to live their lives in comparative anonymity pursuing dedicated careers which outwardly must appear unimpressive, even to their friends. This is no easy vocation.

Now under the specious umbrella of "open government" officers of these services and their work may be open to public scrutiny. It is a dangerous precedent.

The other day I heard a young and rising Labour MP with a shadow portfolio demand that our security services be held accountable to the "elected members" of a parliamentary committee as if the fact of their "election" qualified them uniquely to sit in judgement over these activities. He should read his Machiavelli and thank his stars for the protection afforded him by what are probably the finest security and intelligence services in the world. You might just as well make Lester Piggott accountable to the Automobile Club for all the useful exchange such a proposal would bring.

However well briefed they are, MPs, whether Privy Councillors or no, cannot be expected fully to appreciate the intricacies of this profession, nor where a line of enquiry should cease. Those who spend their lives defending the British interest in secrecy have enough to do watching their front without having to guard their backs as well.

Politics is the business of ideas and in Britain we have an odd paradox. Throughout my time in Parliament and since, both the parties which lay claim to radicalism have never changed. The Liberals, Liberal Democrats or whatever they are currently called, remain rigidly faceless, while the Labour Party is characterized not by new ideas but by a long and so far unavailing struggle to escape from its antediluvian ideological roots, a struggle bravely undertaken by Gaitskell and continued by most of his successors.

The Conservatives, on the other hand, possess an entirely justifiable philosophy of politics and a proven approach to government, yet increasingly and unnecessarily they incline towards populist fashion. The casualties are both dignity and respect.

A damaging example is the current obsession with classlessness. Here is a specious taboo masquerading in the name of equality, an attitude which Oliver Wendell Holmes once described as "idealised envy". No doubt the well-meaning intention is to establish a society in which all reward depends upon merit rather than on privilege or initial advantage. Unfortunately for all of us the effect has been a baneful form of inverted snobbery by which anyone or anything which can be described as upper or middle class is the object of sneering derision. By definition therefore the unspoken common denominator of acceptable class has to be low. This is political correction of a crassly debilitating nature.

The greatest merit of all should accrue to those who overcome relative disadvantage to attain success, for it is they who provide the adrenalin of society. But their direction must be upwards towards a higher and more rewarding life, many of the advantages of which are the fruit of sustained tradition. There can be no incentive if all effort and achievement is to be sunk in some grey stratum of lowly conformity.

Personally I think the only class worth belonging to is one whose adherents judge their fellows by what they are perceived to be, not upon where they come from. Of course it makes sense to provide equal opportunity so far as practicable – though there are blindingly obvious limitations to this praiseworthy endeavour. But to condemn any form of hierarchy in society is to invite an ineluctable collapse of respect for its institutions; for those who hold responsible office, however legitimately; and eventually for authority itself.

Arnold Toynbee, again, convincingly demonstrates that no society has yet succeeded for long unless it is sustained by a "creative minority". Indeed the disappearance or degeneration of this minority leads to breakdown. A creative minority needs to absorb new talent constantly and to discard any unworthy surplus since the standards it develops and sets are its sole condition of survival. I am not referring to a narrow autocracy but to the broad category of those who have attained success and seek to maintain it for their descendants. It is neither strange nor wrong that by a tradition of successful responsibility the creative minority will develop a way of life and a system of education and training which, whether it is acknowledged or no, tends to produce society's leaders. To ignore or condemn this is to deny history and human nature. When capable young people who have enjoyed every advantage and possess the potential to lead, deliberately suppress talent and ambition in order to appear classless, or, worse still, turn their backs on a career in public life because they fear their background would disqualify them before the selection committee; when university selection deliberately loads the dice against candidates with a private education however promising they may be; when even the boy scout and girl guide movement, redolent of so much that is good and true about us, can be condemned as "elitist", then value stands upon its head and aspiration is travelling in the wrong direction.

Strange that this triumph of envy over experience should be accompanied by morose and constant complaint in the media that the quality of Members of Parliament has deteriorated.

But there is a malaise in our society which lies deeper than phobia about class and equality. I feel particularly sad for young people growing up in an atmosphere of comparative aimlessness, in which all misfortune is cushioned by the state, in which all wrongdoing is indulged and moral questions simply degenerate into "problems to be solved" so that the very idea of morality begins to wither away; in which there is no challenge any more, no trumpet call, nothing to lift the heart. At least that is what I believe to be a main cause of the vagrancy and psychological collapse with which we are so sadly familiar.

It was easy for my generation. Religion was impressed upon us as a matter of inevitable discipline as well as required belief. Whether one was a committed Christian or no it gave a shape and dignity to life and death. It drew an immutable distinction between good and evil. We were left in no doubt where we stood. Patriotism was not dismissed as an arcane emotion, it was a vivid driving force. We believed in our country and its destiny. It was axiomatic that we might have to die for it. These values were fixed for us in time of war and ever since they help to resist the onset of doubt and despair. But now it is fashionable to belittle our achievements and to sneer at our imperial history – indeed at all history. It is as though we were in thrall to a cult of the second rate, jealous of a past it cannot emulate, which fears the challenge of its own day, and which seeks to suppress the evidence of its own inadequacy.

"When the Roman Eagles retreated over the Danube it was not the loss of Dacia but the satisfaction of the Roman people at this loss which was the omen of the Empire's fall."

So wrote J. R. Godley, a senior official, in a minute to Gladstone. It is more than an Empire which is at risk for us now.

We have lost the lodestar. The simple disciplines and clear moral constraints which helped to map the lives of my contemporaries are now to be replaced, it seems, by political correctness, an absurd and degrading attempt to control and censor free expression and the truth. It is as though we had fallen victim to some obscure conspiracy, designed to subject what we know to be right to the dictates of a fraudulent code.

I do not know whether within the limitations of our modern media-dominated society it will be possible for a government to develop the strength and determination necessary to rid us of this perverted liberalism. It is notable that so many of our brightest young people seem now to aspire to a career in the media rather than to public service. I understand the reason but if all the talent stays on the touchline, who is going to win the match?

But we are still a powerful people, for the time being lost in an uneasy and debilitating sleep. So much of the decent solid courageous core is still there even if its continued existence is often suppressed by newspapers and television locked in their ceaseless competitive search for horror, failure and distress.

The soul of this country is not dead. Below the surface, like it or not, there beats the heart of a sovereign people, a people which created and maintained for 300 years the greatest Empire ever known, which shaped so much of the world we see and which gave it the only genuine universal tongue. We did not do all this in order to see our ancient liberties eroded and our destiny controlled by a weak and corrupt attempt at supra-national government from Brussels or anywhere else.

I have lived and worked in Europe. It is because I appreciate the rich diversity of the countries I came to know and love that I believe priceless values will be destroyed, not enhanced, by this bureaucratic mishmash. Each nation has its own unique contribution to make. The steadiness, tolerance and political balance which, so far at least, have distinguished the history of this country from that of most other members of the EC can only be sustained by a confidence bred of belonging. Our constitution is a delicate equilibrium, the distillation of centuries and the guarantee of our liberties. It is in itself a mighty contribution to western civilization but it will not survive the imposition of laws and conditions imposed upon us for the express purpose of destroying our sense of nationhood.

To establish by treaty and in practice a system of close collaboration which will guarantee, so far as possible, peace in Europe – yes. To pursue economic benefit by enlarging markets – of course. These are not far from our traditional objectives pursued through the balance of power and free trade. But beyond that lies danger.

The glory and strength of Hellenistic civilization rested upon the integrity of the "Polis", the city state, and it was the centralizing and deadening influence of the Byzantine bureaucracy which became a main cause of its collapse before the barbarian hordes. So could it be with this incongruous and unmanageable amalgamation of European Nation States.

We should not forget that the focus of our vision throughout most of our history was upon the far horizon. We have been notably successful that way. We may no longer aspire to Empire. But to our island's independence – yes. And as those who seek to govern us may have to find out in the end – fiercely so.

Now I come to the question I asked in my letter at the beginning of this book, where did I come from on 4 May, 1921? Or for that matter why did I arrive at all? To what purpose this wandering thread of existence I have tried to describe? Of course it has no intrinsic importance, it is simply the scrap of life I know best. It is the question which matters.

The human condition has changed faster during the lives of my contemporaries than in the course of almost any previous generation and the reason for this must be the bewildering advance of science and technology. Science is a hermetic activity of vast importance to us all, but understood by only a tiny minority. I am not included. Nevertheless there are recent works by distinguished scientists designed to explain the business in terms more or less comprehensible even to the mathematically blind.

We should never deride science. Its benefits are manifest. To fall behind would be fatal for us. To discourage scientific advance would be like trying to halt human evolution. There are scientists who believe there is no limit to the revelatory powers of mathematics, that the code of creation itself will in the end be cracked and the secret of life explained in a "theory of everything". But there are also those who do not agree. Among them is the distinguished Professor of Mathematical Physics, Paul Davies*, who puts it like this: "I am not saying that science and logic are likely to provide the wrong answers but they may be incapable of addressing the sort of 'why' (as opposed to 'how') questions we want to ask."

Later, in his book *The Mind of God*, he quotes a particle physicist who turned to the priesthood: "My erstwhile colleagues are labouring away in the endeavour to produce a theory yet more all embracing . . . I would say that at present their efforts have an air of contrivance, even desperation about them."

Even Stephen Hawking†, hot on the trial of "the theory of everything", admits that "numbers cannot really cope with infinity". And it is infinity which defeats them in the end.

Professor Paul Davies believes it unlikely that science will ever explain the secret of creation. He simply concludes that in some almost mystical way advanced scientific theory indicates that – "we are truly meant to be here".

Jean Guitton, the French Christian philosopher, in a fascinating dialogue with the astrophysicists Igor and Grichka Bogdanov, goes further‡. He and his interlocutors conclude that the laws of classical or objective science from Galileo and Newton have been irrevocably upturned since the establishment of quantum theory, indeed that all nineteenth century concepts of space, time, matter and energy will soon be seen as no more than "anachronisms in the history of ideas".

Try as I may, I cannot truly grasp quantum theory. But I think I follow

---

* Paul Davies is professor of Mathematical Physics at the University of Adelaide. He obtained a PhD from the University of London and held research and lecturing appointments at Cambridge and London Universities before being appointed to the Chair of Theoretical Physics at the University of Newcastle at the age of 34. He emigrated to Australia in 1990. His research interests are in the field of black holes, cosmology and quantum gravity and he has published over one hundred specialist papers, as well as several books.

† *A Short History of Time*, Professor Stephen Hawking, 1988

‡ *Dieu et la Science*, Grasset, Paris, 1991

Guitton's explanation of some of its effects. For instance, the elementary particles of matter are now only explicable as both particles and waves. Yet how can they possibly be both? Guitton and his scientist colleagues see the quantum version of matter dissolving into a haze of probabilities – into "mathematical smoke". Matter is dematerialized. Quantum physics allows no distinction between matter and non-matter or, for Guitton, spirit. The elementary particles/waves are seen as "the dice of God" and *"c'est à nous qu'il appartient à chaque instant de savoir les faire rouler dans la bonne direction"*.

Behind the creation of our expanding universe from the moment of its initial cataclysm, there stands a transcendent creator, a mind. All was foreseen. The universe itself in its initial minuscule form knew *"que l'homme viendrait à son heure"* (a phrase strikingly similar to Professor Davies' belief that "we are meant to be here").

Thus it is the scientists themselves who begin to distil the synthesis of empirical knowledge and faith towards which St Thomas Aquinas strove so long ago.

If these momentous theories are correct, does it not mean that physics must finally acknowledge metaphysics, or what Jean Guitton calls "metarealism", and that science, although it will continue to discover answers to the "how" questions, will never answer the "why"? If this be true, perhaps it is the return of faith which will mark the twenty-first century with incalculable consequences for mankind.

Yet, so far, we wait in vain for a ringing reassertion of authority from the leaders of the Church. The theologians stay silent. Fred Hoyle, the well known astronomer, remarks, "I have always thought it curious that, while most scientists claim to eschew religion, it actually dominates their thoughts more than it does [those of] the clergy."*

Welfare politics has nothing to do with the deity. "Caring" in the modern sense of the term is not the same as the care of souls.

But the needs of the spirit will not be denied. If it is not truly served it will demand attention and get it in all manner of ridiculous guises: mindless evangelistic hysteria, fanatical environmentalism, animal rights, extreme feminism, groping new age mysticism, half-baked and half-understood eastern sects, even drugs.

The Christian faith rests in an ancient story. Clever atheists may revel in the exposure of scripture as archaeologically and historically unsound, but the strength of the story does not lie in this form of description. It represents the eternal strife between good and evil, the mystery of creation, the existence

* There are exceptions. Pope John Paul II clearly understands physics and has addressed a scientific conference on the "drive towards convergence".

of free will and the concept of God in man. Its veracity is a matter of faith and not of reason. It addresses the "why" questions, and not the "how".

I cannot define faith. It is a simple secret quality of mind. But I know that it is here that I must look for the answer to my question. There is no theory, no equation, no exercise of logic which can help me.

I must have come from somewhere on 4 May, 1921, since I arrived with inborn strengths and weaknesses, abilities and disabilities. What I have done with them is my lookout, but clearly I started with a better deal than many.

Before the quantum theory all scientific knowledge was supposed to rest upon causality. This goal was scored because I kicked the ball which attained a certain velocity in a certain direction at a precise moment. The connections can be extended ad infinitum. But I believe there may be another form of causality which will explain the iniquity, the tragedy and suffering of life. Science does not address this question and we may not understand it now for the answer lies truly in the mind of God.

Somehow it must be given to us at the end of the journey, perhaps of many journeys, to escape the vice of good and evil and to pass beyond the need to die.

We need help. Perhaps it is on the way. The scientists trying to conjure God from a computer, needs one or he wouldn't do it. I sometimes think I have a small one of my own, perhaps he is a sort of forward scout. The poor little fellow has had a lot to put up with, but he knows the way I am supposed to travel. His voice is often faint but he is part of the story and I like to think of those he will arrange for me to find at the end if only I can listen, if ever I get there.

And they will have four legs as well as two.

———————|———————

Index